Lighting for Cinematography

The CineTech Guides to the Film Crafts

Series Editor, David Landau

Lighting for Cinematography

A PRACTICAL GUIDE TO THE ART AND CRAFT OF LIGHTING FOR THE MOVING IMAGE

DAVID LANDAU

Bloomsbury Academic
An imprint of Bloomsbury Publishing Inc

BLOOMSBURY
NEW YORK · LONDON · OXFORD · NEW DELHI · SYDNEY

The CineTech Guides to the Film Crafts

Bloomsbury Academic
An imprint of Bloomsbury Publishing Inc

1385 Broadway   50 Bedford Square
New York   London
NY 10018   WC1B 3DP
USA   UK

www.bloomsbury.com

BLOOMSBURY and the Diana logo are trademarks
of Bloomsbury Publishing Plc

First published 2014
Reprinted 2014, 2015 and 2016

Library of Congress Cataloging-in-Publication Data

Landau, David, 1956-
   Lighting for cinematography : a practical guide to the art and craft of lighting for the moving image/David
Landau.
    pages cm – (CineTech guides to the fi lm crafts)
   Summary: "A how-to book on the art, craft and practice of lighting for fi lm & video for students and
filmmakers"– Provided by publisher.
   ISBN 978-1-62892-298-1 (hardback) – ISBN 978-1-62892-692-7 (paperback) 1. Cinematography–
Lighting. I. Title.
   TR891.L36 2014
   777–dc23
2013049287

ISBN: HB: 9781628922981
     PB: 9781628926927
    ePub: 9781628924749
    ePDF: 9781628923629

Typeset by Precision Graphics
Text design by Alisha Neumaier
Printed and bound in China

CONTENTS

THANKS

First, I dedicate this book to my wonderful wife, Wendy, for her encouragement and support and who is my light. Exceptional thanks to my computer animator daughter Tracey who volunteered to do "a few" graphics for me and ended up being pressured into doing 25 lighting plots and a color mixing diagram. This book really wouldn't be as effective without her hard work. And to my younger daughter Alexandra Landau, a talented actress who agreed to sit in for a few lighting example shots and didn't mind having stills with her in them throughout.

Special thanks to the producers, directors, and production companies of the films that allowed me to use stills from their movies for this book:
Geraldine Winters, co-writer/producer, DGW Films – "Dark Tarot"
Nena Eskridge, writer/producer, Nena Eskridge Prods – "Stray"
Paul Williams, Writer/Producer/Director - "Stable"
Chris Schuster, producer & Ryan Kelly, Director, Ellipsis Films – "The Cold Equations"
Matt Mallinson Producer/Director – "Joker's Wild"
Chris Messineo, Writer/Producer/ Director, Offstage Films – "Nine Years Old"
David Carrin, Writer/Producer/Director, UTPA Films – "Waiting for Sandoval"
Don Riemer, writer/producer/director, Airworthy Prods – "Building a Bridge"
Matt Clarke, Producer, Clarke Com – "Luko Adjffi Music Videos," "Stab in the Dark"
Murder To Go/MTG Prods – "Murder at Café Noir," "TV Psychic," "Last Day of Winter", "The Last Duel"

Special thanks to the talented actors and others who appeared in the book:

Michelle Page	Cuyle Carvin	Jonathan Sang
Aaron Lustig	Ashley Taylor	Joseph Molino
Jade Elysan	Jason L. Barrera	Charissa Carfrey
Natasa Babic	Perla Rodriguez	Tina Zoganas
Alexandra Landau	Mitchell Elkowitz	James Leach
Susan Andriensen	Luko Adjaffi	Ira Holzman
Lauren Muraski	Clare Dill	Rich Goldberg
Quentin Fielding	Paul Rivers	Josh Beacon
Jeffery Wisniewski	Joanna Messineo	Bryant Simmons
Joseph Dimartino	Doug Ballard	
Don Singalewitch	Nancy Richards	
Richard Bell	Michael Finkel	

Thanks to the generous lighting suppliers and manufacturers who allowed me to include photos of their equipment and gave me graphics for this book:

Mole-Richardson	Lowel Light
ARRI	Matthews
LitePanel	Rosco
Cineo TruColor	Barbizon
Hive Lighting	Cinelease

And to my lighting class students who allowed some of their work and sometimes themselves to appear in this book. I really wrote this for and because of them.

INTRODUCTION:
No Matter How Good a Camera,
Good Lighting Is What Sells the Picture

We can't make good pictures without good lighting, no matter how good the newest cameras are. Shooting under available light gives exposure, but lacks depth, contrast, contour, atmosphere, and often separation. The story could be the greatest in the world, but if the lighting is poor, viewers will assume it's amateurish and not take it seriously. Good lighting makes things look real, while real lighting often makes things look fake. This book will help the reader create lighting that supports the emotional moment of the scene, contributes to the atmosphere of the story, and can augment an artistic style. Well-crafted lighting helps establish the illusion of reality that is necessary for viewers to forget they are watching a screen and to get lost in the story. So, no matter how good a script, how good a director, how good the actors, the lighting needs to be as good—if not better.

The purpose of this book is to help you, the reader, learn how to execute lighting techniques that will enhance your image and help contribute to the story you are telling. Feature films and TV shows, commercials and industrial videos, reality TV and documentaries, even event and wedding videos tell stories. So the lighting techniques in this book can be just as useful for all types of productions and not just ones telling narrative fictional tales. I will not delve too far into how major feature films are lit. There are many books out there that cover that subject quite well (see Appendix 2 for a list) and *American Cinematographer* magazine does that on a monthly basis. Rather, this book will address how cinematographers on a more limited budget and time schedule can achieve professional-looking images similar to what they see on the big screen.

What I relate in this book comes from my 35 years working on lighting crews as an electrician, gaffer, and cinematographer, as well as from the college lighting class that I have taught for 10 years. Having worked in the lighting business on everything from corporate videos and documentaries to commercials, TV shows, and feature films, I have been fortunate to be able to observe and learn from a wide variety of talented cinematographers.

As this book is geared toward cinematographers just starting out, I have used stills from low- to no-budget productions as examples of the methods and concepts described in the text. I give fair warning that the majority of stills are from a variety of low-budget projects I lit myself and some from the work of my students. These are not being offered for praise or for bragging rights, but rather to make it easier for the publisher to get permission to use the images. Also, since I lit most of them, I know how the lights were set up, rather than going by industry articles, secondhand information, and educated guessing. I have also endeavored to supply lighting diagrams for many setups to better illustrate how the lighting was accomplished.

The techniques here are equally applicable for both studio lighting and location lighting, but as most students, videographers, and independent filmmakers shoot in real locations, this book will be oriented more toward lighting setups applicable to location shooting.

In recent years, some filmmakers have adapted an artistic concept that they want their film/video project to look as real as possible. Often they incorrectly assume that by shooting under available light or with as little light as possible, they will achieve this effect. The fallacy in this thinking is the simple fact that the human eye is a thousand times more sensitive than any HD camera or film stock. The human eye is an amazing piece of genetic engineering that can see an extremely wide dynamic range of light and color. No camera can duplicate that, but with well-crafted lighting, we can make the image captured plausibly pass for what the human eye would see. Without lighting, the camera will record burned-out white areas in which the human eye sees plenty of detail, muddy dark areas in which the human eye can see perfectly fine, and a vast lack of in-between levels of brightness, colors, and contrast that the human eye can naturally detect. Not all lighting setups take a lot of instruments or a lot of time. Each instance is different, and often very much can be accomplished with very little—if you understand what you are doing and how light works.

1 THE MAGIC OF LIGHT:
What Lighting Does and What We Can Make It Do

Before we can sculpt with light, we need to understand it. What is light? What can we do with it? What can it do for us when we are photographing moving images?

Light is life-giving, mood-setting, body-tanning, but it is in itself invisible. It is radiant energy that is all around us and is taken for granted. Light is also an international, transcultural language that we can use to help tell a story. Light is an emotional language—it evokes a common response by all who see it. How we light something is the mechanical craft. It is in the "why" we light something the way we do that the art of lighting lies.

WHAT DOES LIGHTING DO FOR CINEMATOGRAPHY?

Cinematography is the art and science of recording moving images. Through lighting we can create in these images a visual language that indicates time, place, and three-dimensionality. Lighting can do a lot, but it has seven major functions in photographing moving images.

> "Lighting is rarely about just achieving a usable exposure level; that's not why we light a scene."
>
> —DAVID MULLEN, ASC,
> FEATURE /TV SERIES DP

ILLUMINATION AND SELECTIVE FOCUS

Just as light allows us to see, lighting allows us to record the image. Obvious, right? But we need to consider the following. Our eyes register light through rods (brightness on a gray scale) and cones (color values) and transmit images to the brain. They are very sensitive and have a tremendous amount of latitude in what they can perceive and what the brain can then process or "record." At the writing of this book there are a lot of very excellent high-definition cameras being used in the profession. They range from the ARRI ALEXA and the RED to the Sony F55. There is also a wide range of "prosumer" and low-budget professional cameras being used for a wide variety of digital cinema and video production, which includes the Sony NEX-FS700, the Canon EOS C500, and a slew of digital single-lens reflex still cameras that can also record video and that all boast 35mm sensors and high resolution rates. They can record an image under almost any form of available light, even under streetlights outside at night or by the light from a computer screen. Amazing! Yet none of them come anywhere close to what our rods and cones can detect. The human eye can see detail in the darkest shadows in a room with only a single candle. It can see details in the texture of the snow on a sun-drenched mountaintop.

Lighting allows film and video to record an image that approximates what the human eye sees. Without enough light, the image, or parts of it, will be noisy, blurry, burned out, dim, and lacking in detail, if visible at all. While a lot of things can be done to the image in digital postproduction, it takes a lot of time, talent, and money—and can degrade the image quality. Even with the most advanced postproduction coloring software, it is still preferable to begin with a full-range, deeply saturated image—something we used to call a rich negative. That means a picture with a defined contrast, full blacks, clean whites that don't blow out, and a nice full range of in-between levels throughout. We can usually only accomplish this by judiciously adding some of our own lights.

With the new highly sensitive sensors, the need to add light for simple exposure has all but disappeared. That burdensome, nonartistic, technical requirement has been, thankfully, lifted from the shoulders of the director of photography (DP) and gaffer, who can now concentrate totally on the artistic use of lighting. In other words, we now concern ourselves with how much we want the viewer to see and how much we want hidden in the shadows or ignored in burned-out white. In lighting we put light where we want it and take it away from where we don't want it. We now have more ability to be selective in what we allow the viewer to see—selective in the brightness, in the color, in the contrast, and in the detail.

By using this selectivity, we can direct the focus of the viewer's attention to what we want the viewer to concentrate more on within the picture. The human eye is attracted to whatever the brightest thing is in its view. Magicians use this to their advantage all the time. A bright flash of light occurs off to one side and everyone looks at it, giving the stage crew enough seconds to hide an elephant and make it appear to disappear (yes, it's been done). Directors, art directors, and DPs use the same concept. Art directors will give the actress that is the star a more colorful, brighter, or more sparkly costume than the characters surrounding her, thus making her stand out in a crowd. DPs do this with lighting. A great example is Robert Surtees's work in *The Graduate* (1967). In one scene, Ben and Mr. Robinson are in the study having a drink, darkly lit, while behind them is the doorway to the foyer, which is bright white. It's the brightest thing in the frame, and Mrs. Robinson, who has just told Ben she wants to have an affair with him, appears silhouetted in that foyer and slowly walks toward the camera. I've seen this film many times—I show it in Cinematography class. It's taken me years to be able to remember what Ben and Mr. Robinson are actually saying. All I ever do is stare past them at that silhouette of Mrs. Robinson—as the viewer always does. She's not in focus; we can't even see her face. But all eyes are on her as she approaches because she's occupying the brightest part of the frame. The lighting and composition direct the attention of the viewer exactly where the director, a young Mike Nichols, wanted it.

Keeping in mind that the human eye will always be attracted to the brightest thing in the frame, DPs will often try to make the main person or object we want the audience to focus on—such as one actor's face or a weapon in someone's hand or the product on a table in a commercial—the brightest thing in the frame. It might be for only that one shot, but it will selectively focus the viewer's attention to that one detail within the picture. I'm not saying supernova bright, just slightly brighter, sometimes so slight that the viewer isn't even consciously aware of it.

ILLUSION OF REALITY AND MODELING

Movies and videos are two-dimensional images. But everyone working on the project wants to suck viewers into the world being shown onscreen—we want them to feel as if they are looking into another world through a window. We want them to become so engrossed in the story that they feel like they are in the picture themselves. Lighting suggests a belief in the reality of what is on the screen. We use lighting to deceive the viewer into believing what is happening is real. We want viewers to forget that what they are watching has already happened a while ago and isn't happening right here and now, and that who they are watching are actors, that the actors are just reciting written lines, and that they are in sets, not real locations. Good lighting renders an illusion of three-dimensionality to a flat screen, making it feel all the more real and making the viewer feel more present. Lighting does this by providing modeling and depth to an otherwise flat image.

The mind rejects pictures that are false and confusing, thus taking the viewer out of the moment and back into the position of sitting looking at a screen. This causes the viewer to separate from the story and examine the image as an image. When this happens, the viewer becomes detached from the story. While viewers certainly can become reengaged, they will not process fully what was going on or being said while their brain was preoccupied with trying to justify the "reality" of the image.

In order to avoid this, the lighting in the image must look "real" or "natural" or at least story-appropriate. Lighting provides logic. The light seems to be coming from natural or logical sources, making us feel we are in real locations. Lighting utilizes light, shadow, color, texture, and angle to give the audience a perspective on the scene taking place. Shadows must be consistent with the "source" of the light whether seen or unseen. We must be consistent to maintain believability. And believability is key to getting the audience to suspend disbelief and become involved in the story.

In order to maintain an illusion of reality, we will want to light the scene as if it were lit by a motivated light source—something that seems believable, such as a desk lamp, a window, or a fireplace. Thus, the lighting we use should be consistent with its source—in color and intensity, texture and angle. This helps the believability of the image, which helps the believability of the story.

EVOKE EMOTION AND CREATE MOOD

Lighting gives a perception of emotion and invokes a response in the viewer's subconsciousness. Every strong emotional experience we have ever had has a visual connection. We live in a visual world and it leaves emotional imprints from visual scenarios. We even say "I see what you mean" to mean we understand. Lighting allows the viewer to feel the emotional thrust of the image. Dark shadows can create a feeling of loneliness, loss, mystery, or fear, while a bright image can convey happiness. A warm-color, low-angle light can provide a feeling of comfort or romance, while light coming down from directly above can render a feeling of isolation.

> **"Light is the chisel that sculpts the mood of any image on screen."**
> —JOSEPH DE GENNARO,
> INDIE FEATURE DP

Light can convey thought and feeling—as directed by the script. Each scene has a mood or atmosphere, and the lighting is crucial in providing that, surrounding and communicating visually to the viewer that feeling. The same scene, in the same location, with the same lights can be lit so that it is happy, sad, mysterious, romantic, and so on.

PICTORIAL BEAUTY

We want what is onscreen to be something the audience enjoys looking at. So we must compose the scene. While much of this is done with blocking and camera framing, lighting also provides composition—streaks of light can divide the background, highlights can accent something, light and shadow can direct the viewer's attention. All of this is based on the script and the director's vision of the scene. We are asking viewers to watch something we have created, to give us some of the minutes of their limited life span that they will never get back. The least we can do is give them something they enjoy looking at.

WHAT IS LIGHT?

In order to work with light effectively, we need to have some understanding of what it is and how it works. Light is a certain bandwidth of radiant energy that we can see. White light is composed of all the colors of the spectrum equally mixed. Light can be reflected (bounced), refracted (bent), filtered (colored), and absorbed—all things we will do when working with light to create an image. These are all parts of the physics of light. Understanding how we can utilize and manipulate these aspects of light allows us more control, creativity, and flexibility when crafting with it.

INVERSE SQUARE LAW AND FALLOFF

"Radiant" means that as light moves it radiates outward. In other words, light spreads in all directions as it travels away from its source. As it spreads, it decreases in intensity. We call this the inverse square law. The light intensity is inversely proportional to the square of the distance from the source. In plain English, doubling the distance from the light reduces the illumination to one quarter of its brightness. We call this the "falloff" of the light.

Why is this important for us to know? First, if we want the subject to be dimmer, we can easily just back up the light, and if we want the subject to be brighter, we can just as easily move forward the light. Duh, right? Except we have to be aware of how fast the light decreases as we move the light away. We also must keep in mind that the spread of the light will also vary as we move the light closer and farther away. The closer the light, the smaller the spread and the fewer things in the shot that will be illuminated by it. The farther away the light, the wider the spread of light and the more things in the shot that will be lit.

How can we use this to our advantage? The farther away we place the light, the wider the spread and the more even the light will be on two or more subjects standing together. If the light is close to them, say only a few feet away, whoever is slightly closest to the light will be significantly brighter in the shot. But if the light is 20 feet away, the one slightly closer to the light will only be a tiny bit brighter than the others. This is why even with today's highly sensitive cameras, feature films and TV shows are using even brighter lights than ever before: 20,000-watt HMI lights are common on major productions, because if we place the light 50 feet or 100 feet away from the actors, not only will it spread and cover a lot of area, it will be relatively even, since everyone in the shot is so far away from the light to begin with. It's sort of like the sun. The Earth is so far away, someone standing on the roof of a house isn't really any brighter than the person standing on the ground telling him not to jump.

We don't need a 20kW light to take advantage of this aspect of the physics of light. We can do the same thing with a 2,000-watt light positioned much closer but still far enough away from our subjects so that the difference between the distances of each actor from the source is so relatively small they will look the same in brightness. This means actors can walk around without getting visibly brighter and darker in the shot, which they would if the lights were set too close.

LIGHT CAN BE REFLECTED

Light bounces. As a matter of fact, it's almost impossible to stop it from bouncing. The angle of reflection equals the angle of incidence. Think of it this way: light is like a billiard ball on a pool table; it will bounce off a flat surface in a mirrored angle from the way it hits it.

Thus we can reflect and bounce light into the areas we want it. We can direct it. This is put to use in almost all lighting units. Behind the lamp in each fixture is a reflector that bounces light back out the front of the unit, thus increasing the output and brightness of the unit.

The important thing to remember here is that all light bounces, which means that light from a single unit will not just bounce off the subject we are trying to light, but will also bounce off the floor beneath the subject and the wall behind him or her. And since light is radiant, less direct and low-intensity light—which we call spill—will even

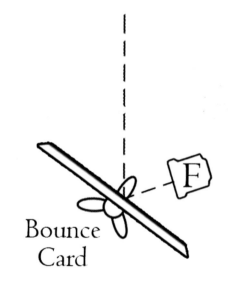

DIAGRAM 1.1 **Light reflects off a white bounce card**

bounce off the ceiling. This simple fact is something many people seem to forget when looking at lighting—especially theater directors. They always seem to be shocked that they can see some other parts of the stage or the set even though there is only one light striking the actor. The floor behind the actor reflects the light that is also hitting the actor—unless we paint the floor totally black, because black absorbs light (we will discuss this in the "Light Can Be Absorbed" section coming up)—and reflects up and illuminates some of the set walls, which bounces light off into other areas. The light gets progressively dimmer the more it bounces, but some of it keeps bouncing, and the human eye can see into very low levels of light.

Go outside and look around. Notice how easily you can see under the trees and in the shade around corners of buildings where no direct sunlight is hitting. Why can we see all of this? After all, we only have one sun—one single light source. So shouldn't all of the areas that are not getting direct rays from the sun be pitch-black? The reason it isn't is because light bounces. Light from the sun bounces off the ground and up under the tree, illuminating the shade. Sunlight bounces off the sidewalk, off the street, off the side of buildings. It is also important to realize that sunlight bounces off the sky and off of clouds. So outside, light is not just coming directly from the sun and from one direction; it is also bouncing off of a wide variety of things and lighting us from a variety of directions.

Why is this important to know? Because if we are shooting someone in the snow, on the sand, or even on a white floor, we often place black cloth down on the ground in front of the person, if it's not in the shot, to cut the bounce light off the person's face—because light bouncing up on someone's face can make him or her look unnatural.

If we are trying to make it look like sunlight is coming in through a window, we have to remember that more than just the direct rays of the sun come in through the window. Light bounces in reflected off the sky. Light can bounce in reflected off nearby buildings, trees, or even the ground. And light bounces up off the floor after it comes in through the window. So if we are trying to design our lighting to look natural and believable—to create an illusion of reality—we must light the scene with more than one light aimed in through the window. Otherwise, the viewer's brain will subliminally recognize that something is wrong with the image—something isn't true to nature. The viewer may not consciously know why, but he or she will feel that the lighting or image looks fake or amateur.

LIGHT CAN BE REFRACTED

Light beams can be bent and redirected, thus allowing us to focus the light and send it where we want it. This is done by sending the light through a lens that bends and focuses the light rays into a tighter beam and out in a straighter line. How can we use this? Lighting units can employ lenses to direct and increase the output of the light. The beam of light from a lighting unit with a lens is more intense and thus travels farther before falling off. We call this the "throw" of a light.

In addition, light is refracted when traveling through almost any piece of glass or any body of water. In these cases, the light beams are scattered or slightly redirected instead of tightened. This is good to know because it means that the light will drop in intensity and usually change color slightly.

LIGHT CAN BE ABSORBED

The surface of any object reflects the wavelengths of light that combine to compose its color. All the other wavelengths of light are absorbed. That's why if you wear a black shirt, you will be warmer in the sun than if you wear a white shirt. White reflects all wavelengths of light, while black absorbs all wavelengths of light and reflects none. How can we use this? We can use black cloth and black "flags" to absorb unwanted light and to cut the bounce, as mentioned earlier.

We see color because the wavelengths of light that combine to make that hue are reflected by the pigment in the object, while the other wavelengths of light (that are in a beam of white light) are absorbed. This is important to remember because if the surface that is bouncing light isn't white, the light bouncing off of it will not be white either. Green light bounces up off of a green lawn, while the other colors of the rainbow are all absorbed by the grass. This means that if you have an actress in a long, white dress standing in a lush, green, grassy field under bright sunlight, the bottom of her dress might appear a little greenish. And in a close-up, you might see green bounce light under her chin. Green isn't a very flattering color, especially for an actress's skin. So you might want to position the actress on a bare spot on the ground that is surrounded by the green grass, and when you go in for the close-up, place something black on the ground to stop the green from reflecting up—or perhaps a white card to reflect white bounce up.

LIGHT CAN BE FILTERED

When light passes through something that is transparent or translucent, it may become filtered. In other words, some color wavelengths of light may be either reflected back or absorbed as the light passes through the material. In the film/video industry we color our lights by placing gels over the front of the lighting unit. Many people call this "adding color to the light," but that is actually incorrect. What a gel actually does is filter out—or absorb—all the other wavelengths of light that are not in the color of the gel, only allowing the wavelengths that compose the color of the gel to pass through it. So, we aren't adding color; rather, we are subtracting it so that the only color left is the one we see.

Why is this important to know? Because anytime we filter a light, we are decreasing the brightness of the light, since we are cutting out (absorbing) some of the light. The richer the color, the more intensity is cut as the more wavelengths of light are absorbed. So if we put a dark blue gel or a bright red gel on a light, its intensity will be greatly diminished. That is something we must keep in mind when lighting and using gels.

Filtering isn't limited to color. Diffusion gels change the texture of the light as it passes through the gel. Both color and texture are attributes of light, which brings us to our next subject.

THE FOUR ATTRIBUTES OF LIGHT

Light has four basic attributes that we can have some control over and use when we paint with light: intensity, angle, texture, and color. The next sections explore these in detail.

Intensity

Intensity is the easiest attribute to comprehend. It's the brightness of the light. The amount of brightness coming out of a light unit is measured in lumens. Household light bulbs even have a lumens-per-watt label on them so you can buy the lamp that gives you the most light for the least amount of electricity. Lumens help us determine the efficiency of a lighting unit.

In film and video we measure the light illuminating our subject by foot-candles. One foot-candle is the amount of light cast on a subject from a single candle 1 foot away. Technically 1 foot-candle is equal to 1 lumen per square foot. The important thing to remember is that for our purposes the brightness of the light in a scene is measured in foot-candles. And that measurement is what establishes our exposure settings on our camera, which we set in f-stops (the aperture opening of the iris on the lens). We use a light meter to read the foot-candles on a subject. We will go into further detail on this topic in the next chapter. We can adjust and manipulate the intensity of the light coming out of a lighting unit in a wide variety of ways. The simplest method is to merely back up the light. Obviously, the farther away from the subject the light source is, the lower the intensity will become. We can also dim the lights—that is, lower its lumen output by decreasing the electricity flowing into the unit that generates the light. We can also scrim the light by placing a metal screen in front of the unit, which lowers the intensity of the light by blocking some of the light.

Angle

The angle is the direction from which the light strikes our subject. We can place the lighting unit almost anywhere and aim it at our subject. The position of the light—its height and where it is placed 360 degrees around our subject—determines the angle of the light hitting our subject. When the light comes more from the side, it reveals the texture of the subject, and it provides modeling—as our brain perceives dimensionality by shadows. The angle of the light provides the angle of the shadows. Shadows are dramatic. In general, the more shadows, the more dramatic a look; the fewer shadows, the less dramatic the look. If the light strikes subjects straight on, they will appear washed out, their dimensionality will be diminished, and the image will look "flat." Also, if the shadow falls directly behind the subject, the shadow will become a black rim that can make the subject look wider/larger than he or she is.

When shooting in a location, we must remember that light will very probably be hitting our subject emanating from things other than our lights. Thus, we will need to turn off whatever is producing that light, or block it somehow, or control it to our advantage. Since every light throws a shadow, we have to look at the angle of all light sources, as they will throw shadows up, down, and across our subject and the shot depending on where the light source is positioned in relationship to our subject.

Texture

Light has texture. Light from the sun and light from a point source has a hard texture. In other words, it will throw harsh shadows on whatever it hits. The harder the light, the further it "travels" before falling off. Hard lights are used in theater all the time, since the lights are routinely hung 25 to 50 feet away from the stage.

A point source is a light bulb or a single candle. It has a center point that is emitting the light. Movie projectors and search lights are very bright point sources. They have high-intensity beams that travel far and remain rather bright. In the film industry we have xenon lights and beam projectors that can send bright, hard, straight beams of light into a set. They are what make those shafts of light shooting in through windows in movies and TV shows.

I worked on a number of commercials with gaffer David Chedd, lighting a Wendy's set inside Silvercup Studios. We had several 4,000-watt xenon beam projectors lined up outside the set windows shining in to give it that early-morning-sunlight feeling. These lights were very bright and very hot, and they took a lot of electricity to power. But they were needed for the desired look, which was hard shafts of light streaming in through the windows. But you don't need an expensive high-powered light to get this effect. You can do the same thing using a theatrical 575-watt ellipsoidal spotlight. (We will talk further about lighting units in the next chapter.) The point is that light can be tightly focused and directed more easily if the light is hard.

Soft light is more difficult to cut and tightly focus. Soft light spreads quickly and produces soft-edged shadows. In fact, soft light bleeds into the shadow areas and wraps around the subject a bit, spreading a small amount of light into the shadows. Thus, it produces a flattering look on the human face. It helps to smooth out wrinkles and blemishes.

Light can be diffused through filtration. We can add a translucent gel that diffuses the light rays as they pass through it to soften the texture of the light. A number of different kinds of diffusion gel are available—frost, white diffusion, opal, grid cloth, and so on—and at various grades—full, half, quarter, and eighth. Also, hard light hitting a flat, white surface will be diffused. In other words, when light strikes the surface of a nonreflective material, it bounces off in all directions because of multiple reflections by the microscopic irregularities on the surface of the material. So we can change hard light into soft light, but as a result, the intensity of the light drops.

Think of the difference between hard and soft light this way: When you place your finger into the stream of water coming out of a hose, it divides on either side of your finger, leaving a dry area behind your finger. That's what hard light does; it creates a hard-edged shadow behind whatever it strikes. But when you place your finger in a slow-moving stream, the water curls around your finger, filling in the space behind it. That's what soft light does.

The texture of the light we use is something we can pick and control. We can choose to use hard light or soft light. We can soften hard light with diffusion gels or make it very soft by bouncing it into a white surface. But one thing we cannot do is make soft light harder.

Color

The three primary colors of light are red, blue, and green. All other colors can be made from a mixture of these three. When these three colors of light are mixed equally, they will render a "full spectrum" white light. Full spectrum basically means all the colors of the rainbow.

Children are taught that the three primary colors are red, blue, and yellow. These are the subtractive primaries—and they are in actuality magenta, cyan, and yellow. These are the colors used in printing and painting. They are subtractive because each of these pigments subtract (absorb) light wavelengths in order to reflect their hue. When equally mixed, they subtract all wavelengths of light and produce black—which is no reflection of light at all. Red, blue, and green light are additive colors, because when they mix, they add wavelengths of light rather than subtract them and produce white.

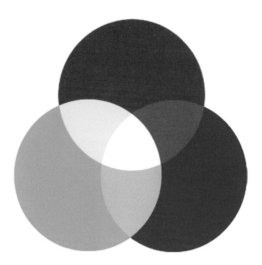

DIAGRAM 1.2 **Additive color mixing, courtesy of Barbizon Lighting**

Why is this important to know? Because we use colored gels often and we need to understand how they will react when mixed with other colors. It also relates to how color will reflect off of costumes and set pieces. Let's say we have an actress in a blood-red dress in the shot. It's a night scene, so we light the entire scene with blue light. If we used a "true blue" gel, that would mean there is only blue-wavelength light coming through the gel and no red wavelengths of light to be reflected off the red costume. So the costume she is wearing will photograph as gray or black. That would really upset the costume designer, and the director, and probably the actress.

We can manipulate the color of our light sources through filtration—placing gels on them. Gels are colored filter sheets of thin material made to withstand high intensities of heat. There is an extremely wide selection of gel colors from a variety of manufacturers. Rosco, Lee, Apollo, and GAM are the most popular. They give away free swatch books with small samples of each color in them, and you can even download apps with all their gels listed (see Appendix 2, "Resources").

A number of lighting units have the ability to change color themselves. These include "moving lights" and many new LED (light-emitting diode) fixtures that allow you to dial in a desired color. Moving lights have graduated color wheels that mix and filter the projected light and decrease its intensity as color is added. LED lights can come with red, blue, and green diodes (most now have amber and white added to help fill out the spectrum—more on this in the next chapter on lighting units), which makes the unit brighter as the colors are mixed.

We can manipulate the color of the light being projected into the scene. Color is a tool for designing with light.

COLOR TEMPERATURE

Each light source also has its own natural color. The color of a beam of light is measured in Kelvin degrees. I'm not going to bore you with the actual scientific definition here; instead, I'll give you a rather simple layperson's version. The color in Kelvin degrees is based on the concept that when a black mass of metal is heated, beginning at absolute zero, it gives off different colors of light as it

Color Temperature Scale

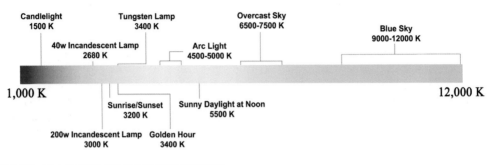

DIAGRAM 1.3 Kelvin degrees chart by Tracey Landau

gets hotter. The Kelvin degree measurement indicates at what temperature the metal glows which color. The lower the number, the warmer or more red/orange the light. The higher the number, the more blue the light. A candle gives off a reddish-orange light that is rated around 1,900 degrees Kelvin, or 1,900K; a desk lamp around 2,800K; a film light 3,200K; noon sunlight around 5,600K; and light from the blue sky 6,400K.

Why is this important? Just because a light might look white to the human eye, it doesn't mean it will photograph that way. We want whatever is white in front of the camera to be recorded as white. We can look at a white shirt and recognize it as white no matter what Kelvin temperature light is hitting it. Our brain just magically adjusts everything we see to make this work.

When I was a kid I would look outside after sunset and everything would look blue outside. I would run outside so that I could turn blue, but once outside I wasn't blue. In fact, nothing outside looked blue anymore. But when I looked back inside the house everything inside looked orangish. My brain was looking at the majority of the color of the light and setting what was white and what was skin tone and shifting everything else to make it work. We call this white balancing. Our brains do this naturally and in milliseconds.

Video cameras and motion picture film cannot do this. Motion picture film is balanced for either 3,200K, known as "tungsten" (which will be explained in the next chapter), or 5,600K, known as "daylight." Video cameras are made balanced for 3,200K with preset 5,600K settings that they can be switched to. But video cameras also have an automatic white balance feature, which allows the camera to set its white balance to whatever color fills the majority of the frame. The camera will digitally set itself to make this color white and shift everything else it sees accordingly.

So, we want all the light sources we use when shooting to be the same color temperature so that the lights will all match. If they don't, each light source will cast a different color that we will not be able to see by the human eye, but that together will make the image recorded look rather ugly and amateurish. This isn't just so that we can white-balance the camera, but also so we can control what color we add to our lights. If we add a red gel to a light that records as a reddish color, it will become even redder. If we add a blue gel to light that records as an orangish color, it will turn white, not blue. In order for us to have any kind of accurate control over changing the color of our lights, we need to know what color they will photograph as to begin with.

We also must keep in mind that with some lights, as they dim, their color temperature changes—it drops, and the light becomes warmer. So placing a blue gel on a light and then dimming it down will not only decrease its intensity but alter its color, making it less blue the more it dims.

METERING

There are two kinds of light meters: incident and reflected. An incident meter reads the light hitting a dome on its front—thus reading all the light coming from every direction that would hit the subject's face. This meter is held in the position of the subject and pointed toward the camera to get a mixed light reading. A reflected meter reads the light bouncing off the subject and calculates an exposure based on assuming the light is bouncing off something that is 18 percent gray. This meter is pointed at the subject or, better yet, pointed at an 18 percent gray card held in the place of the subject.

Reflected meters are in every camera with an auto-iris, and they set their auto exposure. They are also how spot meters work, which are meters that can take readings from long distances. Basically, if you rely on a reflected meter reading, the exposure will be set so that whatever you are aiming the meter at will record as 18 percent gray. That's a problem if you are shooting someone who is light skinned or dark skinned. It's also a problem if you are shooting a very white subject, such as

PHOTO 1.1 **DP Gus Dominguez (Local 600) takes an incident light meter reading during a shoot for** *Project Runway* **in Times Square, NYC.**

snowman. In cinematography, almost everyone uses incident meters, but we also use spot meters for special readings and know how to compensate their reading.

While light meters read foot-candles, all digital light meters have settings that allow them to display the f-stop setting based on the ISO (for International Standards Organization, the governing body that sets standards) and camera shutter speed set into the meter. The ISO is the sensitivity rating of the capture media whether it be photographic film or a light-sensitive digital imaging chip. Film has its ISO ratings on the outside of the can, and digital cameras have a menu setting for their ISO rates. We will discuss selective metering and exposure in Chapter 11. The important thing to remember here is that a light meter is a valuable tool for reading the light values in a shot.

F-Stops

DPs and gaffers talk and think in f-stops, rather than in foot-candles. The DP might say to the gaffer, "Knock that down a stop," or the gaffer might tell the DP, "The background is three stops over and your shadows are a stop under." Speaking in stops is one of the most basic forms of common lighting language and not just a setting for the camera lens. DPs and gaffers know that the f-stop is based on the foot-candles measured by their meter. When the foot-candles double in intensity, the f-stop goes up to the next setting. If it goes down by half, the f-stop drops to the next setting. While many readers will know this already, I will explain f-stops just in case.

An f-stop is a setting for the iris of the lens. The lower the level of light in the scene, the wider the aperture must be to allow more light through the lens to hit the capture medium so it can record an image. The wider the aperture, the lower the f-stop number. The brighter the level of light, the smaller the aperture opening will be to limit the amount of light reaching the capture medium. This becomes a higher f-stop number. The exact f-stop setting for the lens will depend on the sensitivity of the camera or capture medium (rated in ISO) in combination with the foot-candle reading of the light illuminating the subject.

Each standard f-stop setting listed below is double (or half) the amount of light entering the camera. The numbers seem arbitrary, but they are based on a complicated mathematical formula. These are part of every lighting person's vocabulary.

- f1.4
- f2
- f2.8
- f4
- f5.6
- f8
- f11
- f16
- f22
- f32

PRODUCTION MONITORS

In the modern age of digital cinematography, production monitors are almost always on set. Small high-quality high-definition (HD) monitors are often attached to the camera with flexible arms, and larger high-grade flat screens are used by the video engineer or digital imaging technician—if there is one on

CHAPTER 1 : The Magic of Light: What Lighting Does and What We Can Make It Do set—and by the director, producer, script supervisor, and anyone else to view the shot and watch the scene as it's recorded.

Many people now look at the monitor while lighting to see what the picture will look like. If the monitor is calibrated correctly, the image it produces is the image the camera is recording. But, that's a big "if." If you will be using a monitor, it is important to use the camera's color bars to set the monitor before lighting or shooting; otherwise, what you see will not necessarily be what you get. (Several free websites have instructions on how to set your monitor using the camera-generated color bars. I have listed some websites in the appendix rather than write the instructions out here.) While DPs and gaffers consult the production monitor all the time on set, many still rely on their light meter and their eye—a talent that comes from experience.

STUFF TO REMEMBER

What lighting does for cinematography:

- Provide exposure and selective focus.
- Provide modeling and an illusion of reality.
- Evoke emotion and create a mood.
- Add pictorial beauty.

The four attributes of light we can have some control over are as follows:

- Color
- Intensity
- Texture
- Angle

All light has a red to blue color temperature that is measured in Kelvin degrees.

- 3,200K is standard film lighting white, known as "tungsten."
- 5,600K is standard "daylight."
- When we shoot, we want all the light to be the same Kelvin degrees or as close as possible.
- When we dim certain kinds of lights, the color temperature drops and the color becomes warmer.
- There are two kinds of light meters: incident and reflected.
- Standard f-stops are f1.4, f2, f2.8, f4, f5.6, f8, f11, f16, f22, and f32.
- Each standard f-stop setting is double (or half) the amount of light.

PUTTING IT INTO PRACTICE

Take a notepad with you and for one day. Stop and really look at light.

- In the morning, note how the light comes into your room. Note the color, angle, texture, and intensity.

- Do the same for the light in your bathroom, then as you eat breakfast.

- Keep notes all day about the light you see in different places and environments. By actively looking at light, you will begin to realize all the things we usually take for granted that subliminally we recognize as the language of light.

2 WHO AND WHAT MAKES LIGHT?
The Lighting Crew, Lighting Units, Basic Electricity

In the beginning there was darkness. And a voice in the darkness said
"Let there be light"—and the gaffer was born.

THE LIGHTING CREW

The gaffer is the head lighting technician and is in charge of all the lights and supplying all electricity to the set. But it is the director of photography, also called the cinematographer and in the United Kingdom often called the lighting cameraman, who is the creative artist in charge of designing the lighting. For the rest of this book I will use that position's standard nickname—the DP.

Director of Photography

Also referred to as the cameraman or cinematographer (though the terms are not necessarily interchangeable, as described in the next paragraph), the DP is the head of the lighting crew and looks to the director to get an understanding of the mood and atmosphere the director wants for the overall film and each scene. Together they may reference past films, photographs, and paintings to start a dialogue about what kind of look and style the visuals of their project might have. The DP will read and reread the script as often as necessary to get a complete understanding of the intention and emotional moments within each scene, as they will help determine the design of the lighting. The lighting is there to help tell the story, to help support each scene's emotional content. It is from the script, and the director's interpretation, that the DP will decide on such things as the contrast ratio, the depth of field, and the lighting color palette employed in each setup.

The same is true in non-dramatic productions. Whether the production is a documentary, an educational video, a PR film, a sales video, or an internal corporate webcast, the DP (or lighting director, as the position is called in studio video productions with multiple cameras) still will talk with the director about what kind of feeling, style, and overall look he or she wants. If it is a documentary, should it look "unlit" or have more of a slick news magazine look? If the project is for PR or sales, generally the producers and directors will want the visuals and the lighting to have a polished quality in order to give the viewer the impression of the serious professional nature of the subject. In corporate communications, often the desire is to have a look similar to Bloomberg TV or CNN news, as these are stations businesspeople watch and are accustomed to. The lighting should always support the intention of the production.

The DP used to be simply called the cameraman (then later the cinematographer), but times have changed and so has the title, possibly to give the person in charge of creating the look of the film a more authoritative-sounding title. Today the difference between a cameraman and a DP is that a cameraman just operates a camera. They point and shoot. They may be very good at composing an image and picking lenses, setting the right exposure on their camera, and doing all sorts of other things with cinematography, but they don't create the lighting. They find good lighting to shoot under, or at least good enough for the work they are doing, such as documentary or reality TV. Or they are camera operators on live TV shows or at sporting events.

In television productions that have multiple cameras shooting at the same time, such as sitcoms, soap operas, game shows, talk shows, award shows, and many reality TV shows, the lighting will be designed by the lighting director, or LD. The difference between a DP and an LD is that the DP also decides the framing, lenses, filters, and everything else with regard to creating and capturing the image, while the LD concentrates on the lighting only, allowing the cameramen to shoot according to the directions they receive from the director, usually over a headset.

Gaffer

While the DP and LD design the lighting, the gaffer and the rest of the lighting crew make it happen. The gaffer runs the lighting crew and must have a firm understanding of lighting techniques and lighting units, and a basic electrical knowledge. He or she will have to keep track of all the lights brought to the shoot, and also be aware of what equipment is being used where and what is still available to be used. The gaffer assigns the other electricians, if there are any, any additional tasks. Everyone reports back to the gaffer after completing his or her assignment and asks for the next task.

Nothing electrical is ever allowed to be plugged in without permission from the gaffer. This isn't because of some union rule; it's by necessity, as the gaffer is also in charge of the distribution of all electrical power. Here's an example why.

I was working on the lighting crew of *Project Runway* (2011), a reality TV show. On this episode, the contestants were being brought to a private dining room of a chic restaurant in the Meatpacking District in Manhattan. The lighting crew was working as fast as possible to rig lights on the ceiling and above the windows and to power the set dressers hanging lights before the contestants arrived. This was an old building with very old wiring. The gaffer, Tigre McMullan, had scouted the location with the LD, Gus Dominguez, and knew exactly how all these units were going to be rigged and divided between the electrical breakers for the room. Four electricians and two grips worked all morning rigging and lighting the room so it would look "unlit," under Tigre's direction. Thirty minutes before the contestants arrived, everything was up and running and looking great. Gus stopped in and gave it his approval. The moment Gus walked out, half the lights suddenly went dark. Tigre couldn't understand it, as he had calculated the exact amount of electricity we were using and exactly how the cabling was all laid out. And it had just been on. The location producer was panicked. What had happened and how could it be fixed within the next 20 minutes?

Turns out a production assistant had plugged in a coffee pot—which blew the circuits. Tigre was ready to kill him, but lucky for the PA, Tigre didn't have the time. He had to trace the old wiring down to between four different fuse boxes on different floors, as everything was mislabeled. Minutes before the cameras arrived, he found the breaker and flipped it back on—after the coffee pot, and the PA, were removed from the location. The shoot went without a hitch.

This is a perfect example of why nothing can be plugged in, even to a wall outlet, without the permission of the gaffer. This is also an example as to why lighting people need to know math and basic electricity to do their job—and we will cover both topics later in this chapter.

Depending on the size of the production, there could only be the gaffer working with the DP to light each shot. This is more often the case in documentaries and corporate video productions. As the productions get bigger, the lighting crew grows as well.

> **"A good gaffer is incredible."**
> —GUS DOMINGUEZ,
> TV LIGHTING DIRECTOR/DP

Where did the term gaffer come from? There are a few theories, such as that "gaffer" used to mean "boss," or that the stick used to move an overhead light or cloth to block the sunlight was called a "gaff." But the one I like the best, and believe is the most likely, is also the most fun. Back when motion pictures started, movies were thought of as a cheap sideshow. Once silent movies started to add lighting to their productions, they started using lighting equipment intended for the stage. The only lighting technicians movie producers could get who knew how to use electricity and lights were retired theater stage electricians who were too old to work up on the grids of the big Broadway theaters or roadhouses. Back in the early 1900s, "gaffer" was a common affectionate term for an old man. Thus, when a light needed to be added or moved, legend has it, the producer or director, or cameraman would look around the set for the old theater electrician and shout out "can someone get that gaffer to move that light?" Hollywood loves its traditions.

Best Boy

The term "best boy" is the reason I believe the preceding theory. The second electrician works under the gaffer and is called the best boy. Where did this term come from? In the silent film days, the old stage lighting technician would bring his grandson or nephew along to the film set to learn how to use the lights and work with electricity, so that he could then go off and get a real job working in the theater. He was a young apprentice—or his "best boy." That name has stuck.

There are female electricians who are best boys. I worked with one who became upset when the production staff changed the call sheet and wrote her title as "best person," in an attempt to be neutral. She said she had worked hard to become a best boy and was proud of the title. She made them change it back.

On small crews the best boy works with the gaffer to set up all the lights and run the electrical cords, and so on. The best boy is in charge of the electricity. It is the best boy's responsibility to always be aware of how much electricity is being used and how much is left that can be used. On bigger crews, the best boy will have more responsibilities, such as doing the time cards, hiring additional electricians when needed, ordering supplies such as gels and lamps, ordering additional lighting equipment, and performing other similar tasks.

Electrics

The rest of the lighting crew are film electricians, widely referred to as "electrics." An old British slang term is "sparks," but most of us in the United States who do this job hate that name because it implies we've messed up—you only produce sparks if you did something wrong electrically. It's probably best not to use it in the United States or when dealing with an American crew. Electrics set up lights, aim and focus them, place gels on them if wanted, run extension cords, and do whatever is asked of them by the gaffer or the best boy. Everyone in lighting starts as an electric, then works his or her way up to best boy, then eventually to gaffer. Many gaffers enjoy staying gaffers. Some become DPs. Some best boys enjoy staying best boys.

It isn't uncommon in the film business for crew members to move back and forth between these different areas. Gaffers will sometimes hire other gaffers as their best boys or as rigging gaffers or as location gaffers or even as electrics on certain days of a film. There is a lot to know about working as an electric in the film/video business. For those interested in learning more, I recommend *The Set Electrician's Handbook* (see Appendix 2) as a great training guide.

Depending on the project, there may be other positions on the lighting crew, such as generator operator (genie op), shop electric, and lighting board operator (board op). Almost all TV shows and most features films with large sets will employ a dimmer system that allows the gaffer to turn on and off different units and change their intensity quickly. The board op stays at the dimmer board, on walkie-talkie, and makes the adjustments relayed to him or her by the gaffer.

Generators are common on locations, as film crews need a lot of electricity not only for the lights, but also for makeup and hair, for the craft services (catering), for the video playback, and for all sorts of other things and people on set. Someone has to watch over the generator to make sure it runs smoothly, doesn't overheat, and doesn't run out of fuel. That is the job of the genie op.

The oddest position I ever experienced was being the wardrobe gaffer on an episode of *Project Runway Allstars 2* (2012). I was hired to build, wire, and maintain small LED, EL wire (EL stands for electroluminescent), and other tiny battery-operated lights that the contestant designers had to use in making their dresses. I even had a wardrobe electric best boy working with me as well.

CHAPTER 2: Who and What Makes Light? The Lighting Crew, Lighting Units, Basic Electricity

20

Rigging Crew

In some cases there might be a rigging crew, which is a crew that goes into a location while the shooting crew is out filming somewhere else. The rigging gaffer presets the lighting as designed by the DP, runs the cables, and sets up workstations where extra cables and lights are stored ready for use. The rigging gaffer will have his or her own rigging best boy and possible rigging electrics. When the shooting crew arrives, the rigging crew usually leaves and goes to the location the shooting crew just left and cleans up for them while the shooting crew films. This system is called checkerboarding and is common in most big feature films and many TV shows because it allows a production to move faster and get more accomplished in a shorter time.

Some productions will have second unit crews, who will have second unit DPs, camera crews, gaffers, best boys, electrics, grips, props, and so on. These crews often shoot stunts, explosions, and establishing location shots, all shots where the stars aren't seen or needed.

Grips

Grips also work for the DP. They move the camera, move walls, set up scaffolding, operate dollies and cranes, gel windows, and perform other important tasks. They will help rig ways to get the lights where the DP and the gaffer need them. They also do a lot to help control and shape the lighting. They set up butterflies, flags, and nets with grip stands to block and cut light. Some DPs will ask the key grip to work with the gaffer to get things done, while some key grips prefer to take their directions directly from the DP. Grips do not set, hang, or focus the lights. That is strictly done by the electrics, who are trained for that. Grips have many other things they need to do on set. The distribution of work and allowing people to do what they specialize in is what allows the running of a set to be smooth, fast, and accurate.

Very small crews may not have grips. In a three-person crew of soundperson, DP, and gaffer, the gaffer will also serve as the grip. But in these cases there is generally very little grip work to be done other than setting flags and nets.

A lot is involved in becoming a grip, and if that is a career you might be interested in pursuing, I recommend *The Grip Book.* Written by a professional grip, it is an excellent training guide. (See Appendix 2.)

Relationship between DP and Gaffer

The gaffer is the DP's right hand. In feature films, the DP will tell the gaffer how he or she wants the scene lit, laying out which lights should be placed where. Since the gaffer knows all the equipment and electricity available, he or she might make

> **"It's one other person that brings something to the table."**
>
> —ELIA LYSSY, DOCUMENTARY CINEMATOGRAPHER

suggestions based on efficiency of power, equipment, crew, time, and so on. It is always the DP's final decision, but the DP usually listens to the gaffer. After all, the gaffer's expertise is one of the reasons that the DP hired him or her.

I came up through the TV commercial industry in New York City in the 1980s. In commercials there were many director/cameramen hybrids who owned their own companies. Many of these started as still photographers and were very good at framing, lenses, and filters, but were not that experienced in cinematography. They relied heavily on their gaffers to do their lighting for them, while they dealt with the ad agency, talent, and camera. I worked with quite a number of them lighting kids' toys, deodorant, diapers, shampoo, and all sorts of things. The same is often true about cameramen who came up through documentary or industrial videos. I worked with several such cameramen who had me do the lighting for them as their gaffer when they were hired for commercials or TV segments. A gaffer never expects to do the lighting but is always ready to do whatever the cameraman asks. I know of a major TV series where after a few seasons with the same crew, the gaffer did the lighting as the DP worked with the two camera operators and the director, thus allowing the shoot to go faster.

So the relationship between the gaffer and the DP can vary depending on the DP and the situation. No matter the relationship, the gaffer will never supersede the DP—that's who hired the gaffer. But the gaffer is a valuable tool that the DP can use to his or her advantage. Often, new DPs who are getting that chance to do something above what they've been used to doing will seek out a gaffer with more experience than themselves for that project. After a DP and a gaffer have worked together a few times, the gaffer will come to know how the DP wants things done. This is likely to result in the DP giving the gaffer more responsibility and freedom. They become a team that works smoothly and quickly.

On many sets you will find three light meters: the DP has a light meter, the gaffer has a light meter, and often the 1st camera assistant has a light meter. At the beginning of a shoot, everyone gets together and compares their light meters and decides on whose light meter they will go by. Hopefully, all the meters will read the same, or close enough. Many DPs will use a light meter while setting and focusing the lights to read the light levels and determine the contrast ratio between light and shadow areas. In many situations, once the lighting is complete, the gaffer will read the light and tell the DP and 1st camera assistant (called 1st AC) the f-stop setting for the camera. If the DP is unhappy with that f-stop, the lighting may be adjusted. Sometimes the 1st AC will meter the scene after the lens has been changed, camera filters have changed, or the angle has changed.

BASIC ELECTRICITY

Why should you know about basic electricity? Because what you don't know can literally kill you. If you are going to work in lighting, you are going to work with electricity. At this time in humankind's scientific advancements, we can't generate light without plugging something in. So, while this might not sound like the greatest subject to read about in a lighting book, it is perhaps one of the most essential parts, and just might help you live longer and safer.

I was lighting a commercial for a novel, some epic romance between an American sailor and a Chinese woman set during the 1800s. I lit the set of a Chinese rice paper screen bedroom. The set dresser positioned a cast-iron streetlamp in the foreground. The action was simple: Sailor at streetlamp sees Chinese beauty in bedroom, walks back, and joins her. The director wanted to see the streetlamp on. The set dresser plugged it into the wall. The second she did, a 6-inch flame erupted at the base of the cast-iron lamp and quickly burned like a fuse across the floor toward the outlet. I ran over and pulled the plug out just as the flame burned across the palm of my hand. If I hadn't gotten that plug out in time, the fire would have crept right into the wall of the building. The AD (assistant director), being the professional he was, knew there was a hospital only three blocks away and insisted that I immediately go to the emergency room, so long as I had finished the lighting. I assured him I had, and he handed me some money in case I needed it and then asked me to hurry back.

The reason this happened was the set dresser used a 500-watt lamp in the streetlight but wired it with something like speaker cable. The wire gauge was too thin for the amount of electricity being pulled through it, and the wire itself burst into flames. This is why, when working with lights, you need to know about wire gauge, amps, watts, volts, and all sorts of things.

CHAPTER 2: Who and What Makes Light? The Lighting Crew, Lighting Units, Basic Electricity

22

I'm not going to go into a lot of scientific depth. Rather, I will try to boil down what you need to know about electricity to make it as easy to understand as possible. Electricity is the flow or movement of electrically charged particles (electrons), which can be directed through a bundle of wire conductors. Copper and other metals are great conductors of electricity. So is water—and so are humans, as we are 50 to 70 percent water. Wood, rubber, and plastic are insulators—they don't conduct electricity, so they can contain it and protect us from it. That's why extension cords have rubber- or plastic-based coatings around them and why we wear rubber-soled shoes and wear rubber gloves sometimes when working with electricity.

Electricity always flows from negative to positive. The Earth is considered positive, so we should assume that all electricity is trying to find the fastest way it can to get to the ground. Usually, electricity will take the path of least resistance. If a human is a part of that path, it will go through that human—which will usually either burn or kill him or her.

Electricity is either DC or AC—direct current or alternating current. Direct current means the electrically charged particles flow one way—from negative to positive. These are batteries and bolts of lightning. In alternating current, the flow of electrons constantly reverses because the poles are changing back and forth between negative and positive. In the United States, that is 60 cycles per minute, or 60 hertz, while in most other countries it's 50 hertz. This is the electricity that comes out of the wall outlet and from generators. This allows electrical current to be sent much farther before any significant drop in power.

Briefly, here are some technical terms and what they mean:

- Current is the electrical flow of the electrons (speed) and is measured in amps.

- Potential is the difference between the + / – (strength) and is measured in volts.

- Usage of electricity, how much is needed to operate something, is measured in watts.

WAV

The most important thing to remember is this: W = A × V. Watts equals amps times volts. This will be used all the time on sets and when shooting. You can remember it easily this way: Electricity moves in waves, thus WAV.

Why is this important? It allows you to determine how many lights you can safely plug in without setting something on fire or blowing a fuse. Both wire and fuses—although now it's really breakers—are rated by the amperage they can support. Exceed the number of amps they are rated for and the breaker will trip (turn off), while the wire will melt and, in some cases, actually start on fire. So anyone working in lighting, specifically the best boy, will always be calculating how many amps the lighting is taking and how many amps are still available. We do this through simple math: amps = watts ÷ volts.

Almost every light has its wattage listed right on the unit itself somewhere. The lamp has its wattage listed on it as well. We often refer to lights based on their wattage. Standard lights used in the industry are 300 watts (called a 300), 650 watts (called a 650), 1,000 watts (called a 1k, pronounced one-kay, for one kilowatt), and so on. So determining the amount of amps a light is using is very easy. Just divide the wattage by the voltage, which in the United States is 110 volts (in Europe, the standard voltage is 220). So, to determine how much amperage a 650 light is using, we just divide 650 by 110, which is 5.9 amps. Now the easy method where you don't need a calculator—just divide the wattage by 100 (by 200 in England and Europe). You can do that easily in your head. This way you will always have a bumper—a safety net that helps you to not go over the limit of your extension cord or the breaker.

Power Cords

Wires are rated by the AWG—American Wire Gauge—by their thickness and corresponding amperage limit. The thicker the wire, the more amperage it can accommodate without melting and the *lower* the AWG number. You are probably thinking, "Why didn't they do it the other way around?" Well, they just didn't, and that's something you have to remember. Most extension cords have their AWG rating either listed on the cord itself or on the plug—but not all. If you don't know the rating of the wire inside the extension cord, just don't use it. Following are some AWG ratings for cables that we use the most.

Wire amperage (AWG) ratings for copper wire:

- #18 = 7 amps

- #16 = 12 amps

- #14 = 16 amps

- #12 = 20 amps

- #2 = 90 amps (welding cable)

- #00 = 150 amps (really heavy and thick)

In the industry, the standard extension cord is a 12/3, which means three #12 gauge wires—one for the hot, one for the neutral (return), and one for the ground—bundled together inside a rubber or plastic coating. Thus, the extension cord can support 20 amps. The standard length is 25 feet, and they are commonly referred to on set as "extensions," "12/3s," or "stingers."

These cords are much thicker than what you can buy at a hardware store. Most household extension cords are 18 gauge. Some have more than one plug. If you plug in two 650s, the cord will start melting or catch on fire. I've seen students do this. The "heavy-duty" extension cords sold at places like Home Depot are either 16 or 14. It is essential you know what the AWG rating of every extension cord you have is.

It doesn't matter how many open plugs a cord has on it. Most only have one, but some have three at the female end. Some have a "quad box" with four outlets on it. You have to be very careful and add up everything you are plugging into that cord to make sure you don't exceed that cord's limit.

Power Distribution

When shooting, the gaffer needs to distribute the electrical load of all the lights to avoid tripping breakers and losing electricity and thus lights (which will inevitably happen during the best take). When shooting in a real location, the first thing the gaffer must do is find the electrical service box where all the breakers are, which is usually in the basement. If shooting in an office, school, or other public building, find the building electrician or custodian and have the person show you where the electrical boxes are. Often in public buildings there is more than one electrical box, different ones for different sections of the building. Make sure you find out which one is for the area of the building that you are shooting in.

Most breakers in electrical service boxes in the United States are rated at 15 amps in homes and 20 amps in business buildings. The breakers are labeled right on them so it's rather easy to find out which they are by just opening the fuse box. According to electrical code, the lid of the breaker box should have a list of what each breaker is for. But often we find ourselves in a home or building that has had renovations or electrical upgrades and the boxes have been redone. Many times what is written for each breaker is no longer correct, or there are new breakers added with no labeling at all. So, how do we determine which outlets in the rooms we will be shooting in correspond to which breakers in the box? The easiest way is to use a circuit breaker locator, sold in many hardware stores for around $40. You plug a small plug into an outlet and then take the locator to the breaker box and run it up and down the breakers until it lights up or beeps. That's the breaker for that outlet.

If you will be shooting in a house or an apartment, go there a day of two before the shoot with white tape, a marker, the circuit breaker locator or a small light, and a friend. Find the breaker box and have your friend stay at the box with his or her cell phone. If you are using the circuit breaker locator, you take the attachment and give the locator to your friend at the breaker box. You both take tape and a marker. Plug the attachment into an outlet, call your friend at the breaker box, and have the friend run the locator up and down until he or she finds the corresponding breaker. Put a piece of tape beside the outlet and mark it with the breaker number. Repeat the process for every outlet. A "poor man's" method is to plug a small lamp into the outlet, call your friend, and have him or her turn on and off each breaker until the lamp turns off. Your friend can start with trying the breaker labeled for the room you are in, which hopefully will be correct. Remember, you must make sure that all computers are turned off before you begin throwing breakers on and off, as we all know when a computer loses power, it deletes whatever it was working on if it hasn't been saved. Once you determine which outlets are on which breakers, you can now divide the load of your lighting so that you don't trip a breaker during a shot.

There are some fast ways to find individual circuits. Bathrooms, by electrical code, must be on their own breaker. So each bathroom will be on a separate 15-amp circuit. Most refrigerators are on their own circuit, as they draw a lot of power and cycle on and off. Unplug the fridge and use the outlet for another 15 amps. The sound department will love you, as they hate the cycling hum of the fridge. Just remember to plug the fridge back in when you finish shooting. Soda machines in hallways are refrigerators and are usually on their own breakers as well. Unplug them and you'll have more power.

Keep in mind that electrical contractors want to work fast and save money—so they will gang outlets together when possible and run the shortest amount of cabling as possible to get it to the breaker box. Thus, an outlet on one side of a wall will probably be attached to the outlet on the opposite side of that same wall in the next room. You'll find this most often the case in homes, apartments, and offices. To avoid tripping breakers, don't plug into rooms that share the same wall. Rooms across the hall from each other are usually different circuits, as it's faster for building electricians to run cable straight down to the basement than under the floor and over to the room across the hall. Usually, other than the refrigerator, outlets along one wall of the kitchen will all be ganged together and run to the same breaker. So coffee pots, toasters, microwaves, and other small appliances may all be plugged into the same circuit as the behind-the-counter outlets. Unplug them before shooting—or someone will invariably turn them on during the shot and trip the breaker.

Hotel rooms are the opposite. In a hotel room, all the outlets in each room are on one breaker, and each room is separate from the next. The hotel doesn't want someone in one room to lose electricity because the people next door plugged in a computer, a printer, a blow dryer, and a veggie juicer. Bathrooms will still be on their own 15-amp breakers. Also the outlets in the hallway, used by the cleaning people to vacuum the hallway, will be on a different breaker than the ones in the rooms. Remember, in finding electrical power for lights, it's divide and conquer.

Always run extension cables from the source to the light, then plug them in. I have seen countless students pull over lights by plugging an extension cord to a light first, then running the cord to the outlet. They pull on the cord to make it reach, and the light topples over. So, always run an extension cord to the light, and leave excess cord coiled neatly at the base of the stand. Every light should have excess cable by the base because the chances are high that the light will be moved, if not during the fine-tuning of the lighting for the first shot, definitely when the camera changes angles and the lights need to be moved again.

Generators

Big productions have generators on locations that the electrics run the power from. These range in size and output and come usually in their own truck with sound baffling and exhaust fans. But I have had students who went to Home Depot and rented small 6,000-watt generators and used them for shooting at night in the woods. The thing to plan for is that these small generators are noisy. If you decide to use one of these, make sure you hide it around a corner of a building from where you are shooting. It works well to place it on the opposite side of a truck or a line of thick trees as well. Do not, however, leave the generator inside a van and run it that way. This causes two major problems. First, the van becomes a megaphone amplifying the sound, and second, there isn't enough air flow for the

PHOTO 2.1 6,000-watt generator, courtesy of Cinelease NY

exhaust, which can cause the generator to choke and shut down, or burst into flames—something that happened to students at a prestigious film school, who lost the entire van to the fire.

In high-rise buildings where it's too far to run cable from a generator on the ground, the producers have to pay a building electrician to "tie-in" or stand by while the gaffer or best boy ties-in. Tieing-in is attaching special electrical clamps to the bus bars of the inside of an electrical service box to access the power. It is rather dangerous and against all electrical codes. It is part of the film electrician's union test, and I and almost every electric I have ever known has had to tie-in a few times throughout their career. It should only be done by trained professionals. Most small productions use the standard electrical outlets in the hallway, conference room, and down the hall. The gaffer keeps track of how many amps are plugged into which outlet—never exceeding 20 amps, although keeping it under 15 amps is safer, as you might not know what else is on that circuit using power.

LIGHTING UNITS

There are a number of different manufacturers of film lights, and newer units are always being invented. There are also many older lights that have become outdated and no one uses anymore. I'm sure that in the very near future, many lights I include in this section will become obsolete and many new ones will be invented. That's the nature of this industry. What is important to know right now is what the various types of fixtures are and how each has a different function.

Lighting units—which we simply call lights—are our tools in painting the picture with light. The "bulb" inside each unit is commonly referred to as the lamp. So, the light is the unit, and the lamp is the bulb inside. Types of lights included the following:

- Open-faced lights—The open-faced light is a lighting instrument that has a bare lamp with a reflector behind it. This unit emits a bright, hard light that spreads very wide and the falloff is rather fast. These units come in a wide variety of designs, sizes, and wattages. Some

PHOTO 2.2 1,000-watt ARRI open-faced light

of these units can adjusted between spot and flood settings via a knob on the back of the unit that moves the lamp within the housing closer or farther way from the reflector. This allows the operator to tighten the beam, for spot, thereby extending the throw of the light and its intensity, or spread the beam, for flood, which results in lowering both the throw and the intensity but covering a much wider area. The nicknames include mickey or redhead for a 1,000-watt unit and mighty or blond for a 2,000-watt unit. Other units have a single lengthwise lamp in a reflector, which we call board lights or nook lights. Lowel makes a small, lightweight, open-faced light called a Tota-light that is very commonly used in schools and for documentaries, but which Lowel is now replacing with its V-lite.

PHOTO 2.3 **Open-faced Tota-light, courtesy of Lowel Light**

- Fresnel lights—The Fresnel lens was invented for lighthouses and adapted for theater lighting units many years ago. The Fresnel lens is a stepped convex lens in the front of the unit that focuses the light, increasing the output and extending the throw of the light. All Fresnel lights can be focused, spot to flood. Even though the inside flat surface of the lens is a pebbled diffusion, the light is still rather hard. It has a tighter beam spread than an open-faced light, thus having a longer throw. These units come in a wide variety of designs, sizes, and wattages. They are generally referred to by their wattage, such as a 150, 250 (also known as an inkie), 300 (also known as a midget), 650 (also called a tweenie), 1kW (also known as a baby), 2kW (also known as a junior), 5kW (also known as a senior), 10kW, 12kW, 18kW, and 20kW.

PHOTO 2.4 **650-watt ARRI Fresnel**

- Softlights—Softlights are units that either direct all the light into a white reflective surface or through a white diffusion material, with no direct light from the lamp coming out of the unit. The light that emanates is soft; it wraps and falls off very quickly. These units come in a wide variety of designs, sizes, and wattages. But they cannot be spot or flooded. A very popular collapsing softbox unit is Lowel's Rifa light, which has a bare lamp inside a reflective-backed tent with a cloth diffusion front. The 2kW zip light made by Mole-Richardson is a standard on almost all sets and has two lamps hidden below that reflect light up into a coved white reflector.

PHOTO 2.5 **750-watt Rifa light, courtesy of Lowel Light**

PHOTO 2.6 **2kW zip light, courtesy of Mole-Richardson Lighting**

- PAR lights—PAR, for parabolic anodized reflector, lights are units that utilize a parabolic reflector behind the lamp, similar to a car headlight. Some allow various lenses to be placed in front of the unit, and others are sealed with fixed lens on the front of the lamp itself. Both the lenses and the sealed lamps come in spot, medium, flood, and sometimes honeycomb and diffused. Parabolic reflectors reflect more of the light than standard spherical reflectors used in open-faced and Fresnel lights, thus producing a brighter, more narrow beam of hard light with a substantially longer throw. Most PAR lights cannot be spotted or flooded, although a few have a minor ability to do this.

PHOTO 2.7 PAR 64, courtesy of Cinelease NY

- Nine lights—The nine light has nine PAR lamps arranged in three virtual columns that can be switched on and off individually. They also come in 6, 4, 2, and single units. The columns can be swiveled so that the lamps can be focused in three directions if desired. The units can be lamped with either tungsten or daylight. A nine-light Fay has 650w lamps, while a Maxi-Brute has 1kW lamps in it. The Maxi-Brute comes in larger number of lamp units as well.

- Ellipsoidal reflector spotlights—Also known as ERS or Profile Spot and often referred to as a Source Four, which is actually a brand name from its manufacturer, Electronic Theatre Controls (ETC), this unit has a reflector that surrounds the lamp almost like an egg, becoming the most efficient in reflecting all the radiant beams of light through one tight set of lenses. This greatly increases the brightness, tightness of the beam, and throw of a very hard light more than any other design. These lights are used primarily in theater but have become common specialty units in motion picture and video productions, especially for their ability to throw hard patterns, known as gobos, and be cut into tight beams. These lights cannot be spot or flooded, but they do have lenses of varying degrees which can be swapped in and out, which changes the width of the beam spread.

PHOTO 2.8 Nine-light Fay, courtesy of Mole-Richardson Lighting

- Homemade—Many DPs and gaffers like to make their own lights and bring them on shoots, such as bucket lights, which are white plastic buckets or trash cans that have a porcelain lamp socket rigged in the base. The book *Shot in the Dark* is all about making inexpensive do-it-yourself lights and dimmers (see Appendix 2).

PHOTO 2.9 750-watt Source Four ERS, courtesy of ETC

PHOTO 2.10 Homemade bucket light with compact fluorescent bulb

LIGHTING CONTROLS

- Barn doors go on the front of the unit—the exception being ERS lights and most soft lights. The four doors are used to contain or "cut" the light by opening and closing them.

- Scrims are round metal screens that cut the intensity of the light coming out of the unit that slide in behind the barn doors of the unit. These come in four designs:

    1. A single—painted green around the edge—drops the intensity a half stop.

    2. A double—painted red around the edges—drops the intensity a full stop.

    3. A half single—dashes of green—only has the scrim over half the diameter of the frame.

    4. A half double—dashes of red—only has the scrim over half the diameter of the frame.

PHOTO 2.11 **Barn doors**

When a light is brought to set, it should always have the barn doors on it and a full set of scrims with it. Standard practice is to hang the scrims on the knob of the light stand, usually with a binder clip with a piece of black tie-line through it.

When setting the light, the DP or gaffer may say things like "drop a single," which means put in a single. Other common ways of saying it include "slow it down a stop," which would mean a double scrim, or "take it down a half stop," which would mean a single scrim. If the DP asks for a "triple," that means a double and a single scrim. If the DP asks for a "full house," that means two doubles and a single scrim. The most that can fit behind the barn doors of a light are three scrims.

Remember that scrims get very hot once in the light and will burn your fingers, so it's best to remove them with a pair of pliers, the point of a knife, or a wooden clothespin. Most of us just drop the scrim as soon as possible at the base of the light stand. They cool rather quickly, so it is possible to pick them up almost immediately if you hold them by the center screen and not the edges, which retain the heat longer. Dropping them isn't always the best idea, however.

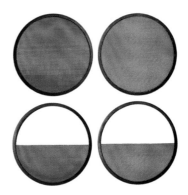

PHOTO 2.12 **Scrim set**

Years ago, I was best boy on a TV commercial in an ice-skating rink. The lights were put on sheets of plywood to stop them from sinking into the ice. We were shooting, and suddenly the DP wanted a scrim pulled from a 5kW Fresnel. I quickly climbed a ladder, pulled the scrim, and dropped it—and missed the plywood. It melted into the ice, around 3 inches deep. The grips were nice enough to help me chip it out during lunch. The lesson here is to always look before you drop. Don't drop a hot scrim onto something that might be flammable, like dry leaves, or on an expensive shag carpet that can get scorched.

- Flags and nets are used by the grips to cut and sculpt the light and are used with grip stands. They come in various sizes: 18 inches × 24 inches, 24 inches × 36 inches, and 4 feet × 4 feet. They come in four basic designs as well:

  1. Black flag—Also called a solid. Opaque black cloth that cuts light fully

  2. Single net—Cuts light a half stop. Green on the edge

  3. Double net—Cuts light a full stop. Red on the edge

  4. Silk—Diffuses the light and lowers intensity. Gold on the edge

  In addition, there are studio flags and nets, as well as collapsible ones for smaller productions made by Westcott and RoadRags. All flags and nets are delicate and can be easily ripped or torn.

- Grip stands—Also known as c-stands and gobo stands. These three-legged, collapsing stands are essential tools in lighting. They come with a grip head (gobo head) and grip arm and are used to position flags and nets, bounce cards, and so on. Be sure to always place a sandbag on the higher leg to stabilize.

PHOTO 2.13 **Single net, double net, flag, and silk**

LAMPS

Each of the units named above is a light fixture that requires a lamp inside that actually generates the light it projects. How these work determines the color temperature of the light being emitted. For the sake of ease and conserving pages, I will briefly summarize how these work as simply as possible. This information is important to know so you can better determine which lamp and which unit will do the best job for the task you want to accomplish. It is also important because of issues such as electrical power usage, color temperature matching, and safety.

Incandescent

The oldest and most widely used method is to send electricity through a very thin wire, called a filament, made of tungsten metal held inside a vacuumed glass globe. The wire is thin and the electricity so "strong" that it heats up the wire and makes it glow, thus giving off light. This is what Edison invented and what is common in almost every household worldwide. This method creates more heat than light, but the light generated contains all the colors of the spectrum and is a single-point source of hard light. The sun and candles both produce incandescent light—light through heating something. So the light from

PHOTO 2.14 **Grip stand**

an incandescent lamp is very natural, warm, and pleasing to the human eye. It is a continuous light source, in that it doesn't flicker, which makes it perfect for motion picture photography.

While your average household light bulb is just made out of glass surrounding a tungsten filament in a vacuum, movie lights have lamps with envelopes made out of quartz and are filled with halogen gas, which helps eliminate discoloration on the inside of the envelope and prolongs the life of the filament by, in layman's terms, pressuring the melting molecules of the glowing filament back onto the wire. Movie incandescent lamps are manufactured to have a color temperature of 3,200K. We call these lamps tungsten halogen, and 3,200K is referred to as the temperature "tungsten." But as you dim the unit, the color temperature will drop and the light produced will become warmer.

IMPORTANT: Never touch the glass envelope of an incandescent lamp with your fingers. Your fingers contain oil and when you touch something, you deposit that oil on it—thus fingerprints. When you touch the glass envelope of an incandescent lamp, the oil from your fingers remains on the

PHOTO 2.15 Tungsten lamp, courtesy of Barbizon Lighting

glass. When the light turns on, the glass gets extremely hot and the oil you left on it begins to boil. This will cause the glass to bubble and eventually burst. This, of course, will break the filament and the light will go out with a bang—invariably during the most serious, quietest, hardest-to-get shot. So, always use gloves to handle and replace the lamps. Also remember that since these lamps generate light from heat, they get extremely hot, very fast—and so do the fixtures these lamps are in. You will need gloves to work with tungsten lighting units.

Also, be careful when lowering the light. The filament is the most delicate during the seconds when it turns on and turns off. Turn it on, wait a beat, then raise it. Turn it off, wait a beat, then lower it. This will extend the life of the lamp.

Fluorescent

First introduced at the 1939 World's Fair, fluorescent lamps send electricity through a vacuum tube with mercury vapor inside. The electricity causes the vapor to emit ultraviolet wavelengths. The inside of the tube is lined with a phosphor paint whose molecules vibrate from the ultraviolet and thus glow, giving off light. This is called generating light through radiant emission. Since the light is generated through vibration, the light source is noncontinuous. In other words, it flickers, generally so fast our eyes can't detect

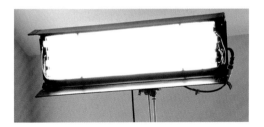

PHOTO 2.16 Kino Flo 4-bank × 4-foot fluorescent unit

it, but it flickers nonetheless. This is important to be aware of because a camera shooting at a high frame rate, in order to play back slow motion, can see the flicker of the fluorescent light, and the shot will be unusable.

This lamp is not a point source but rather a broad soft light. It is missing some colors of the spectrum and often possesses a lot of green. However, it is relatively cool to the touch, doesn't generate much heat, and produces more lumens per watt than a tungsten lamp. So, they are more economical. This is why they are so common in the ceilings of office buildings, schools, and other buildings. In 1989 Kino Flo created the first 3,200K tungsten color-balanced fluorescent lighting units with a more even color spectrum and virtually no extra green wavelengths. They also created 5,600K lamps as daylight-balanced lamps. Today Kino Flo lights are common on most shoots, and now almost all lighting instrument manufacturers make their own fluorescent units.

The warning here is that fluorescent tubes can break rather easily if manhandled. And when they break they shatter, scattering glass and mercury vapor, which are both harmful to humans. I have seen them shatter on shoots and have accidently dropped one myself. It's very messy and embarrassing. So care must be taken when handling and transporting fluorescent units. Also, as they require a ballast to work, fluorescents cannot be run through a dimmer. If you plug one into a dimmer and dim it, you will burn out the ballast. Some units have internal dimmers on the unit, but often as these units dim, they turn slightly magenta.

HMI

Hydrargyrum medium-arc iodide—now you know why we all just say HMI—is basically an internal arch light. The lamp has mercury gas mixed with metal halides in a quartz glass envelope. When turned on, a tremendous surge of electricity runs up the metal poles inside the lamp and an electrical arc strikes between them. It's lightning in a bottle. The mercury gas with metal halides glows—and the light emanating is equal in texture and color to the sun—or a lightning bolt. It is hard, daylight blue light, usually 5,600K. These lights were invented for shooting outdoors or inside in a location with a lot of windows and sunlight. This method of creating light has a very

PHOTO 2.17 1,200-watt HMI Fresnel, courtesy of ARRI

high lumen-per-watt output. So the light is much brighter than a same wattage tungsten unit. HMIs get very hot and require gloves to work with. Also, they cannot be dimmed, as they use a ballast. Some ballasts have dials on them which serve like dimmers but usually can only lower the light output up to one full f-stop.

The ballast is not inside the unit housing but rather a very large metal box attached to the light by a header cable. These ballasts are heavy and have on them breaker switches and on/off switches. It is general practice to set the switch to "on" on the head—the light unit—and operate the light from the ballast using the on/off switch there. This is for a variety of reasons, the most obvious being that usually HMIs are positioned very high up either on high-rising stands or on scaffolding. It's easier and faster to turn the light on and off on the ground than to keep climbing up and down a ladder. Also, the standard practice is to line up all the ballasts next to each other in one place and run header cables out to where each light is positioned. This way the lights can be turned on and off by one person very quickly, and the power distribution can be managed more easily, as any HMI with a wattage above 1,800 watts requires 220-volt power.

HMI lights take a minute to come up to full intensity and color, which we call "coming up to speed." Also, they take a lot of extra electricity to strike (turn on). This means they surge when they turn on, pulling more power than they are rated for when they've come up to speed. A 1,200-watt light will take 15 amps when striking. This is something you have to be aware of when distributing your power when using HMIs. You could trip a breaker—or worse—when turning them on.

HMIs flicker, because it's alternating current. But they have settings on their ballasts for "flicker-free" operation. This is too complicated to explain—it makes the ballast run on a square wave—but the thing to remember is that on this setting the ballasts can sometimes hum. Whenever I'm asked "why do they hum?" I answer "because they don't know the words." All that matters is that they do, and the soundperson might complain. DO NOT ever throw a blanket over the ballast. Ballasts get very hot and require air cooling. Throwing a blanket over it could make it burn out, and possibly start the blanket on fire. The solution is to hang a sound blanket in front of the ballast or move the ballast so that it is behind something, such as the other side of the equipment truck or around the corner of a building, so that the hum sound doesn't get picked up by the soundperson.

Always protect the ballasts from rain and water. Also, it is common practice to ground each HMI light if you are working in a moist environment, as HMI units have a long history of "leaking" electricity, which can shock anyone who touches them. This doesn't happen as often as it used to; the manufacturers have addressed this issue very seriously since the 1980s when a few electricians died from HMI leaks (this was when the technology was in the early stages and usually entailed the lights being on beaches or in puddles) and have made HMIs very safe now. If it begins to rain, we always place rain hoods over the HMIs, which protects them from getting wet and protects the electrics from getting shocked. Also, if a lot of rainwater strikes the lens of a hot HMI, it can shatter the glass. In a light rain the heat from the light evaporates the rain before it can touch the lens, but in a heavy rain with wind, all HMI units are always shut down and unplugged.

LED

Light-emitting diodes are one of the latest developments in lighting technology. Invented in the 1960s, it became common in architectural and display lighting. Only recently has it become a viable source for film, theater, and video lighting. Using LEDs for film lighting was pioneered by Litepanel, but now many other manufacturers make LEDs, and the quality and reliability of these units varies greatly. The advantages of an LED is that it produces more lumens per watt and generates very little heat. Also, LEDs have a very long life span, close to 50 years. They work by sending electrical current into phosphorus encapsulated in a tiny piece of plastic called a diode. The electricity makes the phosphorus give off light—bright bluish light, in fact, although the diode can be colored or covered with a transparent coloring.

PHOTO 2.18 **1 × 1 LED Litepanel**

The disadvantages are that the light emitted from the LED is not full-color spectrum, which means certain wavelengths of light—certain colors—are totally missing. This can cause a problem if you are shooting a set or a piece of wardrobe that has a missing color in it. If there is no wavelength of light for that color hitting the set or costume, it will not reflect that color back. The result will be a different color than what you see with your eyes and what the designer worked so hard to achieve. Some people's skin tone actually looks a little sallow when lit with LEDs, and that affects the makeup artist's work. LEDs also don't mix well with other LED brands, as their color spectrums are often different. LED unit manufacturers are actively developing more full-spectrum LED lights, but the few that are almost there are extremely expensive at this time. In the future, LEDs will become much more standardized and common.

At this time, LEDs are used all the time in situations where there is no attempt of making the subject look glamorous, such as in reality TV or lighting inside cars at night. Daylight-balanced LEDs mix well with HMIs and true sunlight, but the tungsten-balanced units seem to have the most problems with color rendition. Also, LED lights produce multiple shadows, as they are composed of a number of small diodes, creating a field of tiny, hard point sources. Diffusion can help smooth this out, and most LED manufacturers supply plastic diffusion filters for the unit, but using these greatly reduces the intensity.

Remote Phosphor

First pioneered by TruColor, remote phosphor is another form of the LED light. These units have a milk glass panel covering the front of the unit. This panel is coated on the inside with phosphor, which, when excited by the LEDs deeper in the unit, emits light. So in a remote phosphor unit, it is the panel itself that generates the light, rather than light from the cluster of LEDs directly.

The advantage of this design is that the unit now produces a bright, even, broad, soft source of light with no multiple shadows. Also, since it is the panel itself that is producing the light, manufacturers can mix the phosphor on the panel to produce a much wider-color, almost full-spectrum light. The units have different color panels that can be slid in and out so that you can change the unit to the desired color temperature. These units don't get hot to the touch and have a very long life span. At this time they are very expensive but are rentable.

PHOTO 2.19 **Remote phosphor soft light, courtesy of Cinco Lighting**

Plasma

Plasma is sun in a bottle—essentially. This is the newest lighting technology and is quite amazing. First developed by Hive Lighting, the lamps use a single-point plasma source that lasts 10,000-plus hours, are flicker free, and produce a daylight-balanced light with an almost full-color-spectrum spread. Plasma lamps are double the lumen output per watt as HMIs and 4 to 8 times the output of standard tungsten lamps. What exactly is it? I'll have to quote Hive Lighting:

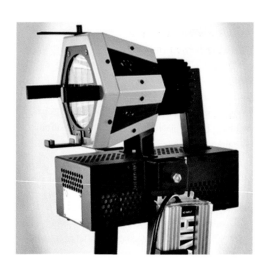

> Plasma emitters use a single point–source bulb, with no electrodes or filaments, just an inert gas fill which is a blend of noble gases and metal salts. When this gas is excited, it shifts its state of matter from gas to plasma, the result being an incredibly powerful light source, essentially a micro-star!

PHOTO 2.20 **Plasma PAR light, courtesy of Hive Lighting**

Right now there are a limited number of fixtures available, which I'm sure will grow, but these units are very impressive in both their output and color. At this time plasma lights are not dimmable. Since these lights utilize a very new technology, like remote phosphor, they are expensive and mainly rented.

SET PROTOCOL

It is important for all crew members to keep their eyes and ears open on set. They should listen and anticipate what is going to be asked for next. If the director mumbles that someplace on the set looks dark, obviously a light is going to be added. The second the DP or gaffer says, "I need an inkie over there," whoever hears it first and goes to get the asked-for light says, "Flying in." This way two people don't go off to do the same function. While one electric gets the light, the other electric will look for the closest place to plug it in. Efficiency is the key to a successful and professional shoot.

Whenever a light is called for, the electric will get it, an extension cord, and a full set of scrims, whether the last two items are asked for or not. Bringing them along is part of the standard procedure of a lighting crew. This way, should the light need to be moved or have scrims dropped in, there is no delay while someone runs off and gets an extension or the scrims. Depending on what has become the standard lighting setup, sometimes the electric will also bring precut pieces of diffusion that he or she will clothespin to the light cord so that it is standing by. The grips will bring a sandbag to bag the light, which is only done after the DP has finished setting it.

Some colleges teach students to yell "Striking!" when they turn on a light. This isn't the standard in the industry, at least not in the greater New York City area. We turn on lights all the time without saying anything. The term comes from working with carbon arc lights, which after being turned on, needed to be struck—the carbon rods inside gently touched together and pulled apart again. This would produce a flash of light; then the light would come up to full strength. Thus we would say "striking" to let everyone know that the flash was deliberate and that the light was beginning to come up and that it would be there soon. Sometimes we say "striking" when turning on HMI lights, as they too give a flash first then slowly build up in intensity. But in my 30-plus years working in the industry, I have never heard anyone say "striking" when turning on a standard incandescent light. In the industry, "striking" means taking down the lights and putting them away. It's only when the light you are about to turn on will blind someone that you might warn people first. If you say "Striking!" or "Watch your eyes," the person you are about to blind will automatically stare right at you and into the light. If you are about to turn on a light that might shine in someone's face, you could tell the person to turn away or close their eyes before you turn it on. But, in general, electrics are not supposed to talk to the talent—that is reserved for the director. So, what we tend to do is wait for the DP to be ready to set the light and then when he or she is watching, turn on the light—because invariably when the DP is watching the subject, the subject will be looking at the DP since he or she is talking. Also, shouting "Striking!" makes the set sound sort of chaotic, which is something to be avoided at all times.

When wrap is called, turn off and unplug every light first. Unplug every extension cord from every light and every outlet. This way anyone and everyone can begin to wrap at the same time. The exception is if sound or video village still needs power to finish up. Also, always wrap whatever you set up first. This way everyone starts wrapping at the same time without needing to discuss who will take down what. Turn off the light, lower the light, wrap up the cable, and carry the light, on the stand, over to the light staging area—the place where all the light kits or bins are stored. Extension cords are almost always wrapped last—because anyone can help with that and wrapping cords can trip people, so if everything else is already put way, everyone is wrapping cords and there's no one moving to trip.

Never run on set—ever. Everyone gets nervous when they see someone run. They think something terrible must be happening. Sets are very tight and crowded, usually with lots of cables stretched all over. Anyone who runs will inevitably trip on a cable, which will either knock over a light, topple a monitor, or yank on a soundperson. Walk quickly and purposefully in as direct a line as possible to where you need to go. But never cross in front of a camera or between the director and the subject— always go around.

Never shout on set. Directors need to talk to the talent, and that takes priority over everything else. Crew members talk softly and tend to use a lot of hand signals.

Always say "please" and "thank you." Film crews and sets try to stay polite at all times.

Always shake hands with every member of your department each morning and say goodbye to everyone each night. It's the civil thing to do, and you get all your work from other people's recommendations. So, the nicer everyone remembers you as being, the more work you might get.

STUFF TO REMEMBER

- The DP—director of photography—designs the lighting.

- The gaffer implements the lighting by running his or her crew of electrics.

- The best boy is the 2nd electric and is in charge of the electricity.

- Open-faced lights are lights without lenses that produce hard light that spreads fast.

- Fresnel lights have a stepped glass lens that focuses the beam of light narrower and thus travels farther before falling off.

- Softlights produce a diffused light that wraps but falls off quickly.

- PAR lights have a reflector that focuses the light to throw even farther than a Fresnel and has lenses or lamps that are interchangeable to spread the beam.

- ERS—ellipsoidal reflector spotlights—are from theater and throw a much brighter and narrower beam than a PAR. They also allow gobos to be slid in that project patterns. They can be defocused and the barrels can be changed, but they do not spot or flood.

- Scrims, which are metal screens, can be placed in lights (except ERS lights) to cut the intensity; a single is green and cuts a half stop; a double is red and cuts a full stop.

- Barn doors are used to cut the light coming out of a unit (except on ERS lights).

PUTTING IT INTO PRACTICE

To work effectively with lights, you will require certain tools. They are rather inexpensive but are essential to being able to move quickly and safely. Anyone working in lighting or with lights must have the following basic items on hand at all times on set:

- GLOVES—Lights get hot, very hot. Use leather gloves and mark them with your initials so that no one walks away with them. Also, cables are on the ground and get stepped on, things spilled on them, and they're run through puddles. I've had to pick up cables from

PHOTO 2.21 **My work gloves, courtesy of ARRI**

puddles in a rainstorm, once through a patch of poison ivy. The worst was when shooting in Times Square late at night and our cables were in the street gutter—you can image what muck they were resting in all night there.

- KNIFE—You will need something to cut gels, showcards, rope, and tie-line with. You can use a pocket knife, a mat knife, or a wallpaper cutter. All work. I have all three.

- C-WRENCH—A crescent wrench, or thumb wrench, is a basic tool that comes in handy constantly throughout the day for tightening and loosening lights and stands. These are required when working in any studio for hanging lights from rigging.

PHOTO 2.22 C-wrench

- CIRCUIT TESTER—Inexpensive circuit testers will allow you to find out if you are getting power. Nine times out of ten if a light doesn't work, it's a lack of power and not something wrong with the unit or lamp. Some will let you know if the power is 110v or 220v, which can be valuable information.

- WOODEN CLOTHESPINS—Also known as pins, C-47s, and #2 wood clamps, we use clothespins to pin the gels on the barn doors of a light. Plastic ones melt; metal binder clips get hot. The industry standard is simple, cheap wooden clothespins. You can always spot electrics on a shoot—they often have clothespins clipped to their shirt or sleeve or on a rope hanging from their belt.

PHOTO 2.23 Circuit tester

- GROUND LIFTER—Also known as a 3 to 2, this allows you to plug in a three-pin Edison plug into a two-pin outlet. Very useful.

- CUBE TAP—Allows you to plug three things into one outlet. Very, very useful.

- BELT PACK—Big enough to hold your tools and C-47s, but simple and small enough that it easily clips and unclips around the waist.

PHOTO 2.24 Diffusion affixed to barn doors with clothespins

PHOTO 2.25 Ground lifter (3 to 2 adapter)

PHOTO 2.26 Cube tap

3 LIGHTING THE SUBJECT:
Motivation and Three-Point Lighting

So, you walk into a set or a location with your camera and lights. You have a fixed amount of time before the eager director wants to shoot. How do you know which lights to put where? First, a lot has to do with the physical location you are shooting in. Following are some considerations:

- How much room you have and how much electricity you have available are factors that will logistically affect how many lights you can use.

- How wide or tight is the shot? This will determine how much area you will need to light.

- What are the actual light sources in the location, or the light sources visible in the set—overhead lights, windows, open doorways, displays? This will give you an idea as to what available light you can use, must block, or must overpower.

LOCATION SCOUT

Hopefully you have done your pre-production work and have answered all of the questions in the preceding list already. Location scouts are essential to creating the lighting.

One of the best things all DPs can do is make sure they have done their advanced homework. It wastes a lot of time to only determine all these things once you show up for the shoot. You should have scouted the location, taken some photos, and done a shot list with the director before the moment of the shoot arrives.

> "My name is on the project and I owe it to the crew, the cast, and the director to be properly prepared for the day."
>
> —JOSEPH DI GENNARO,
> INDIE FEATURE DP

MOTIVATION

Motivation in lighting means justifying why the lighting is the way it is—its angle, texture, color, and intensity. One of the first things a DP does when approaching a lighting setup is to consider what the logical source of the light in the scene would be. Determining this will give a clue as to what angle, what texture, what intensity, even what color the main light should be. The motivation for your light source may be actually seen in the shot—such as a desk lamp, a candle, a TV, a computer screen, a fireplace, or a window—but it doesn't have to be, so long as it is a logical source of light for the setting.

Cinematographer Peter Stein tells his NYU graduate cinematography class every year that it's always a good idea to have a shot at some point in your scene where the viewer can see the

> "I go into a room and let that room inspire me. I look at what I like and how can I enhance, keep, and control it."
>
> —ELIA LYSSY, DOCUMENTARY
> CINEMATOGRAPHER

motivating source of light, be it a floor lamp, a fireplace, a window, and so on. This will usually occur in your establishing wide shot or in your master shot. But once it's introduced, even if it is never seen again, viewers will accept that the light source they saw is creating all the illumination throughout the rest of the scene. Once viewers see where the light is coming from, even for an instant, an illusion of reality is established.

If shooting in a real location, we first start by looking at where all the light is naturally coming from that is illuminating the area. Most rooms will have overhead lighting fixtures of some sort. Unfortunately, overhead lighting is not generally the most flattering, as it casts shadows under the eyes, nose, and chins of our subjects. Often we will unscrew light bulbs or tape black garbage bags or showcards over the ceiling lights that are above our subject in order to allow us to sculpt the light the way we want it and get rid of unflattering shadows. If we are shooting a scene in a factory, or warehouse, or an unhappy claustrophobic office, we may want to have our primary source of light come straight down from above. But we might also decide to place a lamp on a desk, or position the subject to be near a window and turn off or block out the natural overhead lights to make the office light more flattering or dramatic. It all depends on what look you want for the scene.

The major thing to keep in mind is that you should position your subject to the camera, not the other way around. Try to place your subject in the best position to allow you to control the light in the room, allow you to light the subject with your own lights, and make the picture look good. We can have the subject near a window and position the camera so as not to see out the window, just showing an edge of the window frame. Now we can augment that light with our own units just outside of the camera view and make it look like the light from the window is lighting our subject.

If we are shooting in a set, we have to look for practicals—prop lights that are part of the set design and set dressing—windows, doorways, and anything else that could give us a motivation for light coming into the shot. Some sets, such as a store, office, or hallway, motivate overhead lighting even though there may not be any actual ceiling—because if it were a real location, there would be overhead lighting.

Determining our motivation for our lighting is part of creating an illusion of reality for the viewer and gives us an initial approach to how to light a scene. There are times when there may not be a clear motivation for the lighting, such as in dream sequences, fantasies, supernatural events, and of course, music videos. The DP will consider what will work best for the scene—what will best support the director's vision and the moment in the script. If we want the audience to believe what is happening, we have to think about motivated lighting. If the audience is suspending disbelief for this scene, we can do whatever looks cool. But whatever we do, there is a basic method for lighting a subject that we always consider while approaching our lighting.

THREE-POINT LIGHTING

Three-point lighting is a simple theoretical method of lighting a subject. It should be looked at as a foundation on which to work from and not necessarily a rule. Think of it as a guide to beginning to design your own lighting that most fulfills the needs of the scene and your own personal creative design.

The idea comes from the Stanley McCandless stage lighting method that states that each acting area on a stage should be lit by three lights—one 45 degrees to the right of the subject, one 45 degrees to the left, and one directly behind the actors. All three should be aimed down at 45-degree angles.

Why 45 degrees to each side? In theater it allows the entire audience to see the actors no matter which side of the theater they are sitting in. Each light illuminates the face of the actors

> **"Three-point lighting is a concept and a great springboard to lighting."**
>
> —GUS DOMINGUEZ,
> TV LIGHTING DIRECTOR/DP

from each side and puts light into the shadow areas caused by its complement. The light directly behind provides a backlight rim that separates the actor from the background.

Why 45 degrees above? In theater, so that the lights are up and out of the way of the audience (who sit below, equal to and above the stage level), stays away from flying set pieces, and still gives enough spread to light the entire acting area rather evenly, yet doesn't produce too-severe shadows under the eyes and nose of the actor.

In film this method was slightly modified. The lights are positioned not in relationship to the subject, but in relationship to the camera. One light will be your key light—this is your brightest light, your motivated source light as discussed above. Common convention states that this is positioned to be 45 degrees off to one side of the camera and pointed down at a 45-degree angle toward the subject.

The next light is your fill light—to fill in the shadows caused by the bright key light. The fill light is lower in intensity and in practice is almost always softer or fully diffused. This is positioned 45 degrees to the other side of the camera. The fill light should not cast a shadow of its own. We can control our contrast by how bright we make the fill light in comparison to the key light. Common convention also says that this light should be pointed down at a 45-degree angle.

In three-point lighting theory, the backlight is positioned behind the subject opposite the camera, to provide a rim of light on the subject that separates the subject from the background—thus providing depth and three-dimensionality to the shot. To keep it out of the shot, this light is also, in common theory, elevated high enough to point down at a 45-degree angle. From this angle the backlight can wash the shoulders, hair, and top of the head, effectively rimming the person from mid-back up. The farther back the backlight is placed, the more of the entire torso of the subject can be backlit. And when there are multiple subjects, either the backlight can be moved farther back and flooded out or a second backlight can be hung.

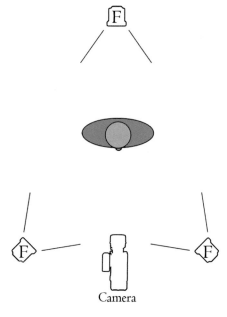

This three-point lighting method is used in multicamera TV studio shooting, such as sitcoms, talk shows, and soap operas. But in most other forms of film and video production such as dramatic TV series, feature films, commercials, documentaries, or location corporate video, this is more often not actually the practice.

In "film" we are not confined by the limits of a theater or a TV studio with a live audience. We can put the lights anywhere we want so long as it is out of the shot. They can come from any angle and any height so long as the light seems motivated or looks right to the eye. And often we don't even use three lights. But we still use the basic concepts of key, fill, and back.

KEY LIGHT

The key light is your brightest light and your motivated light source in the scene, but not always 45 degrees to one side nor 45 degrees up in the air. In fact, it usually isn't. If you are doing a scene in a room with a large window, then your key light would be positioned to aim at your subject from the same side and relative height as the top of your window as in the still below. The fact that the window is behind the actress and couldn't possibly send light on this angle into her face is something viewers never notice. In fact, viewers have been programmed after years of watching movies and TV shows to not only accept, but expect this. Sneaking the key light around to get more light on the camera side of the face has become part of creating an illusion of reality.

In Photo 3.1 from the thriller *Dark Tarot* (2013), actress Lauren Muraski is lit by a 4-bank × 4-foot Kino Flo lamp from the left, a soft bounce fill from the right, and a backlight from behind her, but out of frame camera right. The window behind her provides the motivation for where to position the key light. The brighter part of the window is on the left, so her key comes from the left.

If you are doing a scene lit by a fire, your key light will be down low and aimed up at your subject from the position closest to the fire without being in the shot—or getting burned.

In Photo 3.2, actresses Jade Elysan and Alexandra Landau from the same film burn a book in a fireplace. Their key lights are two 250w Fresnel inkies with two different orange-colored gels, on the floor, aimed up.

If you are doing a scene of someone working by a desk lamp, your key light might be around eye level, positioned to make it "feel" like the light is coming from the desk lamp. That's the function of your key light, to create the feeling that the scene is being lit from a natural or motivated light

PHOTO 3.1 Three-point lighting, Lauren Muraski, *Dark Tarot,* DGW Films

PHOTO 3.2 Low fireplace key, Jade Elysan and Alexandra Landau, *Dark Tarot,* DGW Films

PHOTO 3.3 **Three-quarter back key light on Cuyle Carvin and Ashley Taylor,** *The Cold Equations,* **Ellipsis Films**

source. Most of the time, indoors, that wouldn't be from 45 degrees up and 45 degrees to one side. Sometimes it seems more believable when the key light doesn't come from in front of the subject.

In Photo 3.3 from the sci-fi short *The Cold Equations* (2011), the light from a nearby star is the key light on actors Cuyle Carvin and Ashley Taylor. Knowing that the digitally added sun would be on the edge of frame left, the key light, a 36-degree SourceFour, was positioned off camera left and ¾ behind the actors. The light is around eye height and very sharp. All this combined makes it appear to the average viewer that the light is coming from the star glaring in the lens from the deep background.

Another thing that should be taken into account when setting the key light is which direction the subject will be facing. It is common practice, when possible, to shoot into the fill side of the face. The simple reason for this is that having the darker side of the face toward camera and the key side—the brighter side—of the face turned away from camera adds more three-dimensionality and modeling to the picture. This also holds true for dramatic scenes, interviews, even live documentary shooting. It makes the image more dramatic. The simplest way to achieve this is to position the key light on the opposite side of the subject's nose from the camera. In interviews, we often turn the subject so that they are facing into the key light to get this same effect (more on lighting interviews can be found in Chapter 13, "Nonfiction Lighting").

In Photo 3.4 from *Dark Tarot* (2013), actress Natasa Babic's key light is a 650w Fresnel off frame left, positioned low with light ½ opal diffusion and ½ CTO (color correction orange) gel on it to imitate the warmth of a candle flame. Another 650w Fresnel with ½ CTB (color correction blue) and no diffusion is edge-lighting her, her chair, the napkins, and the chair at the head of the table from off right, as if there is light coming in from a window in early evening or perhaps from another room. Notice how the small stack of mail is positioned on the table to perfectly catch this light. In the scene she has been stood up by her husband, hangs up the phone, then starts to read a mysterious letter from the top of the stack of mail. The lack of fill light on her face and the sharp contrasts of the two colors and angles of the lights left and right help establish what the script called for, a moment of loneliness for the character. This is another example of key lighting the away side of the face to create a more dramatic look. While the actress's face has no fill, some low-intensity soft light was added to

PHOTO 3.4 Natasa Babic, *Dark Tarot*, DGW Films

the front of the table to stop it from going too murky dark and keep the feeling of elegance and wealth established by the art direction. This was done with a 300w Fresnel with diffusion on it.

Sometimes shooting into the fill side of the face simply isn't possible, such as when the subject is up against a wall or the motivation for the light is more frontal. Also there may be times we may not want the dramatic look that shooting into the shadow/fill side of the face gives us.

In Photo 3.5 from a test commercial, actor Mitchell Elkowitz is lit from 45 degrees off camera right, the same side of the frame as the window, with a Chimera Softbox on a 1kW open-faced light. Coming from this side, the lighting helps establish an illusion of reality and lend a natural believability to the picture. The amber color and soft texture of the light helps establish a feeling of warmth, which also complements the wooden surroundings. The hard-edge light hitting the back of his head helps to separate him from the background and gives him some modeling. The light through the back window adds depth and highlights to the image.

The intent of the director was for this to have a happy feeling—a boy at play while his father works in the background. Allowing the key light to be a little closer to the camera warms the feeling of the shot and removes any unwanted drama. The boy isn't about to cut himself or discover anything dramatic. He's just happy playing with pieces of wood, building a toy bridge.

PHOTO 3.5 Mitchell Elkowitz, "Building a Bridge" test spot, Airworthy Productions

FULL FRONTAL KEY LIGHT

There is a school of fashion photography that has seeped into TV commercials and sometimes other media that specifically places the key light directly behind the camera lens, using the brightness to deliberately wash the face and bleach the skin, making the face literally glow. This is how fashion photographers work, with bright strobes allowing them to catch bright, colorful stills of their models as they continuously are moving and posing. Professional actor headshot photographers do beautiful work this way. Actress Alexandra Landau's headshot was done by photographer David Kaptein using this lighting method.

In cinematography this is a very stylized look that is accomplished by using ring lights, which

PHOTO 3.6 **Alexandra Landau headshot, David Kaptein Photography**

are either fluorescent or LED donut-shaped units that surround the lens. This glamorous look can work well in such things as music videos and fashionable commercials. But because of its "glossy" feeling, it doesn't really support an illusion of reality or provide a feeling of time or place. It can be used effectively in a dream sequence or fantasy or to make someone stand out within the frame. This type of direct frontal, bright, soft key lighting is another method that should be looked at as a tool.

DIFFUSED KEY LIGHT

Another common practice is to virtually never light a person's face without some kind of diffusion on the light. Skin and the human face look better in soft light. Softlights can and are often used as key lights, such as in the shots with the boy in the wood shop and with Lauren Muraski, the blond actress against the window. But soft light is harder to control and falls off fast. When a hard light is used as the key, some kind of diffusion, such as a Rosco Opal, Lee 216, or Lee 250 gel, is almost always placed on the light. It looks better, flatters the facial features, wraps around the other side of the face a little, and softens/blends the shadows. This was how Natasa Babic alone at the dining table was key-lit.

Some DPs prefer the diffusion to always be put inside the barn doors of the light. This allows the barn doors to still have some effect cutting the light. Other DPs like the diffusion placed on the outside of the doors, because the farther from the source the diffusion is, the softer the light becomes. Both methods have their advantages, and some DPs will ask for it to be done differently for different scenes. Some DPs will want the diffusion hung off a grip stand and placed two feet in front of the light; others will aim the key light through a 4-foot × 4-foot frame of silk or diffusion. The bigger the frame of diffusion, the softer the light, but also the more it spreads and the harder it is to cut and sculpt.

Another thing to consider is that the closer the diffusion is to the subject, the more it wraps around the subject. Placing a 4 × 4 silk close to the subject and aiming a light into it from a distance back to fill the 4 × 4 frame will produce a brighter, softer light that wraps. The entire surface of the 4 × 4 becomes the source of light. If we place the diffusion back on the light, the intensity of the light hitting the subject also drops, since the diffusion of the light beam begins father away from the subject, thus allowing more light to disperse and not reach the subject.

There are, of course, many exceptions to diffused key lighting as well—such as when the motivated source for the light demands hard light, such as car headlights, flashlights, firelight, and in the earlier still of the actress in the sci-fi film lit by a distant star. Also, when the intention of the scene or the character calls for a harsh feeling, hard light on the face can help support that.

What determines the key isn't its texture or angle or color; it is its intensity. The key light is the brightest light hitting the subject.

FILL LIGHT

The fill light is almost always a soft light, either a softlight unit, a hard light with diffusion gel over it, or a hard light bounced into a white card or other reflecting surface. We can even aim an open-faced light into a nearby white wall and get a very nice soft, wide fill light. Or we can bounce a light into the ceiling if the ceiling is low enough and white. This will produce a soft ambience that will fill in the darkened nooks and crannies. The fill light is most often not positioned at the same height as the key.

In practice, fill lights are most often placed just above eye level of the subject and closer to the camera than 45 degrees. Too high and the fill light will not fill in the shadows under the eyes, nose, and chin. Too low and the fill light may throw shadows up from the nose or throw too much light under the chin. (However, this can sometimes be used to an advantage, which I will discuss in Chapter 13 on lighting interviews.)

Positioning the fill light is best done once the subject is in place and looking in the direction he or she will be looking for the shot. In feature films, stand-ins are used for the lighting, allowing the stars to go into makeup, work with the director, or explore the craft services table while the lighting crew works to light the scene. We cannot light air. Lighting can only be done when we have someone or something in its correct place to light. It should also be noted that the stand-ins are usually the same height, hair, and skin color as the star they are standing in for, and they are dressed in the same-colored clothing as the stars' costumes. This is necessary for the lighting, since a pale blond woman in a white dress will be lit differently than a tan brunette in a dark blue dress—the placement of the lights is not as important as the intensity and perhaps the color of the lights.

A very simple common practice for adding fill light is to aim a hard light into a showcard (an art card that is white on one side and black on the other) on a grip stand. By panning the card toward the subject, we can focus the soft diffused bounce light and change the intensity. Remember, the angle of reflection equals the angle of incidence. This means you have to be aware of where you set your light in relationship to the bounce card and the subject.

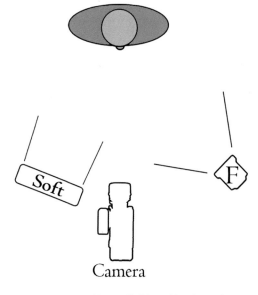

DIAGRAM 3.2 **Key and fill light positions in practice**

"I'm not big on fill light. But some directors will say it's too contrasty, so you put a little white board in."

—ELIA LYSSY, DOCUMENTARY CINEMATOGRAPHER

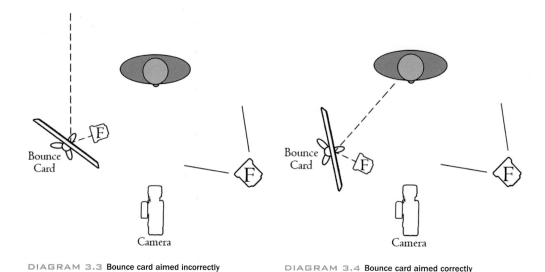

DIAGRAM 3.3 **Bounce card aimed incorrectly**

DIAGRAM 3.4 **Bounce card aimed correctly**

BACKLIGHT

The backlight, in practice, is most often not directly opposite the camera. Rather, it is slightly off to one side, thus providing a little bit of a glint of light off the subject's cheekbone (which we call a kick) as well as serving to separate the subject from the background, such as in the still from the test commercial with the boy. This also makes it easier to rig the light, since if the light were directly opposite the camera, the light would have to be hung somehow from the ceiling; otherwise, the light stand would be in the shot. While we have a wide variety of clamps to allow us to hang lights, it can often be difficult, if not impossible, in some locations.

The backlight, usually a smaller lighting unit, can often be rigged using a grip stand. The grip stand, or C-stand, is placed just off the edge of the camera frame. The backlight is then rigged to the end of the grip arm (whose standard length is 40 inches) and extended out behind the subject. Often the length of the grip arm isn't enough to get the light directly behind the subject in relation to the camera.

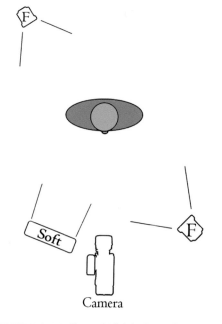

DIAGRAM 3.5 **Three-point lighting in practice**

That's fine, as sometimes if the light is directly opposite the camera, it could get in the shot should the camera tilt up. The light could also shine a flare into the lens, since it's literally aimed directly at the camera. Keeping the backlight ¾ back allows more flexibility for the camera operator

CHAPTER 3: Lighting the Subject: Motivation and Three-Point Lighting

while adding more modeling to the subject by adding a kick to the cheek. Remember, highlights and shadows are what gives us modeling and gives the image a three-dimensional feeling.

Which side of the subject do we position the ¾ backlight? Generally, the side opposite the key light. The side of the face being hit by the key will be so bright that the kick from the backlight will be overpowered and won't be visible. But if we position the ¾ backlight on the fill side, the kick off the cheek will render a nice highlight.

Be careful not to allow the kick or the ¾ backlight to hit the tip of the subject's nose. This calls the viewer's attention to the subject's nose and can become distracting. So when setting the backlight, we must constantly be aware of how the subject turns his or her head during the shot, as we might set the light fine while the subject is just sitting there, but once the scene begins, the subject could suddenly turn to look at something and his or her nose might catch the kick and glare into the camera.

Usually it is important not to make the kick or the backlight rim too bright and overpowering. I say usually,

PHOTO 3.7 **150-watt inkie rigged on grip stand arm for backlight**

as there are times that you might want the ¾ backlight to be the brightest light—say, if your subject has his or her back to a very bright window or a building on fire or some kind of sci-fi portal (see Photo 3.8). In these rare cases, your ¾ backlight may overpower your key or become your key light.

In the example from the sci-fi film *Cold Equations*, Cuyle's face is lit by a softlight low on the ground aimed up from camera right. He is looking down directly into the light. A soft backlight, of a slightly higher intensity, comes from above and off left. His momentary key is the bright white sunlight shining in through the portal on the door—a ¾ backlight.

PHOTO 3.8 **Cuyle Carvin, *The Cold Equations*, Ellipsis Films**

TO BACKLIGHT OR NOT TO BACKLIGHT

In recent years some cinematographers have decided not to shoot with a backlight. They want to stay true to nature and avoid using them. Often it's a matter of whether they can justify a backlight—can it be motivated by a seen or even unseen source so that it maintains the illusion of reality? Light might be coming from a light somewhere else in the room, or coming in through an open doorway or through a window, or bounced off the ceiling or a wall. Light comes from all over and not just from lights. Computers, TV sets, microwave ovens, digital clocks, and cell phones all give off light. In the real world we are surrounded by light coming at us from all different directions, in all textures, intensities, and colors. What these cinematographers are rebelling against is the old Hollywood look of the bright backlight that glows the actress's hair. Yes, that is usually unnatural (but it is glamorous and can sometimes be exactly what the scene calls for). That doesn't mean the subject should be allowed to melt into the background. Rim and backlight, when done in moderation, is natural and serves a needed and important function. The other method is to add a glow or slash to the background to offset the subject in the foreground (more on lighting the background in Chapter 4).

> **"It says something to the audience whether or not you use a backlight."**
>
> —PETER STEIN, ASC, FEATURE DP

DP Peter Stein says a backlight is another tool in the cinematographer's palette. Whether or not the subject has a backlight, and how strong it is, will have an emotional impact on the shot. So, the use of the backlight is actually more important than just a formality of providing separation from the background. It is a decision that should be made depending on what works best for the intent of the scene. Sometimes a bright backlight can give a happier feeling, while no backlight can give a more tense feeling to the shot.

The main concern most DPs have about backlight is not allowing it to look too theatrical (unless that is the desire). One way to avoid this is to not give each person the same backlighting—in angle, intensity, even texture—and to change the backlight when the camera angle changes.

> **"I only use backlights when motivated by sources in the room. So often the backlight will be quite intense if it's supposed to be sunlight; otherwise, it will be a soft backlight coming from a window, and the reverse angle opposite the windows won't be backlit at all."**
>
> —DAVID MULLEN, ASC, FEATURE /TV SERIES DP

MOVE THE CAMERA, MOVE THE LIGHTS

When you move the camera to change the camera angle, you have to move some of the lights. The lighting needs to maintain the basic direction the key light is coming from, in relationship to the subject and the set, and the contrast between key and fill on the face. Once you move the camera, you may end up seeing one of the lights or stands in the shot. Also, you never want to shoot down the barrel of a light—in other words, you don't want to shoot with a light directly behind or above the camera. This will flatten out the image and throw a horrible shadow directly behind the subject onto the set. The shots won't look like they match once in the edit.

So, you have to relight. Tell the director to go get coffee and talk with the actors while you spend some minutes adjusting the lighting so it looks consistent with the last shot. Don't worry if that's not the way it would "really" look. That doesn't matter. What matters is that it looks good and matches enough not to jolt the viewer. Reposition your key light so that the same side of the subject's face is still being hit by it as before. Move the fill with the camera. Swing the backlight around to stay ¾ behind the subject. It might sound like it won't look natural, but if you don't do it, it will look unnatural.

The viewer sees that the right side of Lauren Muraski's face is the brightest area. For the next shot we move the camera 90 degrees to the right, looking directing into what was the right side of her face—the brightest side of her face. If we didn't move our lights, the camera would be looking down the barrel of the key light. The image would have no contrast and be flat and bright. Viewers may not know why, but they will feel something is unnatural because it won't look like it matches; it won't look real to them.

PHOTO 3.9 Lauren Muraski, *Dark Tarot,* DGW Films

PHOTO 3.10 Lauren Muraski, *Dark Tarot,* DGW Films

The key light is moved off to the right more. The fill is moved along with the camera, and since in a previously shot the audience saw a window behind her off left, a bright, hard backlight is added. This helps to maintain the directionality of the key and the feeling that we are in the same place as before.

But sometimes the lights may need to be moved in the opposite direction to maintain the motivation of the key light source. In Photo 3.11, actress Natasa Babic is key-lit from camera right, motivated by the candles seen on the edge of the frame and in previous shots. Her backlight is ¾ back left with a blue moonlight gel, and a ½ blue soft fill comes from front left.

PHOTO 3.11 Natasa Babic, *Dark Tarot,* DGW Films

When the camera is moved 90 degrees to the right to shoot the wide shot, she is in profile. Her key light is switched to the far left to maintain the illusion that she is being lit by the candles, which are now in the middle of the frame but to the left of her.

The fill is moved to the right of camera, and her backlight has been moved to the far right. Even the background light has been moved 90 degrees so that it hits the wall that can be seen behind her—which is a totally different wall than the one in the previous angle.

PHOTO 3.12 Jade Elysan, Alexandra Landau, and Natasa Babic, *Dark Tarot*, DGW Films

This is maintaining consistent lighting. The simplest thing to remember is that whenever you move the camera, you should plan on moving the lights—maybe not all of them, but almost always most of them. You may even add extra lights just to make everything look consistent and matching.

STUFF TO REMEMBER

- MOTIVATION—When approaching lighting a scene, begin with establishing the source of the light in the scene.

- KEY LIGHT—The brightest light hitting your subjects; it will be positioned to act as if it is light coming from the motivated source.

- FILL LIGHT—A diffused light coming from closer to the camera lens and just above eye level that will fill in the shadows produced by the key.

- BACKLIGHT—A light posited ¾ back and opposite the key that will provide separation and a kick off the subject's cheek.

PUTTING IT INTO PRACTICE

Light someone with three-point lighting, but do it the way it's done in common practice.

- Position the person away from a wall. Look at the light in the room and determine which side of the camera the main source of light should come from. Position your key light so that the height and angle seems to fit in and look believable with the surroundings. Add a soft fill, but do it by bouncing a light into a white card and then aiming the bounce off the card into your subject's face. Position this fill light closer to the camera than the key light. Last, position a hard ¾ backlight opposite the key, making sure you get a kick off the subject's cheekbone.

- Shoot this shot two ways. Have your subject turn to slightly face into the key light. Then have the subject turn to slightly look into the fill light. Notice the difference in the modeling and the three-dimensionality of the image between these two shots.

4 LIGHTING THE SHOT, NOT JUST THE SUBJECT:
More Than Three Lights, Three Planes of Lighting

John Alton, a famous and talented DP from the 1940s, once said that
three-point lighting was seven lights. Wait! What? Seven? Everyone says
key, fill, back! What were Alton's additional four lights?

EYE LIGHT/OBIE LIGHT

The eye light is a standard in Hollywood lighting. This is a very small intensity unit placed just above or next to the camera lens that provides a bright twinkle in the actor's eye. It is often called an Obie light, first created by Cinematographer Lucien Ballard for Hollywood actress Merle Oberon, who was known for her seductive eyes. Most Obie lights ride "onboard" the camera, affixed just above the lens. Modern eye lights are now small-wattage LED lights that are dimmable and operate off batteries.

Wait! Didn't I say never shoot down the barrel of a light? Yep. But the eye light is a diffused and dim light that barely shines any noticeable intensity on the subject. It can help wash out wrinkles on the face, fill in deep-set eyes, and add a nice sparkle in the pupils of the actor at the same time, but all very subtly.

Lots of DPs don't use eye lights, probably as many as do. Since the eye light shines in the actor's eyes, it can be a little distracting to them. Also, if the actor isn't looking in the direction of the camera, the eye light won't be seen in the actor's eyes anyway. Also, often the fill light or some other light, perhaps even a window off screen, will be reflected in the actor's eyes, so there would be no need for an eye light, and adding one might produce a double twinkle in his or her eyes, which could look unnatural. So an eye light isn't always necessary or wanted. But it's always a good idea to have one ready just in case, as a person without a twinkle in his or her eye looks less alive than one that does. Someone without that twinkle can look more sad, sick, or unhealthy (or like a zombie) than someone with one—and in certain cases, this might be desired. So the eye light is both an artistic choice and can support the script or character.

In Photo 4.1 from *Dark Tarot*, actress Jade Elysan has a twinkle in her eye, which was provided by the soft fill light reflected in her pupil, so no extra eye light was required.

> "I always have an eye light on the camera. Whether I use it is whether I need it. Generally you want to see a pinpoint of light in their eyes—especially for the stars."
>
> —PETER STEIN, ASC, FEATURE DP

PHOTO 4.1 Eye light on Jade Elysan, *Dark Tarot*, DGW Films

In Photo 4.2 from *Stable*, an eye light was added for this extreme close-up of the swat team member.

KICKER

Alton, and many modern DPs, add a kicker to highlight the actors' cheekbones. This is a separate light than the backlight. But if we use the ¾ backlight method, we can accomplish both of these things with one light—most of the time. There are times the ¾ backlight won't highlight the cheek, such as when shooting a woman with long hair. The hair will block the kick from the ¾

PHOTO 4.2 **Eye light, *Stable*, Paul Williams Productions**

backlight. So a new light, a kicker, will have to be added to accomplish this. The same is true if you have more than one person in the shot. One ¾ backlight for the scene probably won't kick off both people's cheeks. So another kick light might have to be added to help model the other person in the scene. Photos 4.3 and 4.4 are the same shot without a kick light and with a kick light.

PHOTO 4.3 **No kick light**

PHOTO 4.4 **With a kick light from left**

COSTUME LIGHT

Sixth is the costume light. This was more common back when film wasn't as sensitive as it is now or as sensitive as the new HD camera sensors. Dark clothing would just become visually muddy, and the detail and sparkle of the expensive costume would be lost. Alton would add a side light that would only hit the costume and not the actor's face, adding some contrast and contour to the subject's clothing. While not routine in every lighting setup, this isn't forgotten today. If we have one actor in a bright outfit and a man in a dark business suit together in the same shot, we may want to add a side light to bring out the details in the suit a little more.

The caution here is that if the subject moves around, the lighting on the clothing will change and look odd—unless we have a motivation for that light, such as a practical lamp in the frame that could logically throw some light in that direction, or a window through which a streak of sunlight could come in. Every once in a while, I have had to add clothing lights while shooting corporate videos when the subject showed up in a dark suit and white shirt. Somehow we have to lower the contrast between these two extremes. Our eyes see it fine, but on video either the shirt looks too bright or the suit too dark. Adding a side clothing light, at a low intensity, can help equal this out a bit.

But all of this is only to light the subject, not the entire shot. Besides the subject, there is always something seen in the background in every shot.

BACKGROUND LIGHTING

Alton rightfully pointed out that you always have to light your background separately from your subject. That adds at least one background light. It could be just a diffused wash on the wall or a slash of light, or it could be a variety of lights highlighting various different things in the set. The main thing to remember is that you want the background to look real and three-dimensional, and that generally requires lighting.

On the TV show *30 Rock* (2013), I was the best boy on the rigging crew for the first episode of the last season. We spent our second day adding low-intensity downlights above all the practical light fixtures in each set. Each was pointed down and given snoots (small metal cones that look like open-ended top hats, which funnel the light into a small area) to make nice small puddles of light around each of the set prop lights—the bedside table lamps, the desk lamps, the wall sconces, and so on. All of these lights were put through the dimmer system so that the DP, Peter Reniers, could tell the gaffer, Brooke Stanford, what level of brightness he wanted them set at during the shoot. This type of attention to highlighting things in the background is what really sells the illusion of reality and makes the image seem all the more real and natural. After all, every lamp does in reality produce its own puddle of light. And our eyes register it differently than any camera will. So to make it look more like what we see with our own eyes, lights have to be added to augment the effect of the practical lamps on the set.

And this brings us to our next subject.

THE THREE PLANES OF LIGHTING

Wherever the action takes place—where the actors stand, sit, talk, fight—that is the main area you have to light. But as we discussed above, that isn't the only thing seen in the shot. There are basically three planes of lighting, and for best results and creative flexibility, each should be lit separately. Those three planes of lighting are as follows:

• Acting area—Where your subject is, where your actors talk, sit, and do things

• Background—The area behind the actors that is seen in the shot

• Foreground—The area between the camera lens and the acting area

In Photo 4.5 from the festival short *Stable* (2012), the foot stepping on the gun is our foreground plane, actor Jeffrey Wisniewski is in the acting area, and the pulpit and the rest of the church is our background. Each was lit separately.

> **"Shooting in depth means lighting in depth."**
>
> —GUS DOMINGUEZ, TV LIGHTING DIRECTOR /DP

Since the gun is a major story element, it is lit rather brightly to call attention to it, even though the camera is focused on the actor. It is lit as if a shaft of sunlight is coming down into the church and onto the gun, a lighting theme that was established earlier on the actor whose foot is pushing the gun away. A 650w Fresnel hung off a grip arm was aimed almost straight down to light the gun and the leg. Jeff is key-lit by a hard 36-degree Source Four ERS from the right, high up on a highboy stand. He is backlit by a 650w Fresnel with warm gel from ¾ behind, adding a bright edge. Some of his key

PHOTO 4.5 Foreground, Jeffrey Wisniewski, *Stable,* Paul Williams Productions

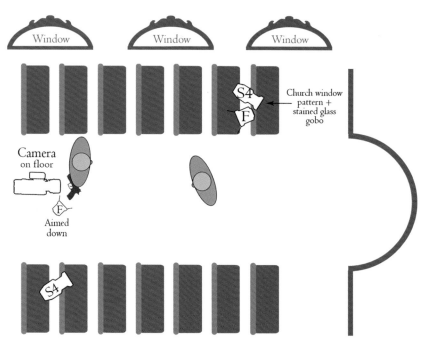

DIAGRAM 4.1 Church scene lighting diagram

light is deliberately allowed to spill onto the pews on the right of frame. The back of the church is lit with a church window pattern and a stained glass gobo in a 50-degree Source Four. Ambient light coming in through the unseen real church windows (which were not stained glass) brings up the overall illumination in the scene.

If the gun wasn't lit with such intensity, the viewer's eyes would be focused more on the cop. Thus the lighting helps focus the attention of the viewer while also providing depth to the image, modeling to the subject, and supporting the emotional intention of the scene. The dimness of the background helps establish that this isn't a happy moment. Even though it's a church and there is light through stained glass on the back wall, it isn't bright or inspiring.

Backgrounds

Lighting our backgrounds, or choosing not to, is an artistic decision. How the background is lit, how it is seen and perceived by the viewer, will help establish not only depth to the shot but also time of day and a sense of place. Dark backgrounds will make the shot feel like night, bright ones as if it's high noon, scattered light and shadow a feeling of dawn or sunset. This is all part of that international language of light. The color of the light on the background will also transmit a subliminal message to the viewer—bluish light has become a worldwide accepted indication of night, while a warm golden color dawn and an orangey color sunset. We will get more into what you can do and indicate with color in a later chapter. What is important to realize is that how your background is lit is almost as important as how your acting area is lit. It's part of the same picture, and thus it is part of the overall message being conveyed to the viewer.

If we do not light the background, it will only be illuminated by whatever ambient light is in the area as well as the bounce and falloff light from how we've lit the acting area. This may, at times, work just fine. If you are shooting in a room full of windows, with the sun pouring in, there may be enough bounce light off the floor to give your background a nice presence. Or perhaps the room is so bright that you barely have to light the shot at all. But even in these cases, a good DP will consider how the background looks and decide whether to augment it in some way. That might include closing window blinds or unscrewing overhead light fixtures or the reverse.

How we light the background can have a major emotional effect on the viewer and thus on how the scene is perceived. Say we have a shot of two people talking on a sofa. First, we light them at the sofa. Now we light the area behind them. If that area is dark and murky, how will that affect the perception of the viewer when listening to the actors talk? The viewer might suspect one of them is lying, or sad, or there is a sinister subtext to the conversation. If we light it bright and warm, it might give the dialogue a different subtext. This is something all DPs are constantly aware of and something they discuss with their director—what is the desired mood for this scene? That will directly influence how the scene is lit, especially the background.

Walls

One thing we try to imitate from nature is the fact that the tops of walls are almost always darker than the bottoms. The reason is that sunlight coming in through windows bounces off the floor and illuminates the bottom half of the wall brighter than the top half. Ceiling fixtures are almost always designed to project as much light directly down as possible. As the light travels down, the light spreads. So again, the middle to bottom parts of a wall will receive more light than the top. And, of course, if we have table lights or floor lamps, obviously more light from them will illuminate the lower part of any nearby wall more than the higher, farther-away top part of a wall.

So, part of working to create an illusion of reality is to light your scene so that the top part of any wall in the shot is dimmer than the bottom of the wall. Doing this will help the image look more real to the viewer and not artificially lit. This graduated background works for both day and night scenes. How we do this is by either cutting or flagging light off the top half of a wall or adding extra light to the bottom half—or a combination of both.

When we set our fill light, it is rather common practice to add a "topper"—a solid black flag positioned horizontally over the top of the unit that cuts light off the top of the background behind the subject being lit. We have to be careful when setting the flag not to cut light off the subjects themselves. So while setting the flag, we have to take into account if the subjects walk around—closer or farther away from the fill light—or if they stand up or climb up anything. Remember, the higher you set the fill light, the easier it is to cut light off the background while keeping light on the subject.

This is another reason for the concept of the 45-degree up angle. A light positioned high enough to tilt down at that angle will be much easier to cut off the background without cutting light off the acting area. Keep this in mind when setting the key light as well. If you want to cut spill light from the key off the background, the higher the light, the easier it is to cut. But also remember that the higher the light, the more shadows under the eyes, nose, and chin.

If there are overhead lights in the location that are spilling too high on the wall so that in the shot the top of the wall isn't dark enough, we can turn them off, unscrew the lamps closest to the wall, or mask them by taping up showcards or black garbage bags over the light fixtures. Sometimes this may make the back wall too dark. So instead of totally cutting the light from the location fixtures, we can partially flag them by taping black cloth called duvetyn, newspaper, or black garbage bags around the side of the fixture frames closest to the wall, and hang it down to cut the light off the top of the wall, while allowing light to spill on the wall lower down. We must be careful not to hang it down so far as to get into the top of the shot.

The second thing we can do is add some extra light to the bottom half or bottom third of the wall. We usually do this with smaller-wattage hard-light units that are positioned off to the sides or from above in such a way to avoid anyone walking through them during the scene. These units are either scrimmed down or run on a dimmer so that the contrast on the wall isn't too severe. The trick is to cover the entire lower part of the wall in the shot evenly. On a recent interview I used a Lowel Tota-light on the floor through a small dimmer and aimed it up into the wall behind the subject. The soft, warm glow (because the light was so far down on the dimmer, its color temperature turned very warm) provided a nice and subtle effect on the wall that helped provide separation and depth.

Another common method is to just aim some hard lights down into the floor and allow the up-bounce light to wash the wall. Of course, the floor must be out of the shot to do this, but it works well. When lighting to imitate sunlight coming in from outside (whether or not a window is in the shot), we often place white cards on the floor and aim lights down into them to get a nice, soft up bounce on the background—as this is what would happen if real sunlight were pouring in through a window. If it's a night scene, often we will aim smaller units down directly onto the wooden floor, which results in a dim, warm upward bounce imitating what light from table and floor lamps would achieve.

Wall Shadows

The next thing to think about is how distracting and unnatural the shot will look if the viewer sees the shadows of the subjects on the back wall. If the subjects move at all, the moving shadow, unless wanted and planned, will be distracting and make the image look amateurishly lit. The higher we set the lights, the more we can direct the shadows of the subjects onto the floor and avoid the wall. The farther off to the side we set the lights, the more we can throw the shadows out of the shot. And the farther away from a wall we place our subjects, the more we can avoid throwing a shadow on the wall. This is why in the vast majority of movies and TV shows, all the sofas and desks are away from the walls, and kitchens all have center island counters. This keeps the actors away from walls and thus avoids distracting shadows in the shot. Remember, position your subject to your camera, not the other way around.

A common misconception by young filmmakers is that they can somehow wash away a shadow on a wall by adding another light. You can't. All lights produce shadows, and by adding another one, you only will end up producing more shadows. I have seen students add light after light, shadow after shadow, and become frustrated and waste a lot of time. Just move the actors away from the wall, or reposition your lights so that the shadow no longer hits the wall. Shadows are part of what gives us three-dimensionality and depth. Use them by placing them where you want them.

Wall Treatment

Another common practice is to add some kind of texture to the background. We do this by adding highlights and shadows to the background. A DP will often say, "I need some kind of wall treatment over there." The easiest and fastest method is to take a hard light, narrow its barn doors, and make a slash of light across the wall. This slash should be motivated—either from a "window" or a "light" that is or could logically be assumed to be in the location. A blue slash will indicate nighttime, a warm one daytime. The trick is to make the slash look as natural as possible, which means not too narrow and not too pronounced or hard-edged. The angle of the diagonal across the wall should indicate the supposed light source. Moonlight and sunlight come in on a high angle, while streetlight comes in lower, and light from a nearby lamp would come in horizontal.

PHOTO 4.6 Cucoloris, courtesy Matthews Studio Equipment

We can also use some kind of breakup on the wall by aiming a light through a wooden cucoloris (commonly called a cookie), pattern cut into a showcard, BlackWrap with different-size holes punctured in it, or through some other object such as a chair back or even a milk crate to throw a pattern of shadows across the background. The trick here is to make the edges of the pattern soft enough that they aren't easily identifiable—unless, of course, you want them to be, such as when throwing a window, venetian blind, or bars pattern on a wall. Something farther from the light source will produce a harder shadow, while something closer to the light source will produce a softer-edged shadow.

In Photos 4.7, 4.8, and 4.9 from the low-budget film *Waiting for Sandoval*, the breakup on the wall above was done by shining a hard light through a milk crate on the floor. The far background was lit with two lights in the back room, one shining through the doorway and another bounced into a white card, adding ambient fill beyond the open door. These add depth to the shot and help the location appear real to the human eye. The breakup on the wall was created by placing a milk crate in front of an open-faced light on the floor off camera left. The bright spot on the frame right wall was created by a 300w Fresnel aimed straight down rigged on the end of an extended grip arm. The grip stand is just off frame right, just out of the shot.

PHOTO 4.7 Wall breakup, *Waiting for Sandoval,* UTPA Films

PHOTO 4.8 Breakup on actors, *Waiting for Sandoval,* UTPA Films

PHOTO 4.9 Jason L. Barrera, *Waiting for Sandoval,* UTPA Films

The breakup falls across the actors as they play the scene, adding drama and a sense of a dingy alleyway, which was described in the script. The pattern was defocused by moving the milk crate closer to the light and positioning it to fall on the wall. It also serves as the key light in this part of the action and for this angle.

As the scene progresses, the key light becomes the 300w Fresnel aimed down into the wall and where the victim ends up being beaten. The light's barn doors were adjusted to create an inverted V pattern on the wall. Notice how the light through the milk crate was used to create the menacing shadow of the assailant on the wall and served to add a back rim on the assailant as well. The milk crate and light on the floor were adjusted when the camera was repositioned so that his shadow would appear on the wall between both actors and not be hidden from the camera. Since the milk crate is right up close to the light and the actor is farther away, his shadow is sharper and more defined than the break pattern of the milk crate. Everything was adjusted to camera to get this image just the way the director wanted it.

Window Patterns

If there is a window in the shot, we often add a slash of light or a glow of light on the wall beside the window, as if a streak of sunlight is coming in. The fun thing is that while this is totally acceptable to the viewer, in the real world this is an impossibility. Light does not come in through a window and then turn 180 degrees around and hit the wall behind it. But none of that matters. What does matter is that the viewer "buys it." Film and TV audiences are so used to seeing this lighting effect over the past 50 or more years that they accept and actually expect to see it. Adding it makes the image look more real to the viewer, and not doing it makes it look like a dull or overcast day outside. Audiences have been programmed to see the slash, so you might as well give it to them.

PHOTO 4.10 **Alexandra Landau and Luko Adjaffi, *A Brand New Day* music video, Clarke Productions**

A simple slash on the wall behind singer Luko Adjaffi in his music video *A Brand New Day* (2012), as well as the burned-out French doors in the background, helps give the image the feeling of early morning sun. The key light, a 4kW baby softlight with only three lamps on, comes from camera right, the same side as the slash. This works well for the image. He could have been lit from camera left, imitating the same angle of light as the slash. But Luko and the tap dancer are not back by the French doors; rather, they are further into the room. So their motivated source would be the bounce of the sunlight off the floor camera right, which would key them from camera right. This is how sunlight works in real life, which is why the viewer buys it. The ambient sunlight (there was no direct sunlight coming through the doors) through the French doors edges Luko and provides a kick on his left cheek, modeling and separating him from the background.

If the window has blinds on it, it is common to shine the slash of hard light through either a real set of venetian blinds hung on a grip stand and positioned in front of the light, or through a showcard with a venetian-blind pattern cut into it on a grip stand. I have cut many a window pattern into showcards, as has every electric and grip in the business. The blind or pattern is tilted on the same angle as the slash. Here the concern is not to make the pattern too sharp but also not so washed out that it doesn't show up. The closer to the light, the more soft and fuzzy the pattern on the wall will become—but the larger the pattern will be. The closer to the wall, the more distinct and sharper the pattern will be—and the smaller the pattern will be. This has to be moved back and forth to get the pattern to look right in relationship to the blinds that are on the window.

An easier way to accomplish all of this is to use a Source Four ERS with a venetian-blind window pattern in it. By adjusting the lens, you can focus or defocus the sharpness of the pattern any way you like. You can also rotate the barrel to tilt the pattern into just the right angle. The thing to consider here is what size lens you will need to get the pattern the size you want it in relationship to how far

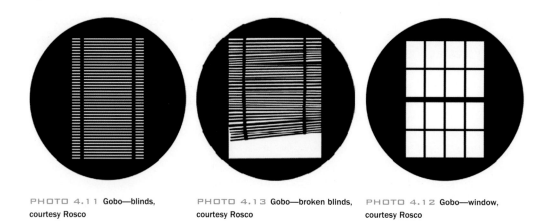

PHOTO 4.11 Gobo—blinds, courtesy Rosco

PHOTO 4.13 Gobo—broken blinds, courtesy Rosco

PHOTO 4.12 Gobo—window, courtesy Rosco

away you have your light. Also, you will want to strike the wall at an oblique angle so that the pattern fans out the way shadows really do, rather than remaining perfectly symmetrical. In Photos 4.11, 4.12, and 4.13 are a few of the numerous window gobos available.

Foreground

Now let's talk about lighting the foreground. In many shots there simply is nothing in the foreground. In these cases, you don't have to worry about lighting anything. But adding something in the foreground helps to establish depth to the shot and a sense of three-dimensionality. Usually whatever is in the foreground is off to one of the edges of the frame and out of focus. But that doesn't mean it doesn't need to be lit. It just doesn't need to be very bright; in fact, it generally shouldn't be brighter or equal in intensity to your main subject. So, whatever is in the foreground usually looks best when lit by sidelight or backlight.

I was the gaffer on an Internet commercial for a major bank. It was one long shot of a retiree sitting in his study with fishing gear while talking to the camera, as it slowly dollied sideways, about how happy he was he started saving for retirement at an early age. The DP, Rick Siegel, choose to start the slow dolly shot with a fishing pole up close to the lens, off to the side, and out of focus. It all looked great and added nice depth to the shot, but the fishing bob was just a little too muddy looking. So I pulled out my LED flashlight, taped on some minus green gel, and we rigged it on a grip arm to shine up on the fishing bob. It wasn't bright, but the side light gave it enough definition that we could tell what it was and it didn't look like an accident.

Deciding to place in frame foreground elements is part of the cinematographer's compositional style—something we call an "obstructed frame." It could be the edge of a door frame or a tree branch or anything. It provides a nice visual element and depth to the shot. An over-the-shoulder shot, a camera framing done very often in scenes with two people talking and especially in interviews, is essentially the same thing. The shoulder of the person we are shooting over is our foreground element. Like any other foreground element, we have to consider how it should be lit. What we don't want is for it to be brighter than the subject we are focusing on. This often means cutting down the light on the shoulder in the foreground, but not allowing it to go black—unless that is the desire, as in the Mrs. Robinson scene in *The Graduate* mentioned in Chapter 1.

Often this means cutting light off the shoulder, allowing it to be only rim or side lit, even if in the previous shot that person's back was toward the light. There is virtually nothing more distracting and visually unpleasant than having a bright white foreground object on the edge of the frame. So we adjust the lighting to keep viewers focused on what we want them to look at and keep the image pretty and interesting. This is all common practice and viewers never notice—they are concentrating on the person the camera is focused on. If they're not, the script and film must be rather boring and you'll have a lot more problems than someone complaining about the lighting continuity. Photos 4.14 and 4.15 demonstrate this procedure.

Susan Adriensen is lit with soft light from camera left, close to camera. A rather strong kicker from camera left highlights her hair and cheekbone, while a ¾ backlight from back right highlights her chin and hair as well. The background is subtly lit but kept dim, while the candelabra is side lit. Alexandra's shoulder in the foreground is left to go dark.

PHOTO 4.14 **Over-the-shoulder shot, Susan Adriensen, *Dark Tarot*, DGW Films**

The next shot is over the shoulder of Susan, and her lighting has changed. Susan's kicker has been moved from behind her shoulder to slightly in front of her shoulder so that the part of her back facing camera will be dimmer. There is still bright light on her cheek and hair, which helps consistency and thus the illusion of reality, but the light is from a slightly different angle. And Alexandra's left shoulder, which was dark in the previous shot, is actually illuminated by her key coming from the right. It isn't bright, but it's not as dark as it actually would have been from the previous shot. The changes here are very subtle, unnoticeable to the viewer, but necessary for the continuity of the cinematography.

PHOTO 4.15 Over-the-shoulder shot, Alexandra Landau, *Dark Tarot,* DGW Films

STUFF TO REMEMBER

- EYE LIGHT—A small-intensity, dimmable light placed just above the lens to add a twinkle to the eye and flatter facial lines.

- KICKER—A side light that adds a kick off the subject's cheek and shoulder.

- COSTUME LIGHT—A side light that rakes the clothing and is cut off the face to bring out the texture and contour of the costume.

- BACKGROUND—The background needs to be lit separately from the acting area and adds depth and indicates time and place.

- ACTING AREA—The area where the subject is lit.

- FOREGROUND—Foreground elements need to be lit, generally by rim light or side light, and almost never brighter than the main subject.

- WALLS—Keep your subject's shadows off the wall. Do this by making sure both the subject and furniture the subject uses are away from the wall. Add some kind of treatment to the wall—a slash or a breakup, or at the very least a low-intensity wash, just to acknowledge it's there. How the background is lit will influence the mood of the scene.

PUTTING IT INTO PRACTICE

Now here is an exercise you can do to apply the ideas and concepts we just discussed.

- Light a person working by lamp light at a desk at night. Position your key light to get the "feel" that the light is coming from the desk lamp. You will have to flag the light off the desk lamp itself—as lights don't illuminate themselves or throw their own shadow. The lamp will be your foreground element, so you will have to light the lamp with some kind of low-intensity fill or ambient light, which could be half blue. You can use a bounce card or a softlight as the acting area fill. Add your backlight ¾ back to add a kick to the fill side of the subject's face. Don't forget to light your background. It shouldn't be black or just murky shadows. It should have some dimension. Add moonlight on a back wall or a light streak from an off-camera open door. Give it a "look."

- Shoot it from at least three angles—the wide establishing shot, a close-up, and a profile shot. Maybe even throw in an over-the-shoulder to see what the subject is working on. The subject could be using a computer, which will give you another light source motivation to work with. Remember to shoot into the shadow side of the face for better modeling. It doesn't have to tell a story, but shooting a variety of angles (coverage) allows you to put into practice the idea that you have to adjust your lights when you change the camera angle.

- After you shoot the scene, cut it together, then watch it and see if the lighting feels like it's coming from the desk lamp and whether the lighting seems consistent from shot to shot.

5 COMMON PRACTICAL LIGHTING SETUPS:
Cross Key, Chicken Coop, China Ball, Bathrooms

Most scenes in a movie are between two people. While three-point lighting is a concept for lighting a single person or an acting area, there are several other standard-practice lighting setups that cinematographers use all the time that allow them to work faster and more efficiently, especially when it comes to lighting two people having a conversation.

CROSS KEY LIGHTING

Cross key is a rather simple and fast method of lighting a wide shot of two people facing and talking to each other. They could be standing or sitting; it doesn't really matter. Simply put, it is a setup where two lights each serve two functions—each unit becomes the backlight for the person nearest the light, and the key light for the person opposite them. The fill light, a diffused source, is then positioned near camera, slightly above eye level and tilted down, with a top chop to flag off any spill light that travels over the actors' heads and might wash the background. Thus we can light two people with only three lights—rather than six as would be the case if we lit each person with three-point lighting.

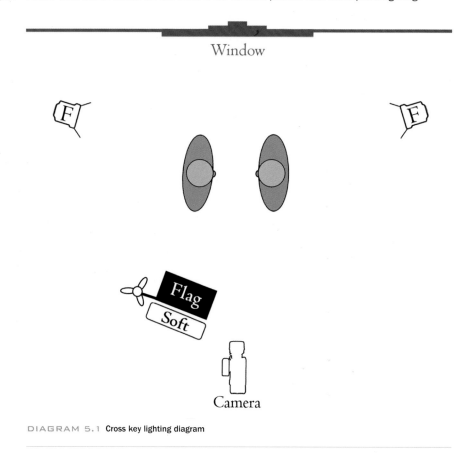

DIAGRAM 5.1 **Cross key lighting diagram**

Why can't we just use three-point lighting to light the entire acting area that they both stand in? Of course, we could. But then one person would have his or her face in shadow, since the person would be facing away from the key light, while the other person would have his or her face very bright, since the person would be facing into the key light. The lighting on the two subjects would be uneven, and the viewer's eyes would be drawn toward the brighter person. Maybe that's what the director wants, so it could work. But often in a two-person scene, both subjects are equal in importance and the director wants the viewer to focus on the lines from each person equally.

What this lighting setup does is give the image some very nice modeling and three-dimensionality with fewer lighting units. Often this lighting setup is used when there is a visible light source such as a window, lamp, or an open door behind and/or between the subjects, thus making it look like the key light is coming from that source. The standard method for cross key lighting is to place the two lights slightly behind the actors in relationship to the camera. Doing this allows each subject to have the key light hitting the away side of the face, maintaining modeling and three-dimensionality, and providing the illusion that the light is coming from the visible source.

Sometimes one or both of the cross keys may work on the camera side of an actor, such as in Photo 5.1 from the festival short *Stable* (2012).

PHOTO 5.1 **Cross key lighting, Joseph Dimartino and Jeffrey Wisniewski, *Stable*, Paul Williams Productions**

Camera left is a 575w Source Four with a 36-degree lens. This unit backlights actor Joseph Dimartino, the man in the jacket, and is the key light for the police officer, actor Jeffrey Wisniewski. It feels like a shaft of sunlight, slightly overexposing the actors' edge, making him stand out a bit more. A 650w Fresnel with a patchwork of colored gel backlights Jeff on the right while key-lighting Joseph. So, different lights were used in this cross key setup. The Source Four imitates the bright sunlight feeling that we see in the back windows, while the gelled 650w Fresnel renders the feeling of light from a stained glass window. Another Source Four with a 50-degree lens and two patterns in it provides the stained glass window effect on the back wall. An additional 650w Fresnel with a patchwork of colored gels was aimed across the pews behind the subjects from off-camera right to stop them from going dark and to continue the feeling of light from an off-camera stained glass window. In fact, this church had no completely stained glass windows in it.

Because this was a tense scene, a standoff in a church, the fill was provided by two LED lights on the floor shining up, subtly casting a menacing look on the actor's faces, while at the same time imitating the bounce light off the floor that would happen if a bright ray of sunlight were coming in on them. (In fact, no direct sunlight was entering the church at all when this scene was shot.) The LEDs were balanced for daylight to match the real light outside the windows. Color correction blue gel,

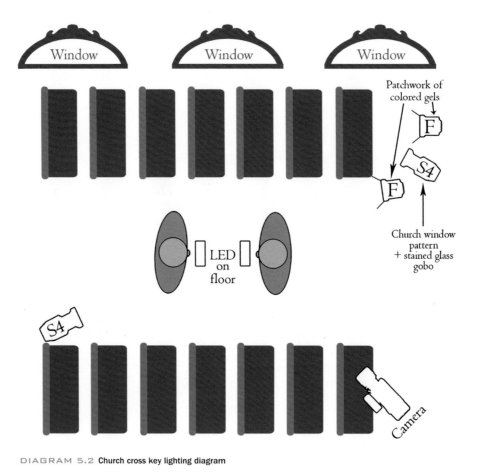

DIAGRAM 5.2 **Church cross key lighting diagram**

known as CTB or Full blue, was placed on the Source Four to make its color temperature match the LEDs and the windows, thus making it "white," while the 650w Fresnel was gelled with orange, red, and yellow gels pasted together in front of the lens to create a stained glass look on the pews.

As mentioned, the background and foreground (if any) still needs to be lit separately from the acting area, but cross key lighting allows a very fast, effective, and unit-efficient method of getting a very nice, believable look. It is commonly done on locations and in studios, shooting inside or outside. (An example of cross key lighting outside is in Chapter 7, "Dealing with Daylight".)

There are a few things to keep in mind when doing cross key lighting. First is that the actors must be aware not to throw their own shadow onto their partner. The actors need to be very aware of where they are and how much space they are taking up. Thus, placing marks on the floor so that they hit the right place is essential, as is asking them not to sway back and forth, which could cast a moving shadow over their partner. Following are some ways to minimize this problem:

1. We can move the lights behind the actors enough so that their shadows don't fall on each other but rather on the floor in front of them. This is generally the best solution.

2. We can set our lights high enough that each person's shadow falls around waist height or below on the other actor. This works when they are standing, but not as well when they are both sitting at a table. Then the shadows fall on the table itself, and that can become distracting.

3. We can ask the director to position the actors far enough away from each other that their shadows don't hit each other at all. This is not usually acceptable to a director, as most two-person scenes require some intimacy, and the lighting should never interfere with the directing of the scene.

In the movie *Annie Hall* (1977), Woody Allen and Diane Keaton walk down a street at night, then stop to kiss. Diane Keaton slightly missed her mark and she blocked Woody Allen's cross key light. Without losing a beat Allen gently places both hands on her shoulders and sways her slightly to one side so that the light hits his face. He says his line, they kiss, and they exit. No normal audience member watching that film will catch what he's doing. But that shows what a truly professional actor Allen is, that he finds his light. This is another solution that you can use to the shadow problem of cross key lighting. Ask the director to tell the actors (or if he or she allows you to talk directly to the actors, you tell them) that if their partner blocks their light, sway to one side or another—or actually gently move their partner within the context of the scene. The main issue is that the actor should be aware of being blinded by a light. If the actor can't see the light, the light isn't lighting them.

The second thing to keep in mind is that in cross key lighting, the backs of both subjects' heads will generally be getting more light than their faces, as they are closer to their backlights than their key lights. If they have dark hair, this may not be an issue. But if one is blond and the other brunette, you may have to use a single or double net to cut down the light hitting the back of the blond person's head while allowing the rest of the light to fully hit the other person's face. If they are both blonds, you may need to partially net both lights. This is something that has to be done by eye.

Netting the light is done with a grip stand and an open net. Open nets have one side that has no hard edge, thus allowing the cut to be more smooth and soft on the subject. The closer to the light the net is positioned, the softer the cut will be on the subject. The farther from the light and the closer to the subject, the more defined the cut will appear.

In order to make the cut work, you will need to look at how the lights are hitting the subjects. The object is to only net the portion of the light that is hitting the back of the near person's head. Depending on where the light is positioned, you will be able to achieve this by either cutting the light from camera side or cutting the light from the bottom. An important consideration is if the subjects will move or not. If not, this will work fine. But if they do move, the edge of the cuts on their bodies might become noticeable. In these cases, a grip stands by each of the grip stands and swings the nets out of the light beam as the actors move, thus eliminating any shadow of the cut.

Another issue to think about is the texture of the light of your keys. The harder the light, the harder the shadow. As mentioned in an earlier chapter, most DPs put some kind of diffusion on any light hitting the actor's face. It looks better, flatters the facial features, wraps around the other side of the face a little, and softens/blends the shadows. Since cross key lighting is all about lighting faces, putting a choice of diffusion gel on the two cross key lights is a standard practice.

Cross key lighting isn't limited to only using hard lights either. Softlights can be used as cross keys as well. This has its own considerations. Softlights are much harder to cut, so netting the back of each actor's head will be less effective. Also, softlights spill more and will wash the background a bit. Sometimes this isn't a problem; in fact, at times it might be helpful. Again, it all depends on the look and the feeling you are trying to build for the scene. What softlight cross keys won't give you is much of a feeling of motivation.

PHOTO 5.2 **Cross key lighting, Natasa Babic and Quentin Fielding,** *Dark Tarot,* **DGW Films**

In Photo 5.2 from the supernatural thriller *Dark Tarot* (2012), actress Natasa Babic touches the ghost of her dead lover. A Kino Flo 4-foot × 4-foot softlight is her cross key (backlighting the ghost), while her backlight and the ghost's key is a 650w Fresnel with diffusion on it. The reason for these choices of lights was predicated upon the script. She is lit in soft white light, as she is mournful, while the ghost is lit with a harder source, as in this scene he is bitter. So the texture of the lighting helps to reinforce the scene. Also notice how the hard light was opened enough to spill on the metal air duct between them and how the stairs in the background were lit with a simple 100w light bulb. This provides both depth and a sense of place—a basement. Also notice the light on the wooden post in the foreground frame left. This is an example of addressing the three planes of lighting mentioned earlier—foreground, acting area, and background.

CHICKEN COOP LIGHTING

Another very common lighting method is what is commonly called chicken coop lighting—also known as bay lights and softboxes. This is rigging a large, square soft light source directly above the acting area. Chicken coops can be very large or rather small depending on the need and the location. The idea is that there is a big, bright soft source of light that comes down and washes over everything and everyone below it. Often there is more than one lamp in the coop, allowing the gaffer to change the intensity of the light according to the DP's wishes by turning on and off the various lamps. Backlights are often added to provide separation from the background and some ¾ kicks off the cheekbone. But if the desired atmosphere is a feeling of isolation surrounded by darkness, chicken coop lighting is ideal.

In Photo 5.3 from the sci-fi short *The Cold Equations*, Cuyle Carvin is lit by a chicken coop, which in this case was a tungsten balanced two-lamp, 2-foot × 2-foot fluorescent unit with a grid to control the spill. Because it was soft already, it didn't require a layer of diffusion across the bottom of the unit.

PHOTO 5.3 Chicken coop lighting, Cuyle Carvin, *The Cold Equations*, Ellipsis Films

In Photo 5.4 from the direct-to-consumer interactive DVD game *Stab in the Dark* (2001), a small chicken coop was hung just behind the hanging lamp, over and slightly in front of actor James Leach's head. A ¾ backlight rims both him and the hanging lamp (hung off a grip arm just above camera framing). An inkie (250w Fresnel) with diffusion was added camera right to only light the side of the hanging lamp to give it some dimensionality.

PHOTO 5.4 Chicken coop lighting, James Leach, *Stab in the Dark*, MTG Productions

The scene was a police interrogation room. The hanging lamp itself had no bulb and didn't provide any light on Jim's face, yet the lighting makes it look like the actor is sitting in a pool of light created by the hanging lamp.

A classic example of how chicken coop lighting can work for a scene, help communicate character, and add drama is Gordon Willis's lighting in the office scene when Marlon Brando is first introduced in *The Godfather* (1972). The chicken coop light box was positioned directly over Brando's head rather than in front of him, so that shadow would fall under his brow, hiding his eyes. As Willis has said in many interviews about this scene, he felt there is nothing more untrustworthy than a person whose eyes you can't see. This lighting gave the audience that exact feeling, by hiding the eyes of the Godfather, making him more mysterious and dangerous—exactly what director Francis Ford Coppola wanted. The irony is that once the studio executives saw the footage, they complained that the scene was too dark and that since they were paying Brando so much money, they wanted to see his eyes. Coppola fought for Willis, and Willis quickly earned the nickname "Lord of Darkness."

Chicken coops are often hung over dining room tables, pool tables, and card tables where two or more actors are seated. In these cases the coop is positioned to not be directly over the actors but rather slightly in front of them, thus allowing the soft light to wrap more into the eyes and under their noses and chins. Light also reflects up from the surface of the tables, helping to fill in the shadows. The next still, Photo 5.5 from the movie *Dark Tarot* is an example.

PHOTO 5.5 **Chicken coop lighting, Jade Elysan, Natasa Babic, and Alexandra Landau,** *Dark Tarot,* **DGW Films**

A large softbox was hung above the three actresses and slightly in front of them. Fill light bounced up off the white marble surface of the island they stood around. A blue kicker was added from camera right to accent Alexandra, the spirit medium, while the other two actresses, Jade and Natasa, do not have any blue on them, making Alex stand out as different. Notice the lighting of the background kitchen walls and the blue pattern thrown across the hallway past the doorway, which all add depth to the image.

Chicken coops can be constructed in any size and often are as big as the table they are hung above. But multiple smaller units could also be rigged, one above each person. Basically, chicken coop lighting is intended to keep the light off the background while providing a puddle of light on and in front of the actors.

Why is this called a chicken coop? Because when it was first done, the softbox had to be constructed by the electrics and the grips using chicken wire, wooden battens, and black foamcore. Sockets were attached to the wooden battens, while the grips made a box out of black foamcore. Chicken wire would be stapled across the bottom of the box, and diffusion gel or tracing paper would be laid down over it. The battens would then be attached across the top with the lamps aiming downward. This construction took a little time, so it was often done during the pre-light.

In Photo 5.6, a men's bathroom set is lit with two large chicken coops built and hung by the grips. In Photo 5.7, local 52 electric Ira Holzman places 250w flood lamps into a chicken coop. Each coop had eight lamps, which were divided into two circuits. So two plugs came out of each unit, allowing their intensity to be more easily controlled. The coops were powered through a dimmer system to give the DP even more flexibility when setting the desired lighting.

PHOTO 5.6 **A chicken coop**

PHOTO 5.7 **Ira Holzman (IATSE Local 52) lamps a chicken coop**

Virtually any open-faced lighting unit can also be used in a chicken coop rig. Lowel Tota-lights are ideal because of how small and lightweight they are.

It is easy to build a small softbox out of foam board available at any art store. Nail- or screw-gun together a square frame out of 1-inch × 2-inch wooden battens, then nail- or screw-gun foam board to all four sides, creating a box. Tape the corners together. Tape diffusion across the bottom, which can be diffusion gel or something as inexpensive as tracing paper or even a cheap white plastic table cloth from the dollar store. Add two struts across the top. Clip onto the struts whatever open-faced lights you have such as Tota-lights, or even clip lights with 250-watt bulbs in them. Use enough units that when aimed down, the entire surface of the white diffusion is lit. Tie rope, sash cord, or twine to the four corners, and attach them to a carabiner or some other hook. Make sure you run extension cords to it before you hang it.

For location shoots and smaller productions, it is common practice to use Chimera or Westcott softboxes, which can be attached to the front of an open-faced light to change it into a softbox, and Lowel Rifa lights, which are collapsing single-lamp softboxes, to achieve the same effect as a chicken coop.

Chimeras, Westcotts, and Rifas come in a variety of sizes, small to large. These are softlight units, but because they have black sides and very wide front translucent surfaces, they can easily be rigged overhead of the actors from the ceiling, from a grip arm, or on a goalpost arrangement. Strips of black cloth (black duvetyn fabric is common practice in the industry) or black trash bags can be taped along the back side of the light to help cut spill from washing the back wall.

In location Photos 5.8 and 5.9 from *Dark Tarot*, the chicken coop is a 750w Rifa rigged on a goalpost over the kitchen center counter. Black cloth is draped down on two sides to cut spill light off the background. One 500 Rifa light and one 650 Fresnel with diffusion were positioned as cross fills to the right and left of the acting area, from about a foot above their heads and at lower intensity than the chicken coop key light. The 500w Rifa has a black card taped to it to flag its spill off the back cabinets, and the Fresnel has BlackWrap on it to do the same.

A 300w Fresnel with ¼ blue was placed just around the corner of the doorway to add a ¾ backlight on the actors. No frontal fill light was used, but light bounced up from the white marble surface of the counter to fill in under their chins and eyes.

PHOTO 5.8 Combo cross key and chicken coop lighting for kitchen scene in *Dark Tarot*.

PHOTO 5.9 Don Singalewitch and Lauren Muraski on set, photo by David Etra

PHOTO 5.10 **Don Singalewitch and Lauren Muraski, *Dark Tarot*, DGW Films**

In Photo 5.10 from the shot scene, notice there is a streak of light on the hallway wall behind them that adds some depth to the image, and notice how the ¾ backlight catches the actress's hair, making her more sexy and feminine, while also giving them both separation from the background and some modeling. All of this works to provide a moodiness, a feeling of an island of light, or that the subjects are a little isolated from their surroundings. In the script, they are meeting away from the others in the story, so the lighting helps communicate this.

China Ball

It is very common practice to use rice paper ball lanterns, with 100- to 250-watt lamps inside, as softlight units in the industry. A piece of diffusion is always taped over the bottom opening so that no direct hard light comes out that could spill on the actor and cause a noticeable streak. In Photo 5.11, Local 52 electric Tom Hamilton assembles several china balls to be used in a bathroom set for a CBS TV pilot.

One was hung in the bathroom itself, and another was hung in the room opposite the bathroom door (see Photo 5.12). The small

PHOTO 5.11 **Tom Hamilton (IATSE Local 52) sets up china balls**

PHOTO 5.12 **China ball in hallway set**

PHOTO 5.13 **China ball with black skirt**

hallway between them was lit with a 4-foot Kino Flo aimed straight down, providing a chicken coop effect, and a 2kW zip softlight was hung in the hallway aimed in through the bathroom door to provide some backlight for the shot in the bathroom.

China balls come in a variety of sizes, and some gaffers will have several of each size on hand just in case. Household bulbs or photoflood lamps can be put in them to make a nice, soft light source that can be hung over tables in diners, over a cash register station, in the center of a small clothing boutique, in a changing room, and in other small quarters. It can work sort of like a chicken coop, except that the light goes in all directions rather than only straight down. However, you can cut and pin black garbage bags or black cloth over the side of the ball you don't want light coming out of. Keep in mind, however, that doing this might make the ball hang unevenly, as there is extra weight from the cloth on one side. Some people build a small wooden frame and hang the china ball below it, and then attach black cloth to the frame for flagging. It usually works best to hang the china ball as low as possible, just above the frame line of the camera. Also remember to add a piece of diffusion inside to cover the open bottom of the china ball, so that no direct light comes out.

Bathrooms

On sets, chicken coops or china balls are often hung in bathroom sets. In real locations, bouncing light off the ceiling with an open-faced light aimed straight up can produce virtually the same visual effect and will imitate how bathrooms usually look. Keep in mind that this will only work if the ceiling is white, and not all bathrooms are nice, white places.

I lit the train bathroom in Photo 5.14 with a 500-watt LED light, rigged off a grip arm above the actress, as close to the mirror as possible, aimed straight down—chicken coop lighting. This provided the depressed and dingy feeling that was called for in the script and desired by the director. A smaller battery-operated LED was placed in the wash basin, aimed up to provide fill under the eyes and nose.

When lighting someone looking in a mirror, it is important to remember that the light must come from above the mirror in order to light the face the camera sees in the reflection.

PHOTO 5.14 Alexandra Landau stands in for lighting of a train bathroom

In Photo 5.15 from *Waiting for Sandoval* (2013), the scene was of two people, both recently beaten, talking in a dingy bathroom. The location was a real bathroom in a public building, so there was no way to rig a chicken coop or a china ball from the low ceiling. Instead, a 4-foot Kino Flo fluorescent unit was rigged over the mirror on a grip stand and aimed down at actress Perla Rodriguez, who is only seen in the mirror. A 650w Fresnel with diffusion was positioned camera left and aimed at actor

PHOTO 5.15 Perla Rodriguez and Jason L. Barrera, *Waiting for Sandoval*, UTPA Films

Jason L. Barrera against the wall, but was flagged off the mirrors and the actress. Both lights were placed as high as possible and aimed downward to give a look similar to a chicken coop. A bounce card was against the right wall just out of frame to bounce some fill onto the back of Jason and the side of his face turned toward the camera. Notice how care was taken to make the top of the walls dark, which helps add both realism and a sense of loneliness to the image. The soft light bouncing off the white tile floor gives the image enough fill to see into the shadow areas, yet the overall feeling of the scene is depressing and dingy. The high contrast, allowing parts of the faces to slightly overexpose, helps reinforce the desired brutal feeling.

Not all bathrooms have to be dreary. Photos 5.16 and 5.17 are from a cinematography class project where the students had to shoot a few shots of a female spy getting prepared in a bathroom. For the leg shot (a tilt up following the garter gun), they used a 300w Fresnel as the side light from the floor and bounced a 1kW open face into the right wall. For the mirror shot, they bounced the 1kW into the ceiling, added steam, and moved the 300w Fresnel as a hard back.

PHOTO 5.16 Bathroom leg shot, FDU cinematography class project

Basically, one bounced light into the ceiling did the job of key and fill. White walls bounce a lot of diffused light, so a nice, even ambiance of soft light bounced all around that small bathroom like a ball in a handball court. The 300w Fresnel was moved around as an accent light to provide depth and modeling. It was simple and fast—and looked much better than using the real light in the bathroom, which was a fluorescent that produced ugly shadows under the nose and chin and was greenish. So if they white-balanced under it, the camera would have added magenta to the backlight.

PHOTO 5.17 Bathroom mirror shot, FDU cinematography class project

STUFF TO REMEMBER

- Cross key light uses three lights to light two people talking, where one person's key light serves as the other person's backlight, and a softlight fill is positioned by the camera.

- Position the cross keys on the far side of the subjects from the camera to throw their shadows down and in front.

- Make the actors aware of not blocking their partner's light and throwing a shadow on each other.

- Cross key light works exceptionally well when there is a visible light source in the background between the subjects, such as a window, doorway, or lamp.

- Chicken coop lighting is a board softlight hung overhead almost straight down, creating a puddle of light that the actors are on the edge of.

- Chicken coop lighting still requires backlight for the subjects and sometimes a little extra frontal or side fill.

- Position the chicken coop over but slightly in front of the subjects so as to fill in some light under the brow, nose, and chin, unless you want them looking mysterious and menacing.

- Use black cloth or black garbage bags to skirt the coop and keep the spill light off the background.

- Light your background and foreground separately.

- Chicken coops can be "homemade," or Rifa lights, Westcotts, or Chimeras can be used for a similar effect.

- Other softlight units can be rigged to render a similar visual effect as a chicken coop when the circumstances make it impossible to hang a softbox.

PUTTING IT INTO PRACTICE

- Find a location where you can stage two people standing and talking to each other with a window, lamp, or open doorway behind and between them. If the latter, make sure there is light in the open doorway. You may have to add some light in that area yourself. Use cross key lighting to light the scene as if the light from the source behind them is lighting the actors. If you have nets, try cutting down the intensity of the light on the backs of each person's head. Don't forget to add some kind of frontal fill softlight. You can do this with a softlight or bounce a hard light into a white card. Also try to add a top chop to flag the fill light off the background. Add some kind of lighting treatment to the background. Shoot a wide shot, then a close-up of each person.

- Find a location where you can stage two to four people sitting around a table. Rig chicken coop lighting above the table, making sure that the light is above but also in front of the main person you are focusing on. Add a backlight and some kind of lighting treatment on the background.

- Shoot one wide shot and then an over-the-shoulder shot of each person at the table. You may have to adjust the chicken coop for each shot as well as move the backlight each time. Also, remember that the shoulder you are shooting over is your foreground (as discussed in Chapter 4), so that needs to be underlit each time. Shoot each over the shoulder with and without a white card on the table under the subject's face, to see how much light you can bounce up from the overhead chicken coop.

6 LIGHTING FOR MOVEMENT: Subject and Camera, Ambient Soft Lighting

We've discussed lighting a single person (three-point lighting), lighting two people talking (cross key lighting), and lighting people seated around a table (chicken coop lighting). Now let's discuss how to light for people getting into these places. Also, sometimes the actors will move around within the scene and the shot. There is nothing worse for a DP than thinking the subjects will be staying put and then see them walk around or change places. The DP must be aware of the blocking before the beginning of the lighting. This is why the standard practice is as follows:

- Block
- Light
- Rehearse
- Shoot

The first order of business is for the director to block the scene, with the DP, boom man, gaffer, and key grip all watching. The director and DP set where the camera will be placed, the 2nd assistant camera places actor marks on the floor, and then the DP lights the scene while the actors depart for makeup, wardrobe, and working with the director. Knowing where the actors will move during the shot allows the DP to light for both their start and end positions and everywhere else that they move.

ROOM TO ROOM

A lot of scenes have actors entering, walking up, and stopping at the place where the majority of the scene will play out. Common practice is to light the ending first—the place where they stop and the majority of the scene happens. Since this is the primary acting area, it gets the most attention in lighting. It can be lit via three-point lighting, cross key, or chicken coop, or by any combination. Since the actors stay here the longest, we need to cater to this image first.

As mentioned, marks are made with tape on the floor for where the actor will stop. Someone must now stand in for the actor—because as mentioned in an earlier chapter, one cannot light air. We look at the framing from the camera—what is in shot and what is out? We look for a motivated source to justify our key light and a way to rig a backlight. We also position our softlight fill near the camera for the end position.

Another thing to keep in mind is when one person joins another, once that person arrives, the lighting needs to look good on both of them. If a person joins someone at a table, when the second person sits down, the original lighting should have been set to include him or her. If the person walks up to someone working in a dark room by a desk lamp, the standing person must be lit as if the light from the lamp is also illuminating him or her. If the seated person stands to talk to the arriving person, he or she too must stand up into light that looks like it's coming from the desk lamp. There should be no shadow cast on either person as the subjects move into their final positions—unless you want that for some dramatic purpose. In other words, the lighting must anticipate where both actors will end up, which might be different from where they both start.

Once we've lit the end mark, we look at the start mark. Where does the moving subject begin or enter from? If the subject just moves quickly from the first position to the end, perhaps it doesn't need a lot of extra lighting. But it will need enough that when they first enter, the light looks appropriate in terms of brightness, angle, texture, and color for its location and surroundings. It may or may not match with the lighting of the end mark. If the subject is moving from one room to the next, we need to light the room the subject starts in to be believable. What is the motivated light source in the back room? What angle would it be coming from? What color, texture, and intensity would it have? If there is another person in the foreground, should he or she be lit at the same intensity? Should the background person be brighter for a second in order to get the viewer's attention? Should the foreground person always be brighter so that the viewer stays more focused on him or her? Where the viewer's attention should be focused is an important question the DP must ask the director before lighting the shot.

After we light the subject's end mark and start mark, we light the path the subject takes to get there. A major way we perceive movement is by seeing someone pass through light and shadow. By seeing light and shadows move across a subject, our brain realizes that the person must be moving through space. This is part of using lighting to provide the illusion of reality and adding depth to the shot. So, as our subject moves from the opening mark to the final mark, it helps if the subject is not evenly lit but passes through some differences of light and shadow. How drastic the difference will be between the light and shadow moving across our subject's face and body is a dramatic choice that should be dictated by the scene and the director.

In the following series of stills from the film *Stray* (2012), actor Aaron Lustig brings a bag of ice from the kitchen, passing through the dining room to actress Michelle Page sitting in the living room. As he does, he moves through several lights. First, we must determine a desired feeling and look based on the script and the director. This is a drama, in which the character is a widower who has a nice,

PHOTO 6.1 **Aaron Lustig's end mark, *Stray*, Nena Eskridge Productions**

quiet life. The intent of the scene was to show how welcoming, calm, and cozy his home was. The time was supposed to be late afternoon, just before sunset. So the lighting had to be warm, soft, cozy, and welcoming. This was a real location, and we were limited to the amount of units we had and the amount of electricity available. Even though we moved the sofa forward into the room, the camera had to be positioned outside on the porch shooting in through an open window in order to get the angle with the view needed.

The end mark was lit first. A 750w Rifa softlight was positioned off left, high up to allow spread to side-light both Aaron and Michelle. We would be shooting over Michelle's shoulder by the end of both their moves. This wasn't gelled, and since we were shooting for daylight balance, it meant that light would record warm amber in color. A 1,200w HMI PAR light with a medium lens was placed on the porch aimed in through a window with blinds about 5 feet camera left. This produced a soft venetian-blind pattern that would fall into the room and on Aaron, but also a nice amount of ambient fill light for the entire living room as the bright light bounced off the floor and unseen right wall. We wanted the blind pattern not to strike Aaron's face but to fall below his chin and over his chest. This worked for the emotional context of the scene. When they walk into the house, Michelle's character says some things that confuse him—his character is in the dark as to what this woman actually wants. Allowing his face to go a little dark subliminally helps communicate this.

No fill light was added, other than whatever ambient skylight filtered in through the open window the camera was shooting through. There were windows on the unseen camera right wall, which were shuttered closed.

A 500w Rifa was placed at the top of the stairs frame left. Eventually in the scene the actress will go up those stairs. But even if she didn't, adding light coming down the stairs makes the room look more real, like there is more of this character's world up there. This light was also ungelled, so it too would photograph warm—matching the walls.

Aaron Lustig's start mark, *Stray*, Nena Eskridge Productions

In Photo 6.2, Aaron is lit by a PAR light coming through the dining room window, which also lights the wall to his right and adds modeling to the knickknacks to his left.

In the kitchen, a 650w Fresnel with half CTB blue gel and diffusion on it was aimed at the open pantry door. Leaving the pantry door open to provide a white background beyond the kitchen's swinging door was a decision made in order not to see farther into the kitchen, which would have been darker. Exactly how far open the pantry door needed to be was set to camera.

The dining room and the foyer were both lit with the same 1,200w HMI PAR with a wide lens (the front door is off right by the small table). It was positioned far enough from the house to allow direct beams of light to travel in through both the dining room window and the front-door window. This unit was positioned not very high, perhaps 6 feet, in order to give a later-afternoon, almost sunset feeling to the image, which was aided by the light's hard texture and its stark whiteness.

As Michelle passes carrying the photo frame, she sweeps close enough to the camera that her head is mostly unseen. But her body moves through the venetian-blind pattern coming in through the window left of camera, and she is side-lit by the warm Rifa light. Thus, she moves through light and shadow as she finishes her blocking and goes to sit on the sofa.

In Photo 6.3, Aaron has moved to the center of the dining room, closer to the light outside, thus becoming brighter in the frame and more side-lit.

In Photo 6.4, he has passed through a short shadow and is now lit by the light coming in through the front door, which is also accenting the stair post.

Notice that as he moves through that light, he throws a soft shadow over the inside doorway edge to his left. Also, as the camera pans to maintain nice framing, the edge of the living room wall appears camera right, revealing the venetian blind pattern and giving a sunset feeling to the image. The bright spot on the wall is camera right, which is where Aaron's key light is coming from. So, even though the light creating the pattern is actually coming from camera left, it helps create the continuity of the sun coming from camera right.

PHOTO 6.3 **Side-lit by HMI coming in through dining room windows off right**

PHOTO 6.4 **Side-lit by HMI coming in through door off right**

In Photo 6.5, Aaron has totally left the hard side white light from the PAR and is now keyed by the warm Rifa light off left. He is starting to become confused by what the other character in the scene is saying.

Now he is walking into the venetian-blind pattern, which can be seen on his lower chest. His intensity has dropped, and he is in warmer light coming from the opposite side. This is his home, his warm place, but this stranger has come in and suddenly said something that puts him "in the dark." He isn't the brightest thing in the frame. The splashes of light on the right and the edge light on the stair post are.

PHOTO 6.5 Lit by warm Rifa light off left

In Photo 6.6, Aaron has reached his end mark. His warm Rifa key is now a side light, and the pattern has moved up to below his chin. Spill light from the PAR on the porch creating the pattern fills in his face, as does the bounce inside the room and some soft skylight ambiance that filters in from the open window the camera is shooting through. Aaron now blocks the bright splash of light camera right. His chest becomes the brightest thing in frame, so the viewer's eyes move to between his head and her head for their conversation.

So Aaron's path has lead him through three shafts of light, two from the right and one from the left, until he ends up at his final mark. The shifts between light and shadow that pass over him are soft and not severe. He never goes dark and never becomes overexposed.

The lighting plan would be the same if this were a studio set instead of a location, with the added ability to perhaps add some backlights. And if it were a lower budget and HMI lights were not available,

PHOTO 6.6 Lit by Rifa off left, and HMI through blinds on porch behind camera

the same thing could have been done with 2kW Fresnels, but filming after sunset so no daylight would come in the windows. Additional ambient light would have to be added to make up for the lack of skylight, so a few more softlight units would have to be utilized. But by and large this is a rather standard-practice method of lighting for someone walking between rooms—he or she will walk in and out of different areas of light.

When a subject moves in the frame and does not move through light and shadow, the viewer is much less aware of the person traveling any distance. In one of the last scenes in *The Graduate* (1967), director Mike Nichols wanted the main character, Ben, to run as fast as possible toward the camera but seem to be getting nowhere. To achieve this feeling, it was essential that the location for the shot was a place where Dustin Hoffman could run straight toward the camera and never go past anything that could cast a shadow over him. If a shadow passed over him, the viewer would know he was moving fast and forward. But because he never passes through any shadows, or any highlights, it feels like he's almost running in place, and it adds to the feeling of frustration the director wanted.

HALLWAYS

In many suspense films, as one person chases another, they invariably end up running down some dark passageways or corridors, passing in and out of darkness and light as they run. This heightens the tension and gives the viewer the feeling that they are lost or frantic. It is common when working to achieve this effect to give the actors pockets of light and darkness to pass through, and often to throw patterns or breakups for them to pass through and to add texture to the walls (as discussed in Chapter 4).

In Photo 6.7 from the film *Dark Tarot* (2013), Bethany, played by actress Natasa Babic, is frightened, confused, and running through a huge, empty house.

PHOTO 6.7 **Natasa Babic in dramatic hallway lighting, *Dark Tarot*, DGW Films**

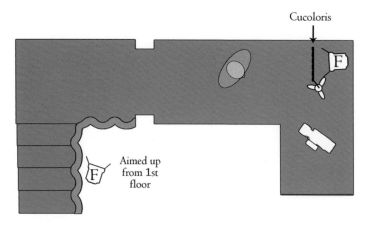

DIAGRAM 6.1 Lighting plot for Natasa Babic running in hallway

A 650w Fresnel throws a pattern on the wall behind her by shooting up through the railing of a staircase off camera left. The pattern not only lights the wall, but also the ceiling that is seen in the shot due to the low-angle camera placement. Another 650w Fresnel was positioned camera right, shooting straight down the hallway through a wooden cucoloris (commonly called a cookie), throwing a pattern on the walls and across her face and body, which she runs through. The angle of the light is such that the camera is looking into the shadow side of her face, giving her some modeling, while her fill comes from the bounce off the wall on the left. The Fresnel's barn doors were open wide enough to allow some spill light to hit the foreground door frame on the left, which added a little definition. She stops momentarily in a predetermined spot where the light will hit her face just right for her to look about in fear.

In Photo 6.8 from the following scene, actress Jade Elysan is also running lost in the house. A 500w Rifa softlight placed in a bathroom off camera left provides a patch of brightness for her to run

PHOTO 6.8 Jade Elysan in different style dramatic hallway lighting, *Dark Tarot*, DGW Films

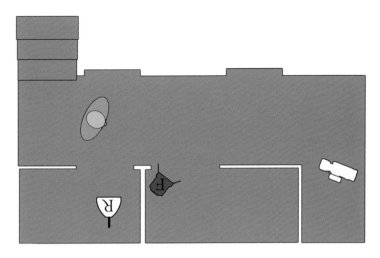

DIAGRAM 6.2 **Lighting plot for Jade Elysan running in hallway**

through. The doorway helps to cut and frame the light, but the soft light coming out bounces and also illuminates the wall behind her. As she runs toward the camera, she becomes silhouetted, until she passes through a 650w Fresnel side light, gelled blue, striking the foreground wall on the right. Both lights are on the left of frame positioned at about head height. There is no frontal light in this shot and no light on the left foreground wall edge, which is left to go black.

These are two different looks for basically the same thing—someone running through a dark hallway at night. One uses patterns for the subject to pass through, while the other uses more radical patches of light and darkness. Knowing that the editor would be cutting between these two shots meant that they had to be lit differently to provide visual variety and to indicate to the viewer that the two actresses are in two different parts of the house. So it was important that they didn't look similar. The DP must always be aware of what will come before and after the shot currently being lit. Some scenes may have to match, while others may have to be different. So the DP must remember how each scene was lit and think about how they might look when cut together.

Placing units off to the side in doorways, behind pillars, or behind furniture that the subject passes by along the path are all ways to hide lights from the camera and give the subject some areas or beams of light to pass through. A perfect example is in the hotel scene of *Catch Me If You Can* (2002), with cinematography by Janusz Kaminski. Leonardo DiCaprio is about to open his door when he sees a beautiful woman down the hall. Look at how Janusz added lights from around every corner. A concern we must be aware of is to never let the subject "burn up"—that is get too bright—as he or she passes by a light unit or through a beam of light. Another concern is to make sure the shadows cast by the subjects themselves as they move along their paths fall out of frame or on the floor. Seeing shadows move across a wall tends to be distracting to the viewer, whose attention we generally want concentrated on the subject—unless we want the shadows in the shot, which can sometimes provide a menacing feeling.

Sometimes both the subject and the camera move together. It is important to plan the lighting so that the camera never casts a shadow on the actor or into the shot as it moves, and that the lens doesn't get hit with any glare.

Aaron Lustig in soft hallway lighting, *Stray*, Nena Eskridge Productions

In Photo 6.9 from the movie *Stray* (2012), actor Aaron Lustig has walked up the stairs and hesitantly walks down the hallway toward the camera. As he does, the camera dollies back. The shot ends with Aaron in a medium close-up. The soft white light in the far room behind him was created with a 650w Fresnel with diffusion aimed at the door, and natural ambient (not direct) sunlight coming in through a window illuminating the back of the room. Aaron's face is being keyed by a 650w Fresnel with diffusion in the room to Aaron's right aimed through the doorway. It was positioned on an angle so that it also would reflect off the white molding of the stairs on the left side of the frame in front of Aaron, thus adding some modeling to the environment and giving Aaron a rim as he walked past the door.

There is a 650w Fresnel with diffusion at the top of the frame left stairs aimed down to edge the railing posts and bring up the wall. Off camera left, on the unseen stair landing closest to where the camera will stop, is a 650w Fresnel bounced up into the ceiling to create ambient fill. Downstairs are actually two lights. The first light is shining up from the bottom of the stairs to light Aaron as he came up, and it illuminates the upper half of the wall between the stairs and Aaron's head. The second light is aimed up from the bottom of a servant's staircase that is virtually unnoticeable; it added more dimensionality to Aaron when he first arrived at the landing.

The camera dollies back as Aaron, in position 1, starts down the hallway (toward the camera). He goes a little darker, only lit by the ambient light from the bounce off the ceiling, until he reaches his end mark at position 2, right outside the bathroom. The door is ajar, allowing some light through and onto his face. He pushes the door open slightly, and the 750w Rifa light inside the bathroom gives him a bright, soft wash.

This end mark was lit first. Aaron was given a mark on the floor, the Rifa was positioned so that the door wouldn't hit it as it opened, and the intensity was set just right to create the contrast we wanted between him in the hallway with the door closed and then with it open. What we didn't want was for Aaron to blow out (become overexposed) as he opened the door.

PHOTO 6.10 End mark for both Aaron and dolly has him in a medium shot

Not finding anyone there, he turns and starts back down the hallway, this time the camera staying where it is and allowing the medium close-up to turn into a wide shot. As the camera pans left to center Aaron, more of the stairs on camera left are seen, which is why it was so important to light those steps from the floor above.

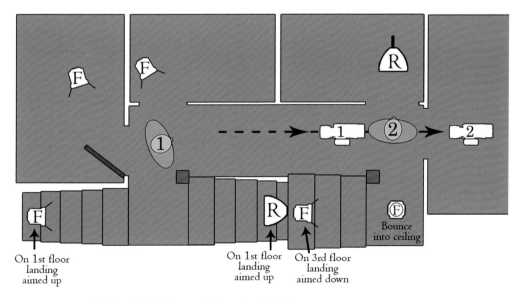

DIAGRAM 6.3 Lighting plot for dolly move with Aaron Lustig in hallway

PHOTO 6.11 Camera remains, becoming a wide shot as Aaron walks away

When the actors or the camera (or both) move during a shot, it is important for the DP to be fully aware of how the framing will change and what will be seen in order to make sure everything will be lit appropriately. Aaron stops back at his first mark now and looks in the room he previously only passed by, finding the person he was looking for. He is lit by the same light as before.

Sometimes we can hang lights above frame to keep them out of the shot. This will, of course, depend on where you are shooting. Scissor clamps allow us to hang smaller units on the crossbars of suspended-ceiling tiles. Don't use any light larger than a 300-w Fresnel, due to the excess weight, with this clamp. Mafer clamps, Matthellini clamps, and studded C-clamps are other devices that can be used to rig lights to posts, pipes, tops of doors, and so on.

PHOTO 6.12
Scissors clamp
(suspended-ceiling clamp)

The main thing to keep in mind is how wide your shot is and what part of the ceiling will be in frame in the background. If the shot is wide enough to see someone walk from front to back, unless you have very tall ceilings, some of the ceiling in the background will probably be in frame. If the camera zooms out or dollies back as the actor moves forward, the ceiling will come into frame in the background at the end of the zoom or dolly. So you have to be careful that no lights or extension cords hanging from the ceiling become visible during the shot.

Another concern with hanging lights is that as the subject moves toward them, the subject will get brighter and brighter, and not at a gradual rate (remember inverse square law?). Then the subject will pass under the light and go dark very quickly. This may be the effect you want, but it can also look like an accident

PHOTO 6.13
Mafer clamp

PHOTO 6.14
Matthellini clamp

PHOTO 6.15
Studded C-clamp

to the viewer. Often when lighting a hallway, we will rig small-wattage lights aiming straight down to form puddles of light for the subject to walk through. Sometimes these will be small chicken coops or softboxes, as ceiling lights are soft sources and not hard lights. Also, using the chicken coop method allows us to cut some light off the hallway walls and keep the light aimed downward. The soft light will wrap somewhat under the nose and into the eyes and give a pleasant, normal hallway feeling. This requires enough height to the ceiling to be able to rig the units out of camera frame. But often on real locations, the ceiling isn't very high.

On the movie *Jumper* (2008), DP Barry Peterson had us rig bare, single Kino Flo lamps to the low ceiling of the hallway of a dive Times Square hotel. Because these were bare fluorescent tubes, if the lamps were ever seen by accident, they would look like they belonged in this junky hotel. Fluorescent tubes are also lightweight, so they weren't difficult to attach to the ceiling using zip-ties and eye hooks. We had to mask the header cables with white gaffer's tape and hide the ballasts on the far side of doorways. We left spaces between the ends of the lamps so that as the actor walked down the hallway, the light would vary up and down a little. The art department painted over the ceiling and our tape, as well as the walls, a sickening lime green, so the image looked truly seedy and rather grungy, even though it was all nice soft light. It worked so well, we felt like we had to go wash after wrapping the lights out.

Depending on the script, perhaps the subject moving through puddles of hard light works better for the scene, providing a feeling of danger to the image, which would be appropriate for a mystery or a horror film. In the classic film noir movie *The Big Combo* (1955), shot by John Alton, the mobster's girlfriend passes through puddles of hard downlight as she runs through the corridors trying to escape her bodyguards. She is stopped in a circle of light that also has a nice backlight for her hair and some fill to bring up her face. She's the "doll" so she has to look good. The two bodyguards are more in shadow than she is, which was deliberate, thus using the lighting to direct the viewer's attention and reveal who is the good guy and who are the bad guys.

I shot a very low-budget film in the late 1970s with a scene where the female hitwoman walked down the hallway of an actual medium-priced hotel we were shooting in. It wasn't possible to turn off the hallway lights and just use our own, which is always the preferred method. So we wedged and taped Lowel clip lights with 250-watt mushroom bulbs into the suspended ceiling and pinned diffusion over the doors to help overpower the real fluorescent ceiling lights in the hallway, which had green in their color temperature. This provided more distinct puddles of light for her to walk through. We should have put minus green gel (magenta) in each fluorescent unit to help cut out the green spikes, but no one thought enough to order it in advance (which shows why a scout is so important). Adding our lights gave the image a more sinister feeling as she walked down the hall, passing under these bright overhead areas, but left the image looking "natural," which was the desire of the director. Actually, the greenish tinge to the image helped it look "unlit" and creepy. The camera was set higher than her eye height, and as she walked toward the camera, we tilted down and panned to keep the lights out of frame.

Today, one can get the same effect by using cheap hardware store clip lights, with the reflector removed to get them higher up against the ceiling, using compact fluorescent lamps rated for 3,000K or the daylight 5,000K lamps. Since they are soft already, you don't need to add diffusion gel over them. And because they are fluorescent lamps, they won't get hot enough to burn or scorch the ceiling. Also, they give more lumens per watt than tungsten lamps, meaning you can use smaller, easier-to-tape-up extension cords. To limit the spread to form more distinct pools of light, the units can be wrapped with BlackWrap or even standard household aluminum foil.

PHOTO 6.16 **Clip light**

Often it isn't possible to rig lights on a hallway ceiling. Either the shot sees the ceiling, or there just isn't any way to safely attach something. But hallways almost always have doorways along them that provide places to hide units and add streaks of light from. In office buildings and public buildings, there might be soda machines in the hallways, which provide great places to hide small-wattage lights behind as well. Also, every soda machine is plugged in, so electricity is right there for each unit. Depending on the emotional feeling you are going for, you can either use hard lights or put diffusion on the side lights to make the variations in intensity not so jarring.

STAIRS

When we discussed the lighting for actor Aaron Lustig moving down the hallway, I also mentioned how lights were placed at the bottom and the top of the stairs. This is even more important to keep in mind when the shot is showing the entire staircase and the movement of the subject going up it or down it. The top and bottom of the stairs are your start and end marks for your subject, even if the subject doesn't actually stop but just passes through these areas. The top of stairway and the bottom are so far apart they require their own separate lighting units. Often two lights will be required at the top of the stairs—one to light the actor and one to light the surrounding area, the wall behind them. The stairs themselves are now the pathway that needs to be lit, and often we rim or backlight the railing and posts to add some dimensionality to them. This can often be accomplished by a light at the top of the stairs aimed down, which will become either the backlight or the key light for our subject on the staircase, thus lighting their path. The concern here is to make sure that the subject doesn't get too bright as he or she approaches the light. Getting less light as the subject moves away isn't very noticeable to the viewer, but the reverse is.

In Photo 6.17 from the music video *Tough Time Lovers,* musician Luko Adjaffi plays as he descends a staircase. The concept was to give this song a 1940s film noir feeling, thus the decision to shoot in black and white. It was also a reason to shoot with so much hard light, as back then films used almost all hard lights. The hard light from a 650w Fresnel hits his back from the top of the stairs,

PHOTO 6.17 Luko Adjaffi, *Tough Time Lovers* music video, Clarke Productions

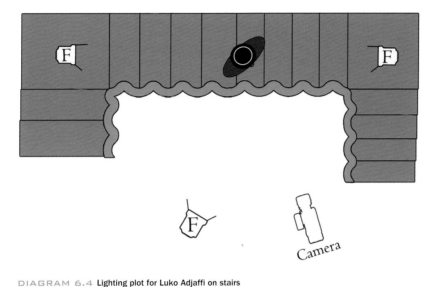

DIAGRAM 6.4 **Lighting plot for Luko Adjaffi on stairs**

giving him an edge, while another 650w Fresnel with diffusion was at the bottom of the stairs aimed up to fill in his face. Both of these lights had their barn doors partway closed to cut any spill off the wall and keep the light only hitting Luko. A third 650w Fresnel was aimed up through the railing from below, camera left, throwing the hard shadows over him and the wall behind him.

While somewhat overdramatic and theatrical, the look here was what the director wanted for the style of the piece. In the finished edit, there are even shots of just Luko's shadow moving across the wall. Aiming lights through railings to create shadows that the subject will move through is a rather standard approach when lighting stairs, but generally not this severe unless it's a horror film or some other suspenseful scene.

Photo 6.18 shows another example of lighting a staircase. A 4-bank × 4-foot Kino Flo with daylight lamps provides the bright soft light coming in through the doorway at the top of the stairs. A 1,200-watt HMI off camera right on the balcony floor set as far back as possible is aimed through a 4-foot × 4-foot opal frame and ¾ backlights actress Susan Adriensen's entire path down the stairs, while also side-lighting the railings and creating the large, menacing shadows on the wall. Another 4 × 4 Kino Flo with daylight lamps is right of camera at the bottom of the stairs, positioned high up and aimed down, providing frontal fill for her once she gets farther down the stairs. We can justify this source as being skylight coming in through the large foyer windows (which were seen earlier in the film and thus established in the viewers' minds). The bright soft light from the HMI also bounced off the white ceiling and helps bring up the ambient light created by the daylight light coming in from the unseen windows behind camera.

This was an early scene in a supernatural thriller, so the intent was to generate a creepy feeling to the image even though it was daytime. The shadows on the wall and the lack of frontal light on the actress at the top of the stairs helped achieve this, as well as allowing the doorway she entered from at the top of the stairs and the room in the far background under the stairs to be the two brightest things in the frame.

PHOTO 6.18 Susan Adriensen runs down stairs, *Dark Tarot,* DGW Films

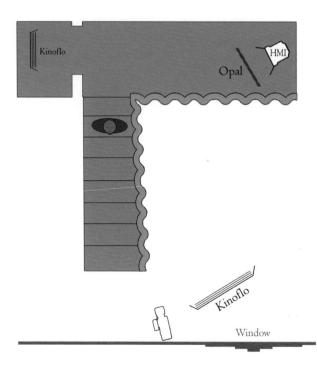

DIAGRAM 6.5 Lighting plot for Susan Adriensen running down stairs

Photo 6.19 is another stairs shot from the same film. A 650w Fresnel in the basement is aimed through the unseen railings at the bottom of the stairs, casting a nice pattern on the wall behind actress Natasa Babic. A bare light bulb in the ceiling at the top of the stairs casts a downward overhead light for the actress to pass through and light her face. A 650w Fresnel is off camera right aimed through a cookie, throwing a soft pattern across the door frame and open door that will catch the actress at her end mark at the top of the stairs. Because it was set far enough away, it spread enough to also light the wall and floor on the foyer side of the wall. A 300w Fresnel off left is aimed into the wall behind the

PHOTO 6.19 Natasa Babic coming up stairs, *Dark Tarot*, DGW Films

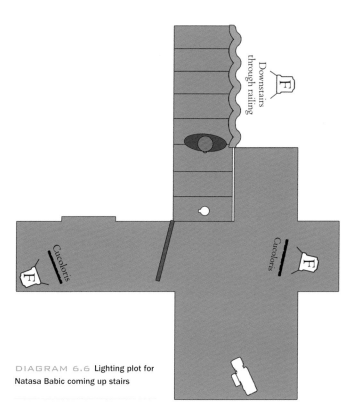

DIAGRAM 6.6 Lighting plot for
Natasa Babic coming up stairs

door on the camera-left side of the frame—with strips of BlackWrap across the barn doors to add a breakup to the light on the walls. The desired effect here was to establish a moody feeling, as she comes up a little disoriented from the previous scene. The shadowy breakups on the walls and door help to support her feeling of being in the shadows emotionally—a little like being lost in the woods.

Not all stairs need to be so dramatic. In comedies the lighting usually doesn't throw any patterns of the railing over the subject or against the wall. But they still have light at both the top of the stairs and the bottom.

CAMERA MOVES

Often the camera will move during a shot. It can dolly in or out, it can track slowly to one side for a better angle, or it can track subjects as they move. When the camera moves, there are several lighting considerations:

- Make sure that no light, grip stand, or extension cord ends up in the shot as the camera moves and changes its angle of view.

- Make sure no lights flare the lens as the camera moves into a new position.

- Make sure the camera doesn't throw a shadow of itself into the shot on the floor, a wall, or over a subject.

- Make sure that the lighting still has modeling and looks good at the end of the camera move, and that the camera isn't shooting down the barrel of a light.

In some scenes the director may want the camera to move back with the actors as they move forward. This could be a dolly back, a handheld shot, or some kind of Steadicam rig. The camera tracks with the subject; in other words, it keeps the subject the same distance in front of the lens. The actor, or actors, could be walking or running, and the director wants to see their faces the entire time. This means we need to keep their faces lit. This can be done a few ways. One is to have an obie light (discussed in Chapter 4) attached to the camera. A number of LED obie lights are on the market now that range in price. The danger is that the cheaper the unit, the more likely it is to have poor color rendition and too much green.

Another well-used method in the industry is to use a china ball hung on the end of a painter's pole (discussed in Chapter 5). Usually a small inline dimmer is attached to the lamp cord so that the electric holding the china ball can adjust the intensity as per the wishes of the DP. Black cloth or a section of a black garbage bag can be taped over the side of the ball facing the camera to avoid lens flare.

The china ball hung on the end of a pole can travel with the actors as they move. This can become a nice, soft light filling in the faces as the actors walk down a hallway or through a store, so it is a valuable lighting tool for documentary and reality TV shooting, as well as a way to just augment the available light.

Keep in mind the following important factors when using china balls this way:

- They are made of paper, so when moving, it is important not to let the lamp touch the paper side, or it can actually burn.

- They can swing, which will cause moving shadows, so it is important when moving them with the actors to move smoothly and stop and start smoothly in unison with the actors.

- The intensity drops off very quickly, so when moving with the china ball, it is important that the distance between the ball and the subject remains consistent.

- The piece of diffusion taped over the bottom opening so that no direct hard light comes out that could spill on the actor and cause a noticeable streak, can shift or fall out if not taped in securely.

Using a china ball to move with the actors does not preclude lighting the acting area and the background. The set still needs to be lit to look believable.

AMBIENT SOFT LIGHT

Sometimes directors will want to give the actors more freedom to move about during the shot. Perhaps it's a wide shot with lots of movement by the actors, or the director wants the camera to go handheld and randomly swing around, following the action or grabbing shots. Maybe the scene will be shot with multiple cameras, so the lighting needs to accommodate more than one angle. Whichever the case, the easiest way to accommodate this kind of "freedom" is to give the entire scene a lot of ambient soft light. Chicken coop lighting can do this, so long as a number of bay lights are hung above the majority of the area the actors will move in.

On the TV show *Sherri* (2009), LD Bill Berner had the grips build softboxes that were hung under a number of 1kW open-faced board lights to provide chicken coop lighting for the reoccurring office, break room, and living room sets. This allowed him to have a nice, soft ambient light for each set that filled in the shadows and made the lighting even on the people but mostly off the walls. In a sitcom, this is usually the desired look, as the actors will walk around a lot and there are multiple cameras shooting from several angles at the same time. It was a nice, pleasant-looking base to build the rest of the lighting up from. But it was also controllable, so that for the "night" scenes, some of the chicken coops were turned off, and only puddles of soft light could be strategically placed throughout the sets.

> "On a sitcom it's a closed environment with multiple-angle cameras and one or more booms that extend far into the set. You have to contend with large sticks coming out over the actors. So the lighting is from the back and sides with softlight frontal light. ¾ back from both sides with 2ks with 250 diffusion and bobbinet on the bottom. Then 2k softlights from both sides in the front and a long bounce along the entire front."
>
> —TIGRE MCMULLAN, GAFFER, REALITY TV AND SITCOMS

The frontal fill was 4-foot × 8-foot sheets of white foamcore mounted above the audience the entire length of each set. Three ETC PAR lights were evenly spaced and bounced into each sheet. In addition, two studio "super softs," which are large 2kW softlights, were hung to the right and left of the front of the set. This allowed the multiple cameras, shooting from various angles, all to be able to shoot with a nice, soft light on the cast members.

On lower-budget projects and on locations, this same kind of effect can be achieved using long bolts of white cloth or bed sheets. The cloth is hung horizontally from the ceiling with spring clamps, or stretched between two grip stands and then raised up as high as desired. Attaching a small chain along the bottom of the cloth with safety pins will help it hang straight and not curl or wave as much when people move about near it. Open-faced lights, raised on stands, are aimed into the hanging white cloth. The object is to totally fill the length of the white cloth with light from all directions, so that the soft bounce will come back over the camera and wash the scene. Fresnels, Source Fours, and PAR lights can also be used to hit the white cloth from farther away. Something to keep in mind is that this will really wash light everywhere.

PHOTO 6.20 Spacelight, courtesy of Mole-Richardson

On big-budget productions, larger units such as spacelights are often used to provide an even overall soft illumination, and on locations, balloon lights are often used. Spacelights are white cloth cylinders with two to eight 1kW lamps in the top that can be turned on and off individually. They provide a bright soft wash of light all around. Balloon lights are helium-filled balloons made of a white translucent material, inside of which are several independently switchable high-intensity lamps, often HMIs.

On the film *Enchanted* (2007), two balloon lights were used to raise the ambiance inside the three-story-tall law firm lobby. This was done to allow the Steadicam more freedom to move around. The bright, soft light filtering down wrapped around everyone and gave the image the feeling that light was pouring in from the big lobby windows. When not in the shot, the grips flagged the windows with 20-foot × 20-foot blacks to cut out the moving sunlight. A few Kino Flo Image 80 fluorescent units (which have eight lamps) were positioned at the start and stop marks for the actors, but by and large the entire lobby was lit with the balloon lights.

In a scene cut from the movie *Jumper* (2008), a balloon light was used to provide a soft puddle of light over the main character reading alone in the empty NYC Library. Balloon lights are also used outside, often to provide a feeling of ambient moonlight. They were used to create soft moonlight during the night battle scene for *The Manchurian Candidate* (2004), and strung between the masts of the ship on *Pirates of the Caribbean* (2003). The difference between these lights and chicken coops are that chicken coops are more directable, shining down and often skirted to stop spill from washing the background, while spacelights and balloon lights are generally used to raise the overall illumination and ambient fill of a set or location by spreading bright, soft light in all directions. Both spacelights and balloon lights have black skirts that can be added to one or more sides of the unit, thus blocking light from traveling in that direction and making them a little more directable. But they were designed for a different function than a chicken coop. Of course, china balls can be used to serve the same function, but on a much smaller scale and at a much lower intensity.

Another simple method for lower-budget productions is to bounce a few open-faced lights into the ceiling to provide a lot of soft ambient light. The units should be raised high enough that no direct light hits the set or actors, and the lights should be flooded out to wash as much of the ceiling as possible. Open-faced lights produce a wider and faster spread of light and thus are perfect for washing a wide area. The wider the area of the ceiling hit by light, the more even and brighter the ambient light will be within the shot. More than one light can be positioned hitting the ceiling in front of or over the acting area from different angles. The barn doors of the light can be adjusted open and closed to change the intensity of the ambient fill light. This works particularly well for shooting inside smaller rooms.

All of the above methods work for handheld and Steadicam shots, where the camera will move more freely with the actors. In these cases, hard light is dangerous, as it can throw shadows of the camera and can glare the lens. The brighter and softer the ambient light in a scene, the easier it is for handheld and Steadicam operators to work.

STUFF TO REMEMBER

- Block, light, rehearse, shoot.

- Light the end mark first, then the start mark, and then the path.

- We perceive movement by seeing a subject move through variations of light and shadow.

- The more drastic the change in light levels the subject moves through, the more dramatic.

- Lights can shine through doorways or windows to give shafts of light to pass through.

- Lights can create patterns for subjects to move through.

- Lights can be rigged overhead to allow subjects to move through puddles of light.

- Stairs require both top and bottom lighting, and often have light through railings.

- Lighting needs to accommodate camera moves to avoid camera shadows and lens flare.

- A china ball on a pole can move with the camera and actors to keep fill on them.

- The more ambient soft light in the scene, the easier for the camera to move around freely.

PUTTING IT INTO PRACTICE

- Find a hallway with a few doors on it. Light the hallway for someone to walk down it toward the camera. Select an end mark for your subject and light that first. See if you can rig a backlight or downlight from the ceiling to accent the ending area. Light the start mark at the other end of the hallway. Use the doors off the hall to allow light to come in. Light it two ways—once for daytime where the difference between light and shadow isn't very severe, and once for nighttime when the difference is much more pronounced.

- Light someone walking down a flight of stairs. Light the top of the stairs, the bottom, and the stairway itself. Shoot it with and without the pattern of the railing thrown across the stairs.

- Light an area where the camera will move with the subject. Use as much ambient soft light as necessary so that the actor is free to move without going too dark. Make sure the lighting doesn't throw a camera shadow into the shot. If you can get help, try shooting the same shot with a china ball on a pole that moves with the subject, and compare the images.

7 DEALING WITH DAYLIGHT 1: Shooting Exteriors

When shooting outside, we must be aware that the sun is always moving (although in actuality it is the Earth that is moving). The sun never stays in the same part of the sky for even a minute, which means the angle of light outside is continuously changing. As the angle of the sun changes, your shadows move and your modeling changes. In the morning and later afternoon, the sun is low, so the shadows are long, adding dramatic highlights and modeling. At midday, the sun is directly above, casting hard downward shadows that are by and large unflattering. Even the color of the light outside changes during the course of the day—starting out warm at sunrise, changing to daylight "blue" during the majority of the day, and then warming again as it sets. So, one of the most important things for shooting outside successfully is advanced planning and sticking to a schedule.

The sun is brighter than any light presently made by humans. This means we cannot overpower or even equal its intensity—on a clear day. On a cloudy day, we can use very powerful HMIs, such as the popular 20,000w Fresnel, to create our own, non-moving sunlight. We can also

use these lights as fill when we use the real sun as our key light. But we often don't need lights to shoot outside. We just need to understand how to best use the light the sun gives us.

The easiest way to get good lighting for shooting outside is to shoot with the sun behind the subject. If we shoot with the sun behind the camera, we will have a number of problems:

- The shadow of the camera may be in the shot, either on the ground or on the subject.

- The actors will be squinting, since the direct sunlight will blind them.

- The lighting will be frontal and flat, hard, and harsh looking.

- Both the subject and the background will be the same brightness.

But if we shoot with the sun behind the subject, the sun becomes our backlight, adding a nice rim that provides both separation from the background and dimensionality to the image. At the same time, it backlights our backgrounds, which are filled in with front bounce light from the sky and ground. This makes their colors rich and soft and stops them from becoming brighter than our subject. A typical example is the work of Bojan Bazelli on *The Lone Ranger* (2013).

In Photo 7.1 from the 16mm festival short *The Last Duel* (2009) was shot just after sunrise, backlit by the sun. Notice the shafts of sunlight on the ground. The low sun also provided a lens flare, which

PHOTO 7.1 ¾ backlight from the sun, *The Last Duel,* MTG Productions

was wanted for the style of the imagery. When you are shooting outside, the placement of the subjects has to be very specific. The actors were all placed mostly in shade. Notice the ¾ backlight created by the sun on the butler (center) and the three women on the left. Also notice how the sun on the duelist on the right provides him with a rim light that separates him from the tree branches behind him. The mansion in the background is also backlit, so it doesn't burn out and lose detail. This allows it to be recognizable but not take focus away from the foreground action. No bounce cards were used in this shot because it was so wide, otherwise, the cards would either be seen or be so far away they would be ineffective. Only the natural skylight and bounce from the ground provided the ambient fill. The intent was to give the image a Dutch Masters painting feeling reminiscent of the Academy Award-winning work of DP John Alcott on the film *Barry Lyndon* (1975). (The Dutch Masters look will be discussed in more detail in Chapter 14.) The image was enhanced by both a diffusion filter and a graduated blue filter on the lens.

CITY STREETS

While shooting on city streets, DPs tend to prefer to shoot on the side in the shade. If we shoot on the sunny side, the sun will move and eventually slip into shade, so the shots done first will not match shots done later. But if we start in the shade and have scouted the location previously, we will know how long we will have to shoot in the same, consistent light. It is usually best to pick streets that don't get a lot of direct sunlight for very long. One thing to watch out for is reflected sunlight from building windows and off passing cars. On more than one occasion, film crews have waited a few minutes for the sun to move enough that a sudden reflected beam of hard light goes away. Or the grips have had to flag it.

On the movie *Jumper* (2008), we were shooting down a shady alley near Wall Street. On the second or third take, the sun came out from behind the tall buildings, flooding the street with bright golden rays. The gaffer told the assistant director to just wait a few minutes and the sun would disappear behind the tall buildings on the other side of the street and the lighting would return to what it had been before. But the AD was from California, as were the director and DP, so they weren't familiar with the light of New York City and were anxious to shoot as soon as possible. They decided the grips should build two 20-foot × 20-foot solids on butterflies (explained later in this chapter) to create a 40-foot wall to block the sun. By the time they had finished setting it all up, the sun had vanished behind the tall buildings across the street and never came back. They spent a lot of time taking it all down again. Sometimes it's better, and faster, to just wait.

DP David Mullen shot a lot of scenes outside on the streets of New York City for the TV show *Smash* (2011)—one of the best-lit TV shows in history. At an industry event on lighting, he said that when lighting close-ups outside, he would have the grips flag off any top sun or skylight from hitting the subject to allow other skylight to fill in the face and provide backlight. By cutting the top light, the light hitting the face becomes more modeled. He also warned that with the increased sensitivity of the new cameras, any minor stray light now can cause problems such as throwing unwanted shadows or kicks on the subject. So more time is needed to flag and cut exterior sources of light, such as reflections of the sun off windows, traffic lights, car headlights, lights from signs, and store displays, to stop too many of them from hitting the actor.

Shooting your subjects in the shade whenever possible is a standard practice in the industry when shooting outside, as it allows more control over the exposure and directing the attention of the viewer. We can do a number of things to bring up the intensity of light on our subject separately from the background—with bounce cards, reflectors, and/or lights.

BOUNCE

When the sun is behind the subject, we can easily bounce or reflect light from the sun back into the scene and our subject's face, which will bring the subject's luminance up higher than the background. It will also help lower the contrast between the brightness of the sun backlight and the darkness of the subject's face in shadow. If we use a white surface, the bounce light will be flattering while eliminating harsh shadows and squinting problems. Bouncing light into the subject's face is the first defense we have against the harsh contrast caused by the sun.

There are basically four standard kinds of bounce devices:

- Showcards—Also sold in art supply stores as art cards, these come in black on one side and white on the other, or silver and white. They are 24 inches × 36 inches and very flexible, which means we can squeeze them into a cove to more easily focus the bounce from the card. A grip or an electric can easily hold the card and adjust it as the subject and/or the sun moves, keeping the bounce light on the subject. They can even walk with this card as the subject walks, thus tracking the soft light with the subject. The limited size makes this basically usable for only one person, so if there are two people in the scene, you would employ two crew members to hold two cards—one for each actor.

- Foamcore—This can also be bought in some art stores as foam board. In the industry, this comes in either white on both sides, or black on both sides. The standard size is 8 feet by 4 feet and is rather stiff but very lightweight. It can be cut with a mat knife rather easily. Art stores usually sell it in small sizes, such as 18 inches × 24 inches. The advantage of the foamcore is its size and stiffness. A large sheet becomes a large light reflector that can easily bounce enough light for two or more people in the same shot. It can also be affixed to a stand. Because of its stiffness, however, it also catches the wind and will sail away if given a chance. Foamcore produces slightly softer light than showcards.

- Beadboard—This can be bought at Home Depot or other hardware stores. It is basically insulation made out of pressed Styrofoam with a sheet of silver paper on one side. This is thicker than either showcards or foamcore, rather stiff, and more difficult to cut, as it will shred and crack easily. It comes in various sizes, but in practice is cut down to almost any size and shape desired. After it is cut, gaffer tape is taped around the edges to stop it from falling apart. The surface is rougher, so the bounce light is much softer than the others and even more flattering. It is very lightweight, and its thickness actually makes it easier to hold on to when it's windy.

PHOTO 7.2 **Showcard (black and white sided)**

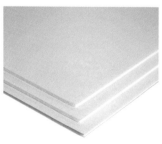

PHOTO 7.3 **Foamcore (white on both sides)**

PHOTO 7.4 **Beadboard**

- Flexfills—Invented for still photographers, these are basically large circular frames with white material stretched across them that collapse by the user twisting them so that they can be stored in small zipped bags. Flexfills come in various sizes and usually have outer sleeves that can be slipped on or off, which allows them to have white, silver, gold, or a silver-and-gold-striped pattern to reflect light off of. The stretched cloth in the frame is usually translucent so that it can also be used as a silk—which we will discuss later in this chapter. Since they are very flexible, they can be bent to direct the bounce light more easily than any of the previous devices. But they are also great at catching the wind, so they require a firm grip. Stands with clips to hold Flexfills are available, but if a wind comes along, they can easily fall over or spin.

PHOTO 7.5 **Flexfills**

In Photo 7.6 from *The Last Day of Winter* (2006) (shot on 16mm Kodak film), actors Don Singalewitch and Richard Bell, playing father and son, are backlit by hard sunlight. A 4-foot × 4-foot sheet of foamcore, positioned low touching the ground on camera left was angled up to bounce soft sunlight into their faces. Don is closer to the bounce and is thus brighter, which helps focus the viewer's attention on him, the main character in the scene. The harshness of the sun on his face helps "sell" the winter feeling, as we all accept that winter is a harsh time of year. Notice how the sunlight also rims and edges the wooden fence behind them. Shooting in this location at this time of day was preplanned, as the small, red barn and shack in the background would be in shadow. Notice also how both their heads are framed to have something other than sky behind them. This helps create more depth and separation than a bright pale blue sky would.

PHOTO 7.6 **Don Singalewitch and Richard Bell, *The Last Day of Winter*, MTG Productions**

For the close up (Photo 7.7) and over-the-shoulder shot (Photo 7.8) of the same scene, Richard, the businessman, was always positioned to be in full shade with a sun backlight and the bounce foamcore filling him. He works in an office, not outside with his hands, so he was lit more softly. Conversely, the camera and Don were positioned so that some direct harsh sun would always strike Don's face, accenting his age lines and giving him a more crusty, farmer look for all of his shots. The bounce foamcore fills the left side of his face. This is another example of how the lighting, even just the manner in which people are positioned outside in the sun, helps communicate the characters and the scene. Because of our schedule, we were unable to take the time to flag the sun off the white barn behind Don, which should have been done in order to not distract the eye. It should have been netted down just to take the edge off it with a butterfly (we will discuss butterflies later in this chapter). But the white is reminiscent of snow, and this is set on the last day of winter, so the bright white element still sort of works for the piece.

In the last shot of the film (Photo 7.9), the father and son have a moment of connection, and so Richard turns and his face becomes struck by harsh

PHOTO 7.7 **Close-up of Richard Bell,** *The Last Day of Winter,* **MTG Productions**

PHOTO 7.8 **Over-the-shoulder of Don Singalewitch,** *The Last Day of Winter,* **MTG Productions**

PHOTO 7.9 **Don Singalewitch and Richard Bell,** *The Last Day of Winter,* **MTG Productions**

sunlight as well—visually showing that despite their differences, they are in fact father and son. Again the lighting subliminally helps tell the story.

ANYTHING CAN BOUNCE LIGHT

I was on a shoot of an educational video for use in divinity schools, filming in a small white-shingled church in the middle of Nebraska. We needed to shoot a number of interviews with parishioners, and doing it inside wasn't going to work, since the walls were all white and there was a noisy breakfast going on. The producer also thought that shooting outside, seeing the endless flat farm lands behind the interviewees, would help set the location. It was a nice bright sunny Sunday, not a cloud in the sky. So, I walked around and found the side of the church the sun was hitting. I was lucky that there was a tree—the only tree in sight, maybe 30 feet away and backlit by the sun—on the other side of a small graveyard. The producer didn't like the graveyard, and I promised it wouldn't be in the shots. I set up the camera only a few feet away from the church, and had each interviewee stand so that the tree was in the background behind him or her, the sun backlighting him or her. The side of the church behind me became my bounce card, reflecting soft white light into their faces.

Remember, the angle of reflection equals the angle of incidence. If the church was directly behind the camera, the subject would squint looking into a bright white wall. Also, the reflected light would be coming from camera and thus not provide any modeling.

I positioned the camera and the subject so that the side of the church was about 30 degrees off camera right. This allowed bright, soft bounce light to come in on the interviewee's face at a slight angle, rendering some three-dimensionality. For fill, I had the producer hold up a white flip chart we found in the church Sunday school room on the left side of the camera.

The church wall became the key, and because it was a very large surface and painted glossy white, it bounced a brighter intensity of light onto the subjects' faces than the 16-inch × 24-inch dull-white paper flip chart. The director and producer both loved the look—especially since it was tight enough that you couldn't see the tombstones.

Even though we only shot outside for an hour, we had to readjust for each and every interview, because the sun was slowly moving across the sky. We had to continuously change both where the subject was standing and where the camera was placed in order to keep the tree behind them, the sun backlighting them, and the bounce from the church lighting their faces.

DIAGRAM 7.1 **Using the church wall as a bounce source**

This was a case where we didn't plan as well as we should have. The decision to shoot outside was made at the last moment. We made it work, but had I known we would shoot outside, I would have brought along some larger bounce cards or a Flexfill. I also would have scouted the exterior of the church the morning before to get an idea of where the sun would be coming from and how the shadows fell. Scouting and planning are crucial for exterior shoots.

REFLECTORS

Reflectors have highly reflective surfaces in either silver or gold that render a harder reflection of light than a soft white bounce. With a hard reflector, the light is more intense and travels farther. Hard 4-foot × 4-foot reflectors, with a shiny silver side and a soft leafed silver side, are standard equipment on exterior shoots. These can be tilted and locked, and they mount on reflector stands, which need to be weighted down with sandbags to stop them from falling over in the wind. Nets can be stretched over these reflectors to cut the intensity if desired, and special reflectors can be rented that have a mirror on one side. But mirrors are usually more trouble than they are worth. The purpose of the mirrored reflector is to direct sunlight into another reflector somewhere in the shade, which in turn is aimed at the subject. The danger is that mirrored reflectors are very heavy and very breakable.

PHOTO 7.10 A Hollywood 4-foot × 4-foot reflector, courtesy of Cinelease NY

I was once an electric on a car commercial, shooting in a working-class neighborhood just down the street from the beach at Coney Island. It was early morning and the DP wanted to use a mirrored reflector to reflect direct hard sunlight onto the porch in the background of the shot. The car was being lit with a tungsten 20kW Fresnel—the biggest Fresnel I have ever seen, and the heaviest. Because we were shooting morning exteriors and the RED camera was color-balanced for daylight, the 20kW tungsten Fresnel produced a bright golden light to illuminate the car. The golden rays of the real sun came streaming down the street from the beach and were being reflected off the mirrored reflector, which had been raised up about 16 feet in the air, onto the family members standing on the porch admiring the car. It looked great. The mirror was lowered until the camera department was ready, as the RED was taking a lot of scheduled time to get set up. Finally the camera was ready, and the producer wanted to roll as fast as possible to make up some of the lost time. The mirror was raised up and had to be refocused, as the sun had moved. The moment it hit the actors on the porch, the AD called roll—never giving the grips the time to tie off the extended reflector stand. After the second take, the reflector caught an ocean wind that, although the stand was heavily weighted down with a dozen sandbags, knocked the stand over. A word of advice here—if you see a large mirror 16 feet in the air begin to wobble, run the other way. It landed facedown on the street, shattering and scattering broken glass in several directions. While the producer paid the price (literally, to the rental company for a new reflector), we were without it for the rest of the shoot, which compromised the DP's lighting. The lesson here is that reflectors on stands catch the wind and need to be properly secured—always.

Many smaller-budget reflectors on the market can be attached to lightweight stands or handheld. As already mentioned, the Flexfill has a sleeve that is reversible and has a gold reflector on one side and a gold-and-silver-striped reflector on the other. Stands with spring clips can be used to secure the Flexfill, but the wind will still catch it and make it spin unless someone is holding it or it's tied down. The silver side of beadboard can be used, held by a grip stand or a grip.

In Photo 7.11, the gold side of a Flexfill was used to add a morning sun accent to actress Clare Dill in the festival short *The Last Duel*. It was held by a grip only slightly higher than her eye height at about

PHOTO 7.11 **Clare Dill,** *The Last Duel,* **MTG Productions**

a 60-degree angle from the camera. Low, gold, and from the side gives the light a dawn feeling. Notice how even though she was positioned in the shade, bounce from the sky adds a nice low-intensity kick to her left cheek and chin, adding some nice modeling and separation from the hazy background.

In Photo 7.12 from the festival short *Nine Years Old* (2008), actor Paul Rivers, sitting in the car, was also lit using the gold side of a Flexfill bounced in through the front windshield. When aiming reflectors or lights in through a car windshield, be very aware of the shadow of the

PHOTO 7.12 **Paul Rivers and Joanna Messineo,** *Nine Years Old,* **Offstage Films**

rearview mirror. If you aren't careful, this shadow can fall on the subject and look rather strange. In some cars you can remove the mirror, which makes it easier. Also keep in mind that sunlight virtually never comes in at such a low angle that it can hit the driver's face directly through any window of a car—unless it's sunrise or sunset. There is some poetic license we take when lighting inside cars, just as we do with lighting windows. Audiences generally just accept what you give them.

The girl, who is a vision played by actress Joanna Messineo, is also side-lit from the Flexfill, and backlit by the sun, with the bounce off the car providing her frontal fill. The strong sun backlight helps give her a more ethereal feeling. The story takes place early morning and is only a 4-minute film. However, the shooting took eight hours beginning at 8 a.m. This shot was actually done in the early afternoon, but the gold reflector added the early-morning-light feeling, and its low angle helped to connect the image to the earlier shots taken outside the car during the morning.

Both of these short fims were set in the early morning, but were filmed over the course of several hours. To match the shots, the actors were often repositioned in relation to the sun to keep them ¾ backlit or side-lit. In the case of *Nine Years Old,* we even moved the car to the opposite side of the street, facing the other direction, once the sun moved to the other side of the sky. Since the country road only had trees on both sides, the move was unnoticable and cut perfectly. The main consideration was to make sure the sun was always hitting the same side of the actors' faces.

This was also true when shooting *The Last Duel.* Once the sun moved to front-light the mansion in the background, all shots had to be done only against a woodsy background. So it was important that all the wide shots and the shots that would require the mansion to be in the background were all filmed in the morning before the sun rose too high. Both of these films required location scouting a few days before shooting so that a shooting schedule could be created before the day of the shoot in order to best use the sun when it was at its lower points.

BUTTERFLIES AND SILKS

In the lighting business, a butterfly is a metal square frame that the grips assemble and then stretch a large silk, scrim, or black solid across, which is then positioned over the talent to intercept the sun. The standard sizes for butterflies are 6 feet × 6 feet, 8 feet × 8 feet, 12 feet × 12 feet, and 20 feet × 20 feet. Butterflies are attached to rolling stands called high boys that can be raised very high in the air. The butterfly can be tilted at various angles in relationship to the sun so that it covers the entire acting area. The DP has the option between a full silk, half silk, or quarter silk depending on how soft a light is desired. A single or double net can also be stretched across the frame, which will cut the intensity of the sunlight by a half or a full stop without changing the light's texture. Sunlight can be totally cut with a black solid cloth or a white reflective plastic tarp like material called a griflon. This can also be used to change the butterfly into a giant bounce card. Since the sun is always moving, the butterfly must be constantly reset and adjusted throughout the shoot.

One thing to always keep in mind is to hide the shadow of the edge of the butterfly from the shot. The butterfly must be positioned so that subjects are fully covered by it, and the edge shadows aren't seen on the ground or on any of the actors. So careful framing is required when you are using a butterfly. The stands can also cast shadows that might fall into frame. Sometimes the grips will be asked to rig tree branches to the stands to help disguise their shadows or even the edge of the stand itself if it can't be removed from the frame.

While they are generally "flown" above the talent, butterflies can also be used to diffuse direct sunlight being used as a side light or frontal key. Sunlight filtered by a silk will produce a beautiful, even, bright, soft light. Never allow a subject to walk out from being covered by the butterfly, as the light hitting them will radically change.

Film crews often use butterflies to maintain an already established look while shooting outside. Perhaps we started shooting with the sun behind our subjects or in shade. But the scene is long or

PHOTO 7.13 **A 12-foot × 12-foot butterfly, photo courtesy of Matthews Studio Equipment**

the actors need a lot of takes. By the time we are ready to start shooting the close-ups, the shade has gone away and the sun has moved to directly overhead and is casting ugly hard shadows down across our actors' faces. Putting up a butterfly over their heads will soften the light back to how it looked during the beginning of the scene. We can use a reflector to bounce hard sunlight behind the subjects as a backlight or however to make the looks match.

It is also rather common to use a butterfly when switching from a wide exterior shot to close-ups. Often when the scene is an extremely wide exterior, a butterfly cannot be used because the stands would be in the shot, so the subjects may be lit with hard sunlight. But once the camera moves in for close-ups or over-the-shoulder shots, it is rather common to use a butterfly with a half silk to soften the sunlight, giving a more flattering look to the subjects. Viewers will usually never notice the difference so long as the key and backlight are both coming from the same directions and the contrast on the face is relatively similar.

Besides softening the harsh sunlight, a butterfly can be used for many other tasks. For example, a butterfly with a griflon is often used to create a tented area to protect the director and camera crew from rain, snow, or bright sun. DP Peter Stein covered his camera with just this setup while filming a rain scene in *Necessary Roughness* (1991). On another film, the director wanted the camera inside as the actress walked out the door onto a porch. Peter had the grips set up a 20-foot × 20-foot double net and stood it upright at the end of the porch, thus cutting the brightness of the exterior seen through the open door as the actress exited.

Butterflies can be quite dangerous, as they are giant sails that easily catch the wind. The grip department sets up, positions, and takes care of all butterflies. Not only do they pile sandbags on the legs of the stands, but they always tie down the corners of the butterfly with tie-lines laced through a pile of sandbags or tied to something nearby such as a tree, lamppost, or fire escape. Also, at least one grip is always required to stand by a butterfly at all times in case it does begin to catch the wind and move. This grip will signal for others to help immediately if needed. Other major concerns when using a butterfly include not setting it up close to tree branches or anything else that could puncture or tear the silk should the wind make it move, and avoiding electric lines. In Hollywood more than one grip has been killed trying to hold down a high boy stand when the wind blew the butterfly into electric lines. Safety must always be the most important thing on set.

The most ingenious butterfly ever created was for the filming of the movie *Memoirs of a Geisha* (2005), which was shot in a constructed Japanese village built in a desert outside Hollywood. Legendary cinematographer Dion Beebe worked with his key grip Scott Robinson and the set construction crew to create a system of rails rigged above the sets so that a giant roll-out silk could be slid over the entire town whenever wanted. This allowed Dion Beebe to silk the sun whenever he wanted or needed to. It also allowed them to change the weather to "overcast" when the script called for it.

We can't all afford town-sized silks. Thankfully, silks come in various sizes, and the smaller they are, the more manageable. Various companies make more economical and easily collapsible 6-foot × 6-foot and 8-foot × 8-foot silks that can travel in 4-foot-long bags. If the shots are tight enough, a Flexfill can easily do the job instead of a butterfly. These can be rigged on grip stands or even handheld.

Clouds are nature's silk. Most DPs get very happy when their exterior shoot turns out to be on an overcast day. Under cloud cover, colors become more pastel, but also a little more saturated, and the light is soft and pretty on people. This also allows the DP to use lights to create a constant, non-moving sun—which brings us to our next subject.

LIGHTS OUTSIDE

The average color temperature of daylight is 5,600 to 6,400 Kelvin, depending on how much blue sky is mixing in with the direct sunlight. Any lights we use outdoors need to be balanced for that color temperature (known as daylight) so that they blend with the natural outdoor light. Tungsten lights will look orange compared to daylight, as they are balanced for 3,200 Kelvin. To use them outside, color correction blue (as mentioned, also called CTB or Full blue) gel needs to be added in front of the light to bring the color temperature up to 5,600K, which greatly reduces their intensity. So, even a 2,000w tungsten light will barely emit enough intensity to be even noticeable outside.

In the old days, arc lights were used for shooting outdoors. These giant lights ran off DC current to create an electrical arc inside a massive housing and needed to have their carbon rods changed every 15 minutes as they burned away. Arc lights were very powerful Fresnel lights but problematic. They have since been replaced with the more reliable HMI lights and the more recent plasma lights, which both emit daylight color temperature light—around 5,600K. Photo 7.14 is a photo of me focusing a 20,000w HMI Fresnel during a shoot for *Project Runway* (2011). Notice the 4-foot × 4-foot silk rigged by the grips in front of the lens and the rain shield over the top to stop any water from getting into the light. Luckily it stopped drizzling before cameras rolled.

PHOTO 7.14 **The author working with a 20kW HMI on an episode of *Project Runway***

While it takes a 20kW HMI to almost equal the lumen output of an arc light, cameras and film have gotten so much more sensitive, and have more dynamic range, now that we can easily shoot many setups with lower-intensity lights. These big lights are used to cover wide areas and are usually positioned rather high. Another common exterior lighting unit is the Maxi-Brute, which has nine daylight-balanced 1kW PAR lamps arranged in a dice pattern. While these are multiple-source lights, they are used often on lifts to flood streets at night or shine in through windows that are gelled with diffusion (more on windows later in this chapter). The smaller version of this unit is the nine-light Fay, which has two plugs on it, allowing it to be plugged into two different circuits, thus making it able to be plugged into household wall outlets if need be.

Staging a scene in a shady area allows more control over the lighting, as we've discussed

PHOTO 7.15 **A Maxi-Brute, photo courtesy of Mole-Richardson**

earlier. Your lights can be smaller and more effective.

In Photos 7.16 and 7.17 from *Stray*, actress Michelle Page sits on a bench at the train station. A 1,200 HMI PAR with a medium lens was aimed through a 4-foot × 4-foot frame of opal gel to give Michelle a diffused-edge light, highlighting her hair and giving her some soft modeling. Notice how the bench was moved out from against the wall so the skylight could give her some nice, soft frontal fill light. Since all the shots from this angle were either close-ups or over-the-shoulder, this repositioning of the bench was never noticeable.

The bench was positioned so that behind Michelle's head was a bright spot of light on the grass and a glint off the train cars, which added depth to the shot. Soft bounce off the back

PHOTO 7.16 **Behind the scenes of *Stray*, photo by Carlin Canfield**

train cars from the sky added a slight edge separating her from the background, so no backlight was needed. Thus, one light was all that was needed to give the feeling of late-afternoon sun. This was an example of using the natural light to our advantage and augmenting it with a daylight-balanced PAR light. It was done simply by positioning the actors and set pieces to what looked best for the camera.

PHOTO 7.17 **Michelle Page, *Stray*, Nena Eskridge Productions**

In Photo 7.18, two 1,200w PAR HMIs with medium flood lenses through 4-foot × 4-foot opal diffusion frames cross-key Michelle and Aaron. One unit was up on a porch camera left shining down from about a 30-degree angle, while the other was off right on the little walkway that went through the front garden that was about halfway up the steps. No frontal fill was added or needed for the wide shot.

PHOTO 7.18 Michelle Page and Aaron Lustig, *Stray*, Nena Eskridge Productions

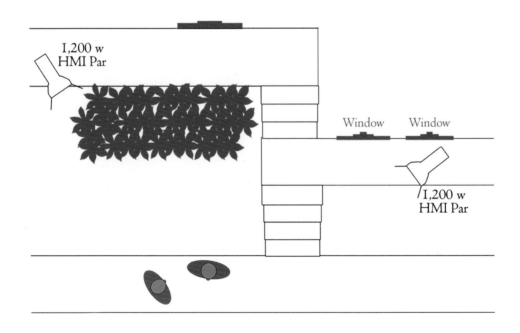

DIAGRAM 7.2 Lighting plot for exterior house, *Stray*

PHOTO 7.19 **Michelle Page and Aaron Lustig,** *Stray,* **Nena Eskridge Productions**

In Photo 7.19, a bounce card adds a little kick to Aaron from camera right, and natural skylight provides the fill. This scene was shot after 6 p.m., so the direct sun had already disappeared behind the treetops. The diffusion in front of the PAR lights softened the light in order to blend it in with the natural ambient light and the suburban surroundings. Notice that although diffused, the cross key ¾ behind Aaron still provides a nice edge to his face and shoulder.

The 1,200w PAR HMI lights worked for us because they were only around 15 feet away from the actors and because we weren't fighting direct sunlight. On a bright sunny day we would have needed 6kW units or more to compete with the sun. Or, we could have flown in a butterfly to silk the direct sun and then use our 1,200w PAR lights with more focused lenses and get a similar look. The difference would have been a much brighter background as direct sun would be illuminating it, which would have created a different feeling for the scene. It wouldn't have been as muted and understated, rather more vibrant. While either may have worked, the look we achieved seemed to fit the intention of the scene better.

Could we have shot it without the lights? No. The sun was behind the trees, which meant the ambient light was constantly changing. We had to shoot the wide shot, his over-the-shoulder, then her over-the-shoulder, and then both of them walking up the steps of the porch and into the house. It was 6 p.m., which meant cars were coming home from work, so takes were often stopped due to sound problems. It progressively started to get a little cooler looking and a little darker looking as we shot. Although we were shooting with two sensitive cameras (Sony PMW F3s), in order to give the editor images that all matched, we needed to have one consistent intensity, color, and texture light source that matched from angle to angle. That was our 1,200w HMI PAR lights, which were plugged into the household outlets.

A number of other lighting units are available that can have daylight-balanced lamps, including LED lights, fluorescent units, and the newest technology plasma lights. These aren't yet made in the same high intensity as HMIs and Maxi-Brutes, so they may not be ideal for lighting larger areas or wide shots. But for medium to close-up shots, these lighter-weight, smaller-sized units work very well.

Larger LED lights that use only 500 watts can put out the same lumens as a 1,200w HMI, such as the Nila SL unit and the BriteShot Luminator. The thing to remember is that all LED units have multiple-point sources, so they emit multiple overlapping shadows. To minimize this problem, most DPs aim them through some kind of diffusion. That will soften the light, but also decrease the intensity.

Plasma lights are all 5,600 Kelvin, and Hive makes a plasma Fresnel that draws 275 watts while emitting the same lumens as a 575-watt HMI and a smaller-wattage plasma PAR light, both single-point sources. They also make a plasma Mini-Brute with four lamps that, with all four lamps on, will output the same light as a 2,500w HMI, but again it is a multiple-point source unit. We could have shot the same way with these on *Stray*, but they weren't on the market yet for rent.

The most economical and easiest to use lighting units outside are daylight-lamped fluorescent units and smaller daylight-balanced LED fixtures. These have less output and fall off rather quickly, but can provide very nice soft key or fill when used in the shade or up close to the subject. On *Project Runway*, oftentimes we were moving so fast that all Gus, our LD, wanted to use outside was a 1-foot × 1-foot LitePanel, to either just add a light kick or a little fill on the close-ups. LEDs are actually tiny hard lights, but when used outside where the ambient skylight actually is brighter, they can be used without diffusion for accenting. News and documentary cameramen often have LED obie lights which run off a battery. Frezzi, LitePanel, Ikan, and others all make small units with camera shoe mounts. Through diffusion they add a nice soft wash that fills in and slightly boosts up the news reporter's or subject's face. Without diffusion they are sharp and often irritating for the subject to look at—like those annoying LED car headlights you see at night. Any lights on the camera can be distracting, as they shine directly into the subjects' eyes. Reporters are used to this, but not necessarily other people who might be on camera.

STUFF TO REMEMBER

- The sun never stops moving, so the angle of the light changes throughout the day.

- The color of the light outdoors changes throughout the day.

- Shoot with the sun behind the subject when possible.

- Bounce cards and reflectors can redirect sunlight to fill in faces.

- Butterflies are large silks that can soften or cut the sunlight, but they require careful attention by the grips.

- Lights used outdoors must be balanced for 5,600 Kelvin, such as HMIs, plasma, LED, and daylight-lamped fluorescent units.

- Shooting in the shade makes using lights more effective.

PUTTING IT INTO PRACTICE

- Shoot outside with the sun behind the subject. Use different-size bounce surfaces to see the difference in intensity they create.

- Shoot outside with the subject in the shade using a bounce card to reflect light onto the face.

8 DEALING WITH DAYLIGHT 2:
Working with Windows

Often we shoot in real locations that have windows that can provide both problems and opportunities.

PROBLEMS OF WORKING WITH WINDOWS

- The sun is always moving, so any direct sunlight coming in through the window will slowly and constantly change, until it goes away completely.

- There is a difference in color temperature of the light outside and the lights used inside. As discussed earlier, standard film lights are 3,200K, while daylight is 5,600K. If the camera is white-balanced to tungsten lights, the light outside will appear blue, and if the camera is balanced to daylight, the lighting inside records amber.

- The sun makes the outdoors so much brighter than lighting indoors, that if a window is in the shot, it can be overexposed and bleached out.

OPPORTUNITES OF WORKING WITH WINDOWS

- Sometimes, but rarely, the light coming in from outside will work as it is to light the entire shot.

- Light coming in from a window can be used as the key light, so only some fill and maybe a backlight need to be added.

- Light coming in from outside will bring up the overall ambient light in the room and can serve as the fill, so just key light and backlight need to be added.

- (In both of these scenarios, we would still have to pay some attention to what the light looks like in the background and make some adjustments with flags, bounce cards, or small lighting units.)

- Windows in the shot add depth and dimension, as well as an illusion of reality.

- What is seen outside the window in the shot can help set time and place.

HOW LIGHT COMES THROUGH A WINDOW

Most people don't stop and consider all the light that comes through a window. If we want to imitate it, we need to really look at it. What most people miss is that almost every window has light of different textures and different colors coming in from a variety of angles, which basically falls into three types.

1. Direct sunlight is hard light that comes in at a downward angle in line with the sun. It is around 5,600K, and slowly moves throughout the day and generally goes away at some point. This beam of sunlight will reflect off of the floor or wall inside the room, producing soft light that bounces up, illuminating the bottom of the inside walls (as discussed earlier in the section on lighting walls). This bounce will get dimmer and go way as the sun moves.

2. Skylight—bounce light off the blue or overcast sky—is soft light that comes in the window from a variety of angles off the sky (straight down, from all sides, from 45 degrees, etc.). Skylight is cooler in color temperature than sunlight—around 6,500K—and remains mostly constant throughout the majority of the day. It will change as the sky changes from clear to cloudy or vice versa.

3. Bounce light reflected off the ground, trees, and other buildings outside the window is soft light that comes in from below, horizontally, sideways, and many other angles. While the light will come in all day, its intensity and color may change depending on when and if any direct hard sunlight hits it and reflects off it.

So, there isn't just a beam of sunlight that shines in through a window; multiple angles of multiple textures and colors are coming in all at the same time. We can use this knowledge to better utilize windows to our advantage when lighting, and to better imitate them.

BALANCING COLOR TEMPERATURE

As mentioned earlier, the light coming in from outside is 5,600K to 6,400K, depending on the weather outside. In order to make sure that all the colors of the set, costumes, and makeup record correctly, we need to set the color temperature of the camera (white balance) to the color of the majority of light. It's always best if we can make all the light match in color temperature, because then we have control over manipulating the colors the way we want (more on this in Chapter 10 on using color). Following are a few methods to accomplish balancing our indoor light with our outdoor light:

- Use daylight-balanced lighting units inside such as HMIs, LEDs, or fluorescent units with daylight-balanced (5,600K) lamps to match the color of the daylight coming in from outside.

- Put CTO (color temperature orange, also known as 85) gel over every window to change the color of the outside light coming in from 5,600K to 3,200K, to match the color temperature of standard tungsten film lights.

- Place CTB (color correction blue, also known as Full Blue) gels on tungsten film lights to change their color from 3,200K to 5,600K and match the color temperature of the daylight coming into the room through the window. (This will drop their intensity quite a bit.)

- White-balance the camera in a mixture of all the color temperatures in the room and hope for the best.

When we have control over the situation and some time to actually light, the first two options are the best. Gelling the windows is very easy and accomplishes two things: changing the color temperature and lowering the intensity of what is seen outside the window. This method is often preferred if there are only a few windows. If, however, there is an entire wall of windows, using daylight-balanced units is the fastest and easiest method, but it's also more expensive because of the cost of renting the units. The last option is the least desirable, but it is what many news and documentary cameramen are often forced to do, as they often don't have time to set up lights.

I was gaffer on an episode of *Models of the Runway* (2010), in which the models would be shopping at a chic SoHo bouquet. I had about an hour before the cameras arrived, and my instructions were to hang a china ball over the cash register and one over the small sofa area in front of the mirrors by the changing rooms (which were more like tiny closets). I hid a daylight 1-foot × 1-foot LED LitePanel on a top shelf behind a pile of blouses directed into this area, and then set up another daylight LitePanel on a stand between the dress forms in the front window. The camera operators set their color temperature to 4,300K as an average between the color of the daylight coming in from the show window, the two daylight LitePanels, the two tungsten china balls, and the normal display lights of the store. Although there were some variations in colors in the shots, it looked rather natural and perfectly acceptable for reality TV (we will discuss lighting for reality TV and documentaries in Chapter 13).

This worked because the DP had scouted the location earlier and had an idea of how he wanted the light mixed. As mentioned throughout this book, scouting locations is vital to lighting.

SCOUTING WINDOWS

If you will be shooting in a room with windows, scout your location a few days before you shoot (or have someone you trust scout the location). Make sure you take the following important notes so you can plan your lighting and shooting schedule accordingly:

• Which direction do the windows face (north, south, east, or west)?

• How many windows are there, and how big?

• When (if at all) does sunlight come directly in which windows, and for how long?

• What is visible looking through the windows?

• What area is immediately outside the window (flower bed, rooftop, balcony, etc.)?

• What kind of window treatments are there (curtains, blinds, shutters, etc.)?

• Something that is very useful is one of those apps for mobile devices that tracks the sun and can tell you where the sun will be at any date and time you input. (For a list of apps useful to lighting, see Appendix 2, "Resources"). Using this allows you to determine when and if direct sunlight will come through a given window.

WINDOWS NOT IN THE SHOT

If the windows in the room are not in the shot, we can black them out using black cloth, and then light the scene with whatever lighting units we have. This may be difficult and time-consuming if there are a lot of windows or the windows are very

> **"The best windows are the ones you block out—then you become the sun."**
>
> —GUS DOMINGUEZ, TV LIGHTING DIRECTOR /DP

large. For large windows, a butterfly can be set up inside with a solid black to block the light. We did this frequently while shooting four scenes in a large empty study with four windows, one of which was very wide. The grips set up an 8-foot × 8-foot butterfly to cut that window when we needed to and used a 4-foot × 4-foot black floppy, which is a 4 × 4 black flag with a flap that opens to become a 4-foot-wide by 8-foot-high flag, in front of another tall window. Other times we used a silk on the butterfly in front of whichever window the direct sunlight came in (when that window was out of the shot). This allowed us to use the sunlight as ambient fill, but not have to worry about hard shadows from bright bounce.

In another room, when we needed to shoot night scenes during the day, we simply blacked out the windows by hanging black cloth over them. The grips spring-clamped the cloth to the top molding of the windows. This way, when we needed light to re-set or take a break, the grips could easily just drop the cloth. Sometimes you may want to rig the cloth on the outside of the windows—just in case one gets into the shot. But be aware that the wind will catch the cloth and peel it off at the worst possible moment—right when you finally are getting the best actor performance.

WINDOWS IN THE SHOT

I was a camera assistant trainee on a movie with legendary cinematographer Haskell Wexler. The first day at lunch he told a story about the film he just finished with a hot, young new director. He said they walked into a cabin that they were going to shoot in, and the sunlight was filtering in through the windows. The director turned to him and said, "This is perfect. Let's shoot available light." Haskell turned to the door and shouted out to his gaffer, "We're shooting available light—so get me every light available!"

The human eye can see easily inside and outside at the same time, because the human eye has a magically wide dynamic range that no camera presently made, nor likely ever made, can match. Not only can the eye see easily both the bright images outside and the much dimmer images inside at the same time, the brain can also mix the colors from outside daylight and inside incandescent lamps without really noticing the extreme difference in color—something no camera can do either. When we shoot a scene with a window in it, we will want to imitate what the human eye sees in order to maintain that illusion of reality, so we have to address both the brightness differences and the color differences.

Interestingly enough, we can now get away with much more than we did 20 years ago, as viewers have become so used to watching their own home videos and seeing blown-out and bluish windows. This doesn't mean we want our images to look like amateur home movies. In fact, we never want that, because then the viewers will think we're amateurs like they are and our film isn't worth spending the time watching—and certainly not worth paying for. But this does mean we can allow our windows to be much brighter than our inside, and we can allow our windows to turn a little bluish. In fact, today's audiences sort of expect windows in the shot to be brighter and bluer than the inside.

As in the story told by Haskell Wexler, sometimes people walk into a location and a shaft of sunlight is coming in at just the right angle, and they think they can just shoot. By then it's already too late. That sunlight is moving away at a slow and constant pace, and by the time the camera is set up and the actors have rehearsed, the light will be totally different, if not totally gone.

Never plan on using actual direct sunlight. A friend of mine was planning a shoot for a festival short with a shot of a child sitting in an empty attic. He scouted his location a month in advance and wrote down exactly when the sun came through the attic window just right, hitting the center of the floor and how long it stayed there. When he came back a month later to shoot, the sun no longer was coming in the window at that angle, didn't hit the same spot, and disappeared sooner. The reason? The sun is never back in the same spot in the sky within the same year. The Earth revolves around the sun, which means each day, the sun moves a slightly different path through the sky. A month is a big difference.

In practice, if the DP wants a ray of sunlight coming in through a window, the gaffer places a bright light outside the window shining in. This way the light is consistent and always under the DP's control. More on this later in this chapter.

If you're suicidal and determined to use the real rays of direct sunlight in your shot, make sure you are set up and rehearsed well before the sun actually starts coming in through the window. Get there hours before you want to shoot. Make sure the AD and your gaffer know exactly how long you will have to shoot once the sun starts coming in, and before it has moved enough that the angle of the rays coming through the window will be so different that the shots will no longer match. Shoot the wide shots first, as you can always fake the close-ups using your own lights. Don't do a lot of takes, and move fast.

Once the direct rays of sunlight have vanished from the room, you will not be able to make a convincing match for a wide shot, but you can use a hard light, such as an open-faced unit or a Fresnel, or better yet a Source Four ERS, to imitate the hard sunlight rays for tight shots. You could even use a daylight-balanced light for this, such as a small HMI or one of the new plasma lights, if you have the budget (make sure you rented them and have them for the day of this shoot).

Some companies such as ARRI and LitePanel have come out with LED Fresnels as well, which are versatile and would work great for this but are expensive to rent. Don't use a daylight-balanced LED light with multiple-point sources, as the multiple shadows will not match the single distinct shadow that is produce by the direct rays of the sun.

You can also use tungsten lights with full CTB (color correction blue) on it. Just remember that once you add the gel, you will cut the lights' intensity. So it is best to use a higher-wattage unit, such as a 2kW Fresnel. It's all a matter of creating a similar contrast between light and shadow on the subject to match what it was when the real rays of sunlight were coming in. This will often require you to lower the overall ambient and fill light in the room, as your tungsten "sun" will never be as bright as the real one was. So close the curtains or blinds a bit on the windows, or put a card over the lower half of the window, or tape diffusion or black cloth over the window—whatever it takes to lower the amount of brightness of the skylight coming into the room compared to the brightness of your fake sun.

If the scene will take some time to shoot, or you just want more control over the look, plan on shooting when there is no direct sunlight coming through the window, and when what is seen outside the window is in the shade for the longest time. Remember that there is plenty of other light coming in through the window from the sky and reflected off of whatever is outside.

Except for predawn and after sunset, the light outside will always be much brighter than we can comfortably make the light inside. Just as lighting our backgrounds is an artistic choice that can affect the mood of the scene, how well we can see outside the windows, and the color of light from the window, are also artistic choices that we want to have control over. We have several options as to how to deal with what we see through the windows:

• Tape thick diffusion, tracing paper, white sheets, white translucent cloth, or even plain white translucent shower curtain over the outside of the window to allow the window to turn totally white and burn out—a look that has become totally acceptable to the average viewer. To accomplish this, we need a consistent light source shining on the outside of the window. So you would need to schedule the shooting in this room for only the amount of time it gets direct sun on the windows. Better yet, know when the windows will get no direct sun, and place a bright light outside shining on the window.

In Photo 8.1 from *Dark Tarot,* tracing paper was taped over the two side doorway windows, and a light was placed outside aimed at them to burn them out. I don't know what my gaffer Conor Stalvey used; I left that up to him. I just told him to burn out the windows, and he did. This is an example of how DPs and gaffers often work together. The actresses were lit by two 4-bank × 4-foot Kino Flos with daylight lamps, 90 degrees to camera each side, to give the feeling of them being lit by the two side windows. This was actually shot after sunset.

PHOTO 8.1 **Papered windows, Lauren Muraski and Susan Adriensen, *Dark Tarot,* DGW Films**

- Tape neutral-density (ND) gel (a transparent gray-tinted gel) over the window. This cuts the brightness outside but doesn't change the color, which allows the camera to be able to see better what is out there. ND gel comes in three grades—ND3 (one f-stop), ND6 (two f-stops), and ND9 (three f-stops). It also comes mixed with CTO (orange 85 gel) to allow us to change the color temperature of what is seen outside, so that it matches the color of tungsten film lights, at the same time as cutting the intensity. That also comes in three grades: 85ND3, 85ND6, and 85ND9.

In Photo 8.2 from *Dark Tarot,* the windows behind Natasa Babic in the far room were gelled with ND6 so that the green of the trees outside would read on camera and not bleach out.

Gels are usually taped outside a window when possible, since it allows the gel to be pulled tight, and the window can be covered with one large section. But sometimes that isn't possible. The location was on the second floor, and we didn't have a ladder high enough for the grips to gel the window from outside. So our key grip Nick Greenfield carefully cut the gel to the exact size of the window and then taped it into the frame with black gaffer's tape. He knew it would be in the background and out of focus enough that the black tape would read as a black window frame. The window frames are actually white in the entire house, but he covered it completely to turn it black.

PHOTO 8.2 **ND gelled windows, Natasa Babic,** *Dark Tarot,* **DGW Films**

PHOTO 8.3 85 gelled windows, Jade Elysan and Alexandra Landau, *Dark Tarot,* DGW Films

In Photo 8.3 from *Dark Tarot,* the scene takes place during sunset, but was shot during midday. In another room on the second floor, Nick taped CTO gel to the inside of the window using white gaffer's tape over the entire window frame. Real sunlight warmed by the gel strikes the wall behind Jade Elysan, adding a nice natural streak. Since the sun is shining in, what is seen outside is actually in shade, being backlit by the sun, yet it still washes out as being bright sun outside.

Both Jade and Alexandra Landau, seated on the floor, are key-lit by a 4-bank × 4-foot Kino Flo in the room off to the right, which is mostly edge-lighting them, but imitating the direction and feeling of the window. A Diva light, which is a smaller, soft fluorescent unit made by Kino Flo, lights them from the hallway just above and off left of the camera. The Diva is flagged off the camera right hall wall. The Diva has a dimmer built into it and was set at a lower intensity than the 4-bank × 4-foot Kino Flo. Both units had daylight lamps.

It's often best to shoot when whatever is seen outside is in shade and thus not so bright that it burns out or overexposes too much. Bring up the intensity inside so the contrast isn't too wide.

In Photo 8.4 from *Stray,* the sun had already gone behind the rooftops, and the trees in the shot were in shadow. Daylight-balanced LED lights were used inside to light both Michelle and the door in order to bring up their intensity and get them closer to the intensity outside, which still was overexposed somewhat.

Lighting a person through a window is not the preferred method. As you can see from the photo, a lot of light still ends up on the window itself. We need some light there to provide definition, but it's usually better to have the face behind brighter than the window frame. This was a short shot that started on the door handle then tilted up to the lock, ending on her face—so we needed light on the door itself. We also didn't have a lot of time to get the shot, as it was the end of the shooting day. The best way to light someone the camera sees through a window is to place lights on the actor side

PHOTO 8.4 **Clear windows, Michelle Page,** *Stray,* **Nena Eskridge Productions**

of the window and side-light the subject. That wasn't possible here either, as the door was inset, and there was an exterior screen door that was propped open to get it out of the shot.

- Totally overexpose the windows so they completely burn out by shooting inside at a wide-open f-stop.

In Photo 8.5 from *Last Day of Winter,* a Chimera on an open-faced 1kW was used inside the kitchen (you can see its reflection in the tea kettle), but the exposure was very wide open to get the window

PHOTO 8.5 **Burned-out windows,** *The Last Day of Winter,* **MTG Productions**

to burn out. There was no direct sunlight coming through the window, only ambient skylight, but it was bright enough to add a nice kick to the pots, backlight the coffee, and flare out the window.

Photo 8.6 shows Luko Adjaffi in the music video *Secret Window,* a white pro-mist diffusion filter was added to the camera to help flare out the window and provide the halo look to the highlights. The piano was moved into the corner flanked by the two windows so that the one on the left could become his key, while the one on the right behind him could serve as his ¾ backlight. A 750w Rifa without any color correction gel on it was used as a fill light off right, which only had a minor effect, as the real daylight overpowered it.

PHOTO 8.6 **Flared-out windows, Luko Adjaffi, *Secret Window,* Clarke Productions**

LIGHTING THROUGH WINDOWS

Aiming lights from outside in through a window is a standard practice in the industry. When bright light comes in through the window in the shot, not only does it establish motivation and give the image a great amount of believability, it simply looks good. Creating our own sunlight replaces the ever-moving sun with a constant light that can be relied on take after take, hour after hour. In big-budget productions, DPs will have large, powerful lights set up on scaffolding outside windows shining in. The sun never moves, and the crew can shoot all day and even all night, and it will all look the same.

For the last scene of the movie *Michael Clayton,* DP Robert Elswit had six scissor lifts lined up outside the New York Hilton with three Maxi-Brutes on each one (that's a total of 27,000 watts per lift) all shining in through the windows of the second-floor conference center lobby, which were all covered with tracing paper by the grips. It looked great.

On the movie *The Shining,* legendary DP John Alcott had a wall of PAR lights rigged on swivel poles outside the hotel lobby windows that could all be pivoted so they could be aimed any direction through the lobby windows. He even had them all move once during a shot, tracking Jack Nicholson as he walked through the lobby to produce a truly subliminally creepy effect.

Not everyone has these kinds of budgets. But that doesn't mean you still can't do a lot by shining lights through windows. You can get really great effects with smaller and fewer lights, especially when your shot is tighter.

The following stills are from an internet commercial for a bank shot on location. The scene was of a mother coming into a kitchen with her young son, talking to the camera about saving for his future. DP Rick Siegel wanted to use the window as a motivated light source. So outside the window we placed three HMI lights.

In Photo 8.7, the light on the left is a 1,200w PAR with a medium lens aimed straight in through the window to mimic the sun. It has a ½ CTO gel on it to warm it up, and is scrimmed with a double and a single, known as a triple, which takes its intensity down 1½ stops. This light was the subject's key light, and provided a nice slash on the back kitchen cabinets.

A second 1,200w HMI PAR with a medium lens, but no gel, is to the right of the window, up against the house, aimed into a 4-foot × 4-foot sheet of beadboard that bounces soft light back in through the window. This provided a motivated soft ambient fill. A flag was rigged above the window to cut any real direct sunlight that might dare to try and come through the window. (The silk over the PAR on the right was being used as a rain hat to protect the light when it drizzled. The other lights also had rain hats, but they were removed by the grips after the light rain stopped so they could use the stands inside.)

PHOTO 8.7 **Three HMI lights through a kitchen window**

Last is a 575w HMI Fresnel with ½ CTO that was precisely positioned near the window so that the shadow of its stand from the first PAR falls on the window frame and not through the window. This light is aimed at the kitchen island, highlighting what the actress will pick up in her hand. The PAR light couldn't spread wide enough through the window to hit both there and the subject's face. If we moved the PAR back, it would spread wider, but the window would cut a smaller portal. So the 575w Fresnel had to be added to help augment the sunlight-through-the-window effect.

PHOTO 8.8 Kino Flo, flags, stands, gobo inside kitchen setup

But the lights outside are only for coming in through the window. Two more lights needed to be added inside. The main fill light was a 4-bank × 4-foot Kino Flo with daylight lamps set inside the room to the left of camera, raised up to the ceiling, with both a top chop to flag light off the background and the tops of the back wall and a bottom flag cutting light hitting the stools in the foreground. This way the light only fills in the front of the subject's face and adds some wash to the kitchen.

The stools were lit separately by a small "joker," which is a 300w HMI PAR light aimed through a window pattern cut into a showcard, with opal diffusion taped over it. This provided both modeling to the stools and a soft breakup of light and shadow on them. This light was also gelled with ½ CTO.

In Photo 8.9, notice all the grip stands. One was needed to add a double net to "slow down" (lower the intensity) of the joker on the stools. Another stand was used to hold the window pattern. Another was used to hold the top chop, and still another to hold the bottom cutter. Someone once told me that you can tell how good a DP is by how many grip stands are being used. The more in play, the better the DP is at lighting, because the more care has been taken to sculpt the light.

PHOTO 8.9 HMI joker, flags, nets, and stands inside kitchen setup

In Photo 8.10, my buddy Stephen Scotto (a great LD himself, who was the production manager on this shoot) is standing in for the actress in the final lighting. Notice how the 575w HMI Fresnel outside the window highlights the peppers and the milk but blends in, looking totally natural.

We don't always have to use this many lights for a sunlight-through-the-window setup. It all depends on the mood that is required for the scene. This was a commercial featuring a mother and son

PHOTO 8.10 Stephen Scotto stands in for the kitchen lighting, lit by DP Rick Siegel

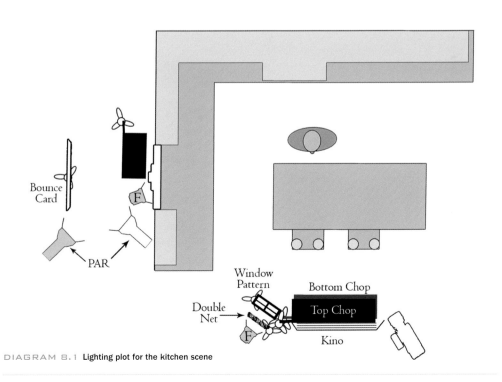

DIAGRAM 8.1 Lighting plot for the kitchen scene

returning from grocery shopping, so the desired look was happy and fresh—wholesome, in fact. But if the scene was supposed to be more dramatic, the lighting would be different.

In Photo 8.11 from *Stray,* both Aaron Lutig's and Michelle Page's key lights were two 1,200w HMI PARs with medium lenses set up outside the windows on the roof of the porch. This was a real location, and all the bedrooms were on the second floor, as is typical of most homes. I had scouted the location a few weeks before and picked this bedroom over a different choice because this one had a place to put lights outside the windows—on the roof of the front porch.

PHOTO 8.11 **Michelle Page ¾ backlit by 1,200-watt HMI through the window, *Stray,* Nena Eskridge Productions**

One light was aimed at Michelle and the other at Aaron. This provided our direct early-morning-sunlight look, with light coming in low and hard across the bed. A 650w Fresnel with ½ CTB on it was positioned 90 degrees to the right, aimed directly at the lamp in the background. It didn't hit either of the actors. The HMIs outside couldn't hit the lamp due to the angle required to hit the actors, so the Fresnel needed to be added to help flesh out the lighting and give the background some dimension. Notice the bounce of light off the white sheets onto the back wall, casting a shadow on the piles of books behind the lamp shade. Our fake sunlight did that all on its own. If it hadn't, it would have been a good idea to stand some white bounce cards along the far side of the bed to accomplish this.

Since this was a bittersweet moment and a heart-to-heart talk in bed, I chose not to add any fill light. The bounce within the room was enough to bring up her face, but keeping her face edge-lit helped the emotional moment of the scene. She's shy and hesitant at this moment, and the lighting works for it—she's barely coming out of her own shadow. Sometimes less is more.

While HMI lights are daylight-balanced and produce much more light per watt than tungsten units, a similar look could have been achieved without the use of these expensive lights. If I didn't have the HMI lights available, I could have used other lights, such as three Source Four units with 36 lenses through each window. The total wattage of those six lights—575 watts each—would have been only slightly more than the HMIs, but they rent for much less, as they are theater lights. They would all have to have been gelled with ½ or full CTB to match the daylight, which would have cut the overall intensity inside the room, but the sharp beams would have made a nice pattern coming through the blinds and would definitely have given the actors that edge. There are always a number of ways to light a scene, which will all work. Each DP may well light the same room totally differently.

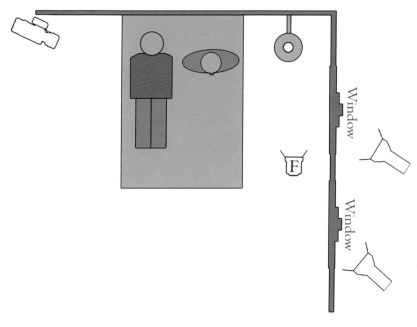

DIAGRAM 8.2 **Lighting plot for bedroom scene**

This couldn't have been done relying on the real sun, which did start the day coming directly in through the windows. When the sun came in, we didn't use the HMIs. But very soon the sun moved during the three hours it took to shoot this sensitive dialogue scene, and the HMIs took over, keeping the look exactly the same. As the sun moved, we had to keep changing the blinds on the window, as it was highlighting them. We wanted a burned-out-window look, but also to have a tiny bit of color outside. While our fake sun through the window never changed, the intensity of what could be seen through the window did. So the blinds on the window also became our way of adjusting the intensity of what was seen outside by opening and closing them to camera.

That is another thing to always consider—your window treatment. Sheer curtains look great on windows in the shot. They catch the light and allow it to soften while being backlit. Heavy curtains just cut the light and can work if the scene calls for a feeling of confinement or severity. Blinds have more of a middle-class (because of wooden shutters) or office-like feeling to them. A window with screens in them cuts the brightness of what you see through it. So, often we remove the window screens when shooting a window we want to burn out. Also, be careful about windows with the screens up or only covering half the window. This will record the window as being two-toned, one half brighter than the other. That looks a little odd in the background.

Photo 8.12 is from a cinematography class group project. Their assignment was to shoot a short, no dialogue, one-page script, but in this room, which was almost all windows. Instead of trying to avoid or shoot around them, the students quickly learned to incorporate the windows and the natural light into their shot by closing the sheers and balancing for the outdoor light, allowing the tungsten units inside to go warm, which helped them achieve the early-morning look that the script called for.

In Photo 8.13, a still from student Michelle Perkowski's lighting final, the window has translucent curtains and is lit with a 2kW Fresnel from outside. This was actually shot at night after dark, but the light

PHOTO 8.12 **FDU cinematography class location shoot**

PHOTO 8.13 **FDU lighting class final lit by Michelle Perkowski**

PHOTO 8.14 Aaron Lustig and Michelle Page, *Stray*, Nena Eskridge Productions

striking the curtain sells the feeling of an early-evening, romantic dinner date. Notice her use of lavender-colored light under the table, which she saw in a painting she used for inspiration. This added a nice dimension and romantic feeling.

Shooting with windows doesn't always mean shooting in a normal room. In Photo 8.14 from a scene in *Stray*, Aaron and Michelle are in a train car. Although lined with windows, train cars really don't get much sun, especially when they are parked in a train yard surrounded by other train cars. Direct sunlight never came into this car, and the ambient light was also always dim, made even dimmer by the fact that for the two days we shot there, it was overcast. That meant there was no ambient skylight fill inside the train. So we kept all the shots as tight as possible,

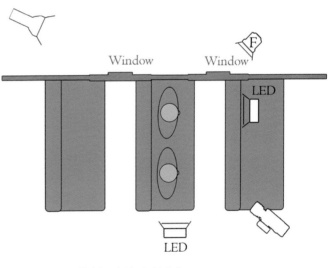

DIAGRAM 8.3 Lighting plot for inside train

not showing the rest of the train car because we simply didn't have enough lighting units to light the whole thing. Sometimes you need to pick your angles based on what you can and cannot light well.

Inside the train car were two daylight LED lights shining down through the luggage racks, one 50 degrees off to the right of camera and one about 45 degrees off to the left of camera. Both were diffused with opal gel. The backlight was a 1,200w HMI PAR with a medium lens set outside the train car window, behind them and out of the shot. In other words, three-point lighting. A very big green screen was set up by the grips outside the two windows in the shot that was lit by the ambient skylight. (We will discuss lighting for green screen in Chapter 12.) To aid the after-effects artist's work with the green screen, a 650w Fresnel with CTB and light diffusion was placed outside the window to soft-rim Michelle. The exposure was set so that the backlight would be very hot on them, giving the feeling of bright direct sunlight in the late afternoon.

Even on a very low budget, you can still have light coming in through the window to provide that feeling of reality and depth. In a previous chapter, I used the boy in the woodshop as an example of three-point lighting. This was a small location with not much electricity available, and because it was a test commercial, there was no budget. Since I knew what the location was, I knew that I had a window and planned accordingly.

In Photo 8.15, the boy, Mitchell Elkowitz, is lit with a Chimera on a 1kW open-faced light 45 degrees off camera right—the same side of him as the window in the background. The viewer just accepts that this may be soft skylight coming in through an unseen window.

A 300w Fresnel is off camera left ¾ backlighting him without diffusion. The sharpness of this light has the feeling of a ray of direct sunlight through the back window.

A 2kW tungsten Fresnel is shining in through the back window aimed to rim the window frame and Mitchell's father in the background. This provides modeling and depth to the image—but also the illusion of reality. The 2kW Fresnel outside the back window allowed us to shoot all day without having to worry about losing the sun. We were lucky that it was overcast, which was what we wanted, as it brought down the intensity of what was seen through the window. This meant I didn't have to gel it with ND. That would have cut the intensity of the light coming in from the 2kW.

PHOTO 8.15 Mitchell Elkowitz, "Building a Bridge" test spot, Airworthy Productions

A 650w Fresnel with diffusion was set off camera right, as high as the roof would allow, aimed into the background to bring up the shadows and imitate how ambient skylight from the window would bring up the overall level inside. I only had that one 2kW and an ARRI light kit, so there was no way to bounce another bright light into beadboard outside the window to get this effect. Nor could I just bounce a light into the ceiling, as the ceiling was dark wood.

The wood shop was located in a garage, and the door was open in order to set the camera back far enough to get the angle and framing the director wanted. A white card was used to bounce skylight to fill the left side of Mitchell's face. If we didn't have an open garage door, I would have had to add his fill by either bouncing a light into the card or adding a low-intensity softlight. The camera was white-balanced on a white card, mixing the tungsten light from the Chimera with the skylight ambient fill. This allowed the image outside the window to not turn too blue, and it warmed up Mitchell's face to give him a childlike glow, which the director liked.

This is an example of using the same concepts as the bigger budget shoot with a low-budget amount of equipment. This was a commercial, so the desired look was a happy one, not an overly dramatic feeling, so the contrast on Mitchell's face was very low and pleasant.

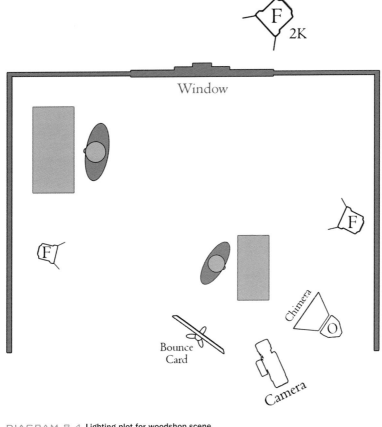

DIAGRAM 8.4 Lighting plot for woodshop scene

AMBIENT SKYLIGHT POSING AS DIRECT SUNLIGHT

Sometimes we just can't place lights outside that will come in through the windows. Maybe the room is on a floor too high up, or there's a ditch right outside the window, or for some other reason you can't place a light outside and get it to aim through the window. In these cases we can balance our indoor lighting so that the light coming in from outside remains the brightest and serves as our key. It is always best to do this when only skylight and bounce are coming through the window, not direct sunlight, for reasons discussed earlier. But we can still make this ambient skylight appear on camera to be bright "sunlight."

In Photo 8.16 from *Dark Tarot,* the trees outside the windows are actually in the shade and not being hit with direct sunlight, yet they photograph bright. Natasa Babic is back-lit by skylight and from bounce off the ground 18 feet below. The only direct sunlight coming in barely rims the left edge of the back window, but it does provide bounce light, which reflects up and adds some glow to the lower half of the wall with the window and in the corner.

PHOTO 8.16 **Windows in shade, Natasa Babic,** *Dark Tarot,* **DGW Films**

We planned on shooting these shots in this room after the sun passed over the house and when we knew we wouldn't have to deal with direct sunbeams coming into the room.

Natasa's face is lit by a 4-bank × 4-foot Kino Flo with daylight lamps set 90 degrees off to the right, but the trunk is lit with a Source Four with a 50-degree lens and a sunset-colored glass gobo in it from about 30 degrees left of camera (explained further in Chapter 10, "Working with Color"). We wanted the outside to be overexposed, but still get the color of the trees to come through. This combination of lighting and colored light renders a sunset feeling to the image. The camera is exposing for the trunk, allowing Natasa's face to be slightly underexposed and the back of her arm slightly overexposed. Picking your aperture is important—remember that the viewer's eye will go to the brightest thing in frame. The lighting and aperture setting for this shot sends the viewer's eye to the trunk, which was the director's desire (in the scene the trunk has moved by itself to get closer to her while her back was turned).

Simple can often work great. In Photo 8.17, also from *Dark Tarot,* Lauren Muraski and Susan Adriensen are both lit by the bright skylight from outside.

PHOTO 8.17 **Ambient skylight, Lauren Muraski and Susan Adriensen,** *Dark Tarot,* **DGW Films**

No gel was put on the window, no outside lights were added, and the sun was not shining directly in the window. But the look on camera was very nice, because of how bright the exterior light was compared to the light level inside. A 4-bank × 4-foot Kino Flo with daylight lamps was the only light used besides the actual light from outside. It was positioned about 60 degrees off left, rimming Lauren's face and Susan's back. It was set vertical and raised up to imitate skylight from a second window in the room.

The AD planned when this scene would be shot based on when that room wouldn't have any direct sunlight coming in. It was a short scene, but still took some time to get all the angles. If we didn't have the Kino Flo, this could have been lit with any softlight unit (a 2kW zip light, a 1kW Rifa, a Chimera on an open-faced 1kW, etc.), with ½ or full CTB gel on it to match the daylight Kelvin temperature. If one light was too dim, a second could easily be added right above or below the first to double the intensity.

Both of these lighting setups could have been shot using tungsten film lights by simply gelling the windows with CTO (full 85). In modern houses like this one, the windows can be tilted inward to allow easy cleaning. This also allows us to tape gel to the outside of the window even though we might be on a higher floor. And if it was very bright outside, taping 85ND3 would have helped cut down the brightness of what is seen outside as well.

THE VIEW OUTSIDE

What we must be careful of is never cutting down the brightness of what is outside the window too much. If the light inside is the same as the light outside, the brain realizes something is wrong with the picture. Something isn't true to nature, and for a moment, the suspension of disbelief will be lost. Viewers will become aware, if only for a moment, that they are watching something that has been faked—and they will be removed from being absorbed in the story. There is no basic rule of thumb, but on average, most DPs like what is outside the window to be around three stops brighter than what is inside, if not totally burned out. If this appears distracting, sheer curtains or blinds can be added to the window.

Another thing done often in practice when shooting windows is to ask the prop department to put a branch outside the window to break up the view. The grips usually will attach the branch to a grip arm and then be able to adjust it up and down, closer and farther away according to camera. This is done both on location and in studio shooting. In a studio, a light unit needs to be added to light the prop branch—sometimes two, one from above and one as a backlight. Of course, this wouldn't make sense if it's a window of a high-rise apartment or office. What this does is help break up the bright square of light in the shot and add some texture to the background.

STUFF TO REMEMBER

- Light coming in through windows is a mixture of textures, angles, and colors.

- When shooting in a room with windows, you must either gel the windows with CTO, gel the lights with CTB, or use daylight-balanced lighting units—whether the windows are in the shot or not.

- Audiences expect what is outside the windows to look brighter and slightly bluer than what is inside.

- We can burn out windows by covering them with white cloth, tracing paper, or diffusion.

- It is always better to shoot in a room with windows when no direct sunlight is coming through them.

- Shining lights in through a window is a common standard practice that provides a constant sun as well as exposure, motivation, modeling, depth, and an illusion of reality.

PUTTING IT INTO PRACTICE

- Scout out a room with windows on a first floor. Plan to shoot when no direct sunlight is coming through the window. Decide how you want to treat the window—burned out, with set light coming through, or use the skylight as if it were sunlight. Color-balance your lights. Shoot it.

9 NIGHT LIGHT:
Lighting Night Exteriors and Interiors

One of the most common mistakes made by people trying to shoot a night scene is to make the scene too dark. All that does is make viewers irritated because they can't see what's going on. It removes them from the story because for a few seconds they wonder if it's their eyes or the screen, or if it's supposed to be that dark. The human eye can actually see really well in very little light. So radically underexposing or making a scene dark is unnatural and not at all what the human eye sees. Our eyes adjust and can usually see just fine at night, except for details in the shadow areas. So that is how we should light our night scenes, outdoors and indoors.

Earlier in my career, I was lighting a commercial shooting in a greenhouse in the Brooklyn Botanic Gardens. I had six HMI lights, a range between 575w to 4kW Fresnels, a 4-foot × 8-foot foamcore, and some other bounce cards to work with. Everything was looking great, until the sun set and we were still shooting. We narrowed the angle of the remaining shots, and I pounded every light that wasn't used to light the subject into the greenery in the background. It never looked like the daytime shots we did. I soon realized why. No skylight—not enough ambient fill light. This meant that all the shadows were going very dark, and the more lights I added, the more dark shadows I produced. By the time I figured out what I should be doing, bouncing the brightest light into the foamcore to add ambient fill, the shoot wrapped because they were too far into overtime. It wasn't a disaster, but I doubted the editor could use much of the last few shots we did.

This made me realize what makes the biggest visual difference between day and night. It isn't the exposure; it's the contrast. More specifically, it's how dark the shadows become. We see this every time we go to an event held outside, such as a football game or a concert that goes into the night. The bright lights turn on and wash everything with light, from all directions. Yet without ever looking up at the sky, we still can feel that it is nighttime. That's because there is no skylight, no abundance of ambient fill light that is bringing up the illumination in the shadows. Even with the bright lights of the stadium, it becomes dark and murky under the trees and around corners.

Unless you are in a cave, there is always light. Often, outdoors there are more sources of light than indoors. Streetlights, light from the windows of buildings, car headlights, traffic lights, and bounce off the moon all produce light pollution that can sometimes make watching the stars difficult. Clouds reflect light back down, as does the humidity in the air at times. So outside at night is never really that dark—and exterior night scenes shouldn't be either. Having no lights or ready electricity is no excuse.

I had students that did a shoot at night on a country road. They had no generator, so they used two of the crew's cars to light the trees along the road with their headlights. They used the two cars from the scene to light the actors, having the actors stand between the facing cars—cross key lighting with car headlights. It looked great.

Unlike shooting outdoors during the day, we do not need extremely bright lights and expensive HMIs to light at night. We can very easily work with standard lower-wattage tungsten units. However, when the budget does allow, DPs will prefer to place large lights up high on lifts to cover wide areas with hard backlight. This produces a separation and feeling of depth—and allows the camera angle to be wider, since much more is lit. A similar effect can be achieved with a lower budget. I have seen students place 2kW Fresnels on a balcony, a fire escape, and even on top of a van to get a higher spread of light. This light can be motivated by streetlights or by the moon, depending on the environment.

At night, almost all light is hard. Streetlights produce hard light. Porch lights produce hard light. Traffic lights produce hard light. Moonlight is hard light. Light coming out of house windows is either hard or soft, depending on whether the curtains are open or closed. Hard light produces darker shadows, as it doesn't wrap the way soft light does. For all of these reasons, working with hard key lights for night scenes usually works best.

What about fill? Often, we don't add any for night scenes. But other times we will add diffused fill but at a very low intensity in order to keep the contrast more severe and "night-like". Peter Stein says he likes to put a bright light up on scaffolding in the back as the moonlight. Then he has a large butterfly with a white griflon on it set on end standing upright just off to one side of the camera, and he bounces a large HMI into it. This provides a wide, general, soft blue light that can fill in and help carry the action in front of the camera. On a low budget, the same kind of thing can be accomplished by using a 2kW or even a couple of 1kW open-faced lights bounced into foamcore. The moon backlight can be a 1kW PAR aimed out a window, off a balcony, or on a high-boy stand.

EXTERIOR BACKGROUNDS

Remembering to light separately the three planes of lighting is just as important, if not more so, when shooting night scenes than at any other time. Totally black backgrounds outside at night look fake. While there isn't any ambient fill from the sky outside at night, our eyes can see pretty far into the darkness. The camera cannot. So when shooting outside, always consider making some kind of background slightly visible. It doesn't matter if the background will be totally out of focus or not. There still needs to be something there. Otherwise, the viewer feels like the scene is taking place in a void (unless that's what you want). The illusion of reality will be lost, and so will depth to the image.

The easiest thing to do is to position the subject so that whatever is behind him or her is already somewhat lit. This could be a building with lights on in its windows far off in the background, or a shopping center or parking lot with lots of lights across the street. Planning where to film at what angle has a lot to do with lighting, so a scout is required to find out what lights might be on for how long into the night.

In Photo 9.1 from my student Dan Inzitar's lighting final, Dan picked a location with a building and parking garage in the background that had lights that he knew would be on all night. Notice how Dan used hard side lights and high contrast between light and dark to achieve this film noir look. The subjects are not in the dark, nor is the shot. It's not underexposed, but rather overexposed on the away side of the main subject's face—the key side. The shadow side toward the camera is slightly underexposed. We can even see the texture of the trash can in the shadows. But the image is obviously late night and has a great amount of atmosphere.

Often it will be necessary to add light to the background. If the scene takes place in a backyard or on a farm, the DP will light the trees in the deep background and add a light to hit the outside of the house. These lights could be motivated by moonlight or a porch light. Lighting the trees and any other pieces of architecture outside at night will help provide depth and the illusion of reality, and make the picture more dynamic and interesting.

PHOTO 9.1 **FDU lighting class final lit by Dan Inzitar**

Photos 9.2 through 9.7 are from an exercise I do in my lighting class. We meet for three hours one night and light a series of shots outside. Due to the time limit, the lighting wasn't refined, but it was enough to demonstrate the concepts behind lighting night exteriors. This was all shot on Betacam a number of years ago, but while the cameras have changed, the lighting techniques have not. So if the images look a little old-fashioned, it's because this was shot on analog tape. The first shot was of student Bryant Simmons walking out of a room and over to a balcony banister, where another student attempts to climb up. The shot was set up to pan with Bryant as he exited the building and walked to the banister railing.

PHOTO 9.2 **Bryant Simmons walking for exterior night lighting class**

For the beginning of the pan shot, four lights were set up inside the room that Bryant exits. One was bounced into the ceiling to provide overall ambiance so the room won't go dark inside. Another was set as his backlight, shining through the door he exited. Two more lights were set high up shining out the side windows of the room, producing window patterns on the balcony floor and banister outside in the background that he would walk past. The bright intensity of these two lights helps establish the feeling that the outside is dark night. They also provided a nice visual breakup in the background.

Directly outside the door Bryant exits was a Chimera on a 1kW open-faced unit with half CTB (half blue). This soft light was his key, which the camera was exposed for, allowing the inside and the light through the windows to overexpose. This soft light was flagged off the top of the door and the side wall. The light was panned as Bryant walked from the doorway to the balcony banister to keep some fill on him as he moved, and so that he didn't quickly step from light into darkness.

Around the back of the building was a 650w Fresnel with full CTB on it aimed to both hit the ground and hit Bryant at his end mark as a backlight. A 300w Fresnel with full CTB backlit the banister at the far end of the balcony. Both of these lights were to provide a feeling of moonlight. An open-faced 1kW was also hidden around the back of the building aimed into the trees past the end of the balcony to give some depth to the background and give the effect of light coming from windows of the building.

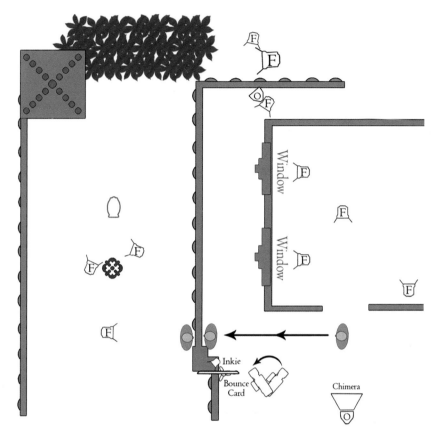

DIAGRAM 9.1 **Light plot for exterior night lighting class**

As Bryant reaches the banister in Photo 9.3, the gazebo comes into view. So it had to be lit as well, along with the banister and whatever else would be seen once the camera comes to rest at its final mark. The gazebo was lit with a 2kW Fresnel set about 70 feet away, hidden around the back of the building, striking the gazebo at a side angle. The motivation is "indoor" light coming from the building and illuminating the gazebo. While this is a stretch, the human eye would be able to see the gazebo with the low amount of light emanating from the building. The camera would not, so a light needed to be added.

Down below the balcony, out of frame on the grass, next to the real streetlamp, was a group of lights set to augment and imitate the effect of the real streetlamp. A 650w Fresnel was aimed at the urn statue on the lawn. Another 650w Fresnel down there was aimed at the cement railing and grass behind student Josh Beacon climbing up. A 650w Fresnel from below is shining up, backlighting the balcony railing and rim-lighting the two subjects with a hard edge. Although it burns out in frame and flares the lens, the real streetlamp only dimly lit Bryant's face. The rim seen by the camera on both subjects is being created by a film light.

PHOTO 9.3 The gazebo comes into view as camera pans with Bryant

PHOTO 9.4 Josh Beacon rim-lit as if from street lamp reaches for help from Bryant

Bryant's fill light was a 300w Fresnel bounced into a white card off camera left, and the Chimera that was panned after him from camera right. The bounce became Josh's key light as his head appears over the banister. If we had had more time, I would have had the students flag the bounce light off the top of the cement railing in the left foreground and scrim down the intensity of the light on the gazebo to create a more balanced night look.

WHITE REFERENCE

The streetlamp gave us a nice bright "white reference," which is a bright light in frame that establishes in the viewer's mind what is "normal" illumination and "normal" color. Many DPs do this by making sure there is a streetlamp or bright house window or a car headlight in frame and overexposed. Subliminally, the viewer interprets the overexposed white light as being normal brightness, and then accepts whatever else is lit in the scene as taking place in the shadows. Even if we expose correctly for the subject, the use of a bright, burned-out "white reference" will make viewers feel like they are looking into the dark—as if their eyes have adjusted and they can now see into the shadows.

In my opinion, the acting area of this shot should have been a little dimmer only because the motivation for Bryant's key light is the streetlamp. Light from the room's windows would fill his back, but it should have been at a lower intensity. The way to have fixed this would have been to have set up a net on a grip stand that would have cut down the light from the Chimera at Bryant's end mark as the light panned. The bounce light into the card was still needed to be bright enough to let us see Josh's great expressions, but that too should have been flagged to take some of the light off the foreground stone. But this was a class, and we had several more setups to do.

Setup number 2, Photo 9.5, is of Josh after he has fallen, staggering up a staircase to seek his revenge. Here two lights are being used to imitate what the streetlight would do. One is aimed into the ground behind the lamppost, and a second is aimed into the bush at the base of the steps. A light with ½ CTB is aimed into the side wall between the bush and the lamppost to add the feeling of moonlight. A 300w Fresnel is rigged on a double grip arm and extended out from the balcony, aimed straight down to provide the puddle of light at the bottom of the stairs—where Josh began before he starts to stagger up the steps. This becomes another "streetlight," although unseen.

PHOTO 9.5 Josh staggers up the steps after falling into puddle of light at the bottom

PHOTO 9.6 Josh staggers up into side lights

A 650w Fresnel with ½ CTB off left is aimed sideways through the stairs, casting the banister pattern on the frame right wall. Camera right is a 650w Fresnel, without gel, aimed sideways through the balcony banister, backlighting the posts and side-lighting Josh as he moves up the staircase. This is his key light for most of his climb, and it allows him to move in and out of shadow as he approaches the camera. Last is the Chimera on the 1kW open-face light with half CTB at the top of the steps off camera right.

If we had had more time, I would have had the students flag this off the frame left banister closest to camera, as it is too bright. But flagging softlights takes time and a number of flags. Notice the streetlight remains in the frame, providing the white reference.

MOONLIGHT

As stated earlier, outdoors there are a number of sources of light, including incandescent light from the windows of houses and buildings, sodium vapor pinkish/orange light from streetlamps, headlights from cars, which vary according to manufacturer of vehicle, light pollution bounced off the sky if is humid or cloudy, and, of course, moonlight. Our brains do the best they can white-balancing all this mess, and the majority of the time, moonlight will still seem blue. If we are out on a mountaintop or a wide-open desert, or on the deck of a ship at night in the middle of the ocean, moonlight might not look blue to our eyes, since our brain has nothing to compare it to. But basically, it is part of the worldwide, cross-cultural visual language that moonlight is blue—that night is blue. So, when lighting night scenes, it is common practice to add some blue light.

PHOTO 9.7 Josh rim-lit behind column

Photo 9.7 is a simple shot, but it has depth. Foreground is the pillar, student Josh Beacon is hiding in the acting area, and the stone balcony wall and the trees behind it are the background. The trees were light by one 650w Fresnel off left on the balcony. A second 650w Fresnel lit the balcony wall from the right at a side angle. Josh was key-lit from the left by a 650w Fresnel with half CTB, adding a moonlight rim to his face and side. His fill was from a 1kW open-face bounced into the white cement floor. A 300w Fresnel with half blue side-lights from the right the pillar he hides behind.

The contrast is what sells the picture. The rim light is overexposed, while the fill is underexposed. The back cement banister is correctly exposed. We can see something in the darkness frame left, but the lack of any texture in the background behind Josh makes his rim stand out even more. Thus it has a feeling of suspense. If this was supposed to be a romantic evening, we would light more of the background, lower the intensity of the backlight, and bring up the fill. We might even add twinkle Christmas lights in the trees in the background. The lighting is there to help tell the story, so the emotional context of the scene is essential to know and support.

CITY STREETS

City streets are full of light. Streetlights and store windows provide a tremendous variety of colors, angles, and intensities. If you are going to shoot a scene on a city street, pick a street that has a few store windows that leave their lights on all night. Set your camera on an angle where you don't see too far down the street—less to light, more control. Now, remember that at night, light comes directly down from the streetlights over a person, but also on an angle from the streetlights across the street, behind the person and in front of him or her. The downlight should be your strongest, as it would appear that way to the human eye. You can pick a spot for the subjects to stand based

Mike Finkel lit by street light, *Murder at Café Noir,* **MTG Productions**

on where there already is a puddle of light from a streetlamp, or you can easily create your own streetlight effect.

On the film *Murder at Café Noir* (2004), we shot a bunch of quick shots for a montage in Atlantic City on the streets at night without any lights. Every location was selected based on the amount of light being given off by the casino signs—which are really bright. The camera was always positioned to show a lot of other lit-up buildings in the background. This was a fast montage, so it worked fine.

They did something similar on *Project Runway* once at dawn with the contestants walking past Times Square. The segment producer, the director, and the camera operators picked the route in advance based on how the group would be passing the neon lights on Broadway. The cameras were balanced for 4,300 Kelvin to mix the streetlights, the neon signs, and the light of dawn.

On the opposite end of the spectrum was the lighting on the movie *Sorcerer's Apprentice* (2010). New York City's 6th Avenue was lit up from 14th Street through 23rd Street for a car shot. Lifts that were 140 feet high were positioned at each cross street, and three Maxi-Brutes were rigged in each bucket. We rigged 1kW PAR can lights under every small tree along the street, and hid 650w Fresnels behind mailboxes and trash cans to shine up, illuminating various storefronts. Six generators were parked around every other corner, and miles and miles of cable was run out. All of this was for a shot inside a car as it drove down the street. The car itself was on a flatbed trailer and towed. On the car were rigged lights to shine in through the front windshield, and LED Color Blasters were rigged outside the back side windows and programmed to keep changing colors to get the effect of neon light coming in from outside. They shut down the street at 3 a.m. for shooting to begin, and wrapped at dawn. The street was reopened around 7 a.m. the following morning—which was a Sunday. No one is up at 7 a.m. on Sunday in New York City. The rigging crew came in to wrap out beginning at 8 a.m.

PHOTO 9.9 Jonathan Sang and Mike Finkel lit by casino signs, *Murder at Café Noir,* MTG Productions

PHOTO 9.10 Jonathan Sang and Mike Finkel lit by street and car light, *Murder at Café Noir,* MTG Productions

Streetlights

When shooting a scene on a city street at night, we often want the effect of walking under streetlights. The common practice of rigging lights high up, usually 1kW open-face units, aimed down to create a puddle of light, works well. These can be rigged on telephone poles, off fire escapes, on top of tall street signs, or even on real lampposts. Keep in mind that real streetlamps are usually sodium vapor discharge lamps, which produce an amber/orange-like color, or mercury vapor, which produce a murky green/gray color. We can attempt to overpower these with our own lights or just mix them to keep the strange but familiar streetlight color. Rosco makes gels to simulate these two streetlight colors, so we can create our own streetlight looks whenever and wherever we want. One consideration when rigging a film light as a light post, is running the cable to power the light and keeping it out of the shot.

China Ball

If you have a person or a couple walking down a city street toward the camera, the fastest and simplest way to light the scene is with a china ball on a pole. First, pick your location so that you have a series of windows of shops along the path, to help motivate the china ball soft light. Just as we discussed in Chapter 5, the china ball can be held just in front and out of frame of the subjects and can move with them as they walk toward the camera. The caution here is to make sure the china ball doesn't throw a shadow from any real streetlights the actors walk under.

Glare and Flare

Another standard practice in shooting night exteriors is to wet down the street. The reflections and glare off the wet surface add a nice nocturnal feeling to the image. Wetting the street makes it read blacker on camera, and wetting a sidewalk also makes it turn darker and not read so white. The glare from the wet surface can often provide the white reference for the shot.

PHOTO 9.11 Jonathan Sang steps into the Café alley, lit by Stephen Scotto, *Murder at Café Noir,* MTG Productions

In Photo 9.11 from *Murder at Café Noir* (2004), gaffer Stephen Scotto placed a 1kW open-faced light at the far end of the alley to backlight the sailor and edge-light the storefronts on the right. Notice how the light glares off the door frames along the alley way. He placed a second 1kW open-faced light closer to camera but out of frame left to continue the effect and rim-light both the blond streetwalker and the detective, actor Jonathan Sang, exiting the café. The bright glare off the wet ground became our white reference, along with the real wall sconces under the awning.

A light inside the café's doors off frame right rim-lights the door window frames and side-lights Jonathan. A light inside the café is bounced into the ceiling to provide an inside ambiance. His key is a 300w Fresnel off right, and his fill is an open-faced 1kW bounced into a 4-foot × 4-foot foamcore sheet just right of camera.

PHOTO 9.12 Josh Lowey approaches Tina Zoganas, lit by Stephen Scotto, *Murder at Café Noir,* MTG Productions

In Photo 9.12, the femme fatale, Tina Zoganas, exits as the detective hides off left to watch. His end mark on camera left was lit by a 650w Fresnel off camera right with ½ CTO (half 85), and backlit by a 300w Fresnel with ½ CTB hidden behind the tropical plant on the left. Tina walks into the same lights that lit Jonathan before—front-lit by the 300w Fresnel, fill by the bounce, edge-lit by the light through the café door, and backlit by an open-faced 1kW in the back left.

Note the little red light in the background shining straight into camera and how it gives the image some depth. This was a happy accident, but it could have been rigged simply by using an inkie (250w Fresnel) with red gel and aimed directly into the camera. DP Peter Stein says he likes to add small lights with colored gel on them set far away in the background shining directly into camera for night scenes. These will be totally out of focus but will add depth and variety to the background. In the

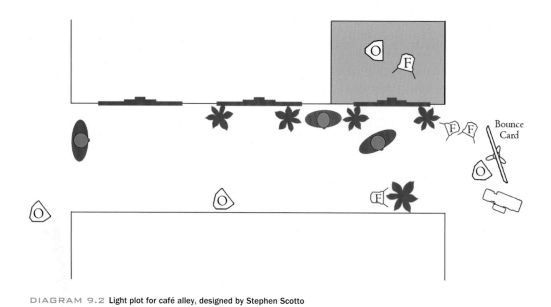

DIAGRAM 9.2 **Light plot for café alley, designed by Stephen Scotto**

sci-fi film *Super 8* (2012), DP Larry Fong added tons of gelled lights aimed directly into the camera throughout almost the entire movie. He deliberately created flares in the lens as part of the visual style that he and director J. J. Abrams came up with. The bright backlight, glare off the dark ground, red light, and lavender color on the edge of the building in the background all help project the feeling that this is a dingy, seedy area.

When wetting down the street, one thing to remember is that water evaporates, so there is a need to re-wet the street after a number of takes or when changing angles. Also, all electrical cable connections need to be wrapped in plastic and elevated so they don't get wet. Water is an electrical conductor and it easily seeps between the plugs. So if you reach into even a tiny puddle to unplug two cables, you will get shocked. This happened to me (and every electric I know) on more than one occasion. Remember that electricity is still flowing into the extension cord even if it isn't plugged into a light. On *Jumper* (2008), we were wrapping up a night street scene, and I picked up a cable that was in the wet gutter and got zapped through the insulation. No one had unplugged it from the generator. In a moist environment, it is imperative that before you wrap your cables, you make sure that everything is unplugged from the electrical source first—whether a generator or a wall outlet. Place all electrical connections and distribution boxes on wooden apple boxes or plastic milk crates off the ground. You can even use plastic light cases. Don't use anything metallic or with metal trim that will conduct electricity—like most camera cases. Always be safe.

THEATRICAL NIGHT

Sometimes there is a call to go overly theatrical with the nighttime look. This could be for a dream sequence, a surreal moment, a comedy horror film, or the average music video. In these cases it is common to overdo the blue effect, such as in Photo 9.13 from *TV Psychic Party Game* (2006), an

PHOTO 9.13 **Exterior night lit with blue gels, *TV Psychic Party Game,* MTG Productions**

interactive fortune-telling DVD made as a direct-to-consumer Halloween gift. The DVD opens with a few shots flying over tombstones in a foggy cemetery at night, then glides up to this creepy stone tower.

The tree and the front of the tower are side-lit by 1kW Fresnels with a heavy theatrical blue gel. The fog is backlit by a 300w Fresnel. Inside the door is a 650kW Fresnel with full CTO on it aimed out the door window, from a low angle in order to rake the underside of the roof over the doorway.

Nothing about this lighting setup relays an illusion of reality—rather the spirit of Halloween, which was the production's entire intent. This could work for a music video, or perhaps a kids' Halloween special, as the vibrant colors make it over-the-top. If I had lit this more realistically, it wouldn't have worked for the project or pleased the producer. The lighting must always complement the intention of the project (we will discuss this further in Chapter 11).

NIGHT INTERIORS

The concept of high-contrast, low ambient fill and a touch of blue light works nicely for interior night scenes as well. Basically, how you light a night scene outside can work for lighting a night scene inside—hard, brighter backlight edging the subject, murky shadows but some definition in the background, and a white reference such as a desk lamp or an open door to another room where a light is on.

In the opening bedroom scene of the movie *Body Heat* (1981), DP Richard Kline used the light from the open door to a bathroom as his motivated key and white reference. Both hard and soft light comes into the bedroom from the bathroom direction, side-lighting star William Hurt standing at the window. On the reverse angle, the

bathroom door can be partially seen. The light from it now backlights Hurt, side-lights the actress in the scene and casts a streak across the bed, while soft slightly blue "moonlight" fills in the shadows. It's a great, modeled night image.

In the film *Erin Brockovich* (2000), DP Ed Lachman uses hard light from the open door to a hallway to key star Julia Roberts as she talks to her son in his dark bedroom. The hallway behind her is the white reference and the brightest thing on-screen, but Julia Roberts' face is only slightly underexposed. The effect on the viewer is as if their eyes have adjusted to the dark. It also helps support the feeling of intimacy the scene called for.

NIGHT WINDOWS

DP Peter Stein recommends that when shooting a night scene it helps to, at some time during the scene, show a dark window in the shot. He feels this helps to establish that it's night outside and not just a dark room. Shining bright lights in through windows works just as well for nighttime scenes as it does for daytime scenes. Instead of sunlight, this light becomes moonlight, or in city stories, this could be streetlights. When shining moonlight in through a window, Peter likes to net the light down on the top of the window so that the blue light drifting in is brighter on the bottom than on the top. The reason is that almost all buildings have some kind of roof overhang that would naturally cut the moonlight. There could be trees outside that also could cut the light. Another thing Peter prefers is to always put lacey curtains on the windows to be backlit by the moonlight. They can be mostly open, but if there, they provide a nice accent of blue on both sides of the black window and can gently move in a breeze—provided by the prop department placing a fan just outside the window.

PHOTO 9.14 Dark windows at night, Jade Elysan, Alexandra Landau, Natasa Babic, *Dark Tarot*, DGW Films

Dark windows appear in the background of Photo 9.14 from *Dark Tarot*. The key light was a chicken coop above the counter, and a 1,200w HMI was outside the French doors off to the right, aimed in to give the actresses an edge, while also bouncing off the outside of the building, providing some blue ambient light on the porch. This light on the underside of the porch roof helps to give more depth to the scene, while the darkness outside and the dark windows on the left read nighttime. A light blue streak is on the back wall created by a 300w Fresnel off right. The deep color blue used was a repetitive thematic element. This is a supernatural thriller, and once the ghost becomes in control, there is always this same color blue somewhere in the shot. Because the color is unnatural, it subliminally reminds the viewer that what is going on is also unnatural—supernatural, in fact. If this were not a supernatural story, I would have used either full CTB or ½ CTB for that streak, and not something as theatrically blue.

Something to always be careful of when shooting a night scene with dark windows is to keep checking to see what, if anything, is reflected in the window panes. With black behind it, a glass window becomes a mirror, and it's easy to accidently get the reflection of a light or a crew member in the window pane in the background and not notice until the edit.

Photo 9.15 from the same scene demonstrates how even if the windows glare, they still can read as nighttime. The HMI outside is 5,600 Kelvin, which means the light is blue compared to the 3,200 Kelvin inside, for which the camera was white-balanced. The lack of ambient fill, the blue

PHOTO 9.15 Lit windows at night behind Alexandra Landau, *Dark Tarot*, DGW Films

breakup on the out-of-focus back wall, as well as the very bright kick in Alexandra's hair, all help to relay a nocturnal feeling. She isn't underexposed, nor is there a big contrast on her face. Rather, it is the contrast between her and her surroundings that renders the night look.

The decision as to how blue to go is an artistic one. The richer the blue, the more theatrical we risk making the image appear. But sometimes that is the desired effect, such as in a dream sequence or a surreal moment in a horror film. Lighting night scenes that are more theatrical is actually much easier than lighting realistic night scenes and can often be a lot more fun. Therein lies the danger—that we might overdramatize the lighting for a night scene when it isn't appropriate.

Photo 9.16, from *TV Psychic Party Game,* is the fortune-teller's chamber. This was actually shot during the day, with a clear sky and bright sun outside. Blue fabric was stretched over the windows in the room, which can be seen in the background. The sun striking the material made the windows blue. This opening angle was shot when we knew there would be direct sun hitting the windows in the back, which faced south. It was only one short shot where the gypsy fortune-teller walks in and talks to the camera. The rest of the DVD is her sitting at her fortune-telling table in front of the fireplace, dealing cards and telling fortunes.

PHOTO 9.16 **Blue cloth over windows makes them night for** *TV Psychic Party Game,* **MTG Productions**

Notice the warm light glowing on the back wall, so that it doesn't go totally dark. This was done with a 300w Fresnel with ½ CTO on it hidden around the corner of the fireplace. The motivation is to imitate how the light from the candles, both on the table and on the wall, would illuminate that wall, which adds some nice depth to the shot. If that light wasn't added, that wall would become as dark as the wall in the far corner. The chairs were lit by a 650w Fresnel with theatrical blue on it off left. This same light washes the front of the fireplace. There are three 150w Fresnels in the fireplace. Two strike the inside fireplace wall and alternate diming to create a fire-like effect (which we will discuss further in Chapter 12 on lighting effects), and one is aimed out, striking the edge of the chair and the table lighting the candelabra. The beautiful dabbled-light effect on the fireplace mantel was a happy accident, created by the glare of all the candles off the shine of the marble. The overall ambiance is raised slightly because we added fog to the room, which lowers the contrast by dissipating light rays. Like the outside night shot of the tower for this same project, the colors used in this shot send the image over-the-top and into the world of Halloween party rather than realism.

When shooting a night scene during the day in a room with windows, you have various options on how to deal with the windows:

- Block out the windows. This can be done a variety of ways. If the windows are in the shot, black cloth can be taped over the windows on the outside. If not in the shot, black cloth can be taped over the windows inside, or large sheets of foamcore or butterflies or anything else that can block the light from the window can be utilized.

- Tape black cloth over the windows on the outside or inside, and then close the blinds or curtains to hide the cloth. Just closing the blinds or curtains will still allow light to seep in around the edges, which will be very bright and will change during the day as the sun moves outside.

- Tape translucent blue cloth over the windows as in Photo 9.16. The light shining through will still allow the pattern of the window frames to be seen. For this to work, it is rather important to make sure the windows are out of focus.

- Tape Neutral Density gel (3, 6, or 9) with or without a layer of CTB (Full blue) over the windows to make what is seen outside darker or bluer, then balance for tungsten inside.

- Don't show the windows, and use the light through the windows as moonlight by color-balancing for tungsten. To make this work, the shoot must be planned accordingly to film all the desired footage before the sun moves too far and the light no longer matches—the same as if shooting a daytime scene using the real sun.

STUFF TO REMEMBER

- Night scenes are not dark. They are contrasty. Use a hard-edged bright rim light to help achieve this look. Slightly overexpose the rim and slightly underexpose the face.

- Always light the background to provide depth and an illusion of reality.

- Provide a "white reference" to help create a feeling that the viewer's eyes have adjusted to the dark and can now see into the shadows—both for exteriors and interiors.

- Use blue gel to add the feeling of moonlight, but be selective as to how blue you make the light.

- China balls can provide an easy moving fill light for moving shots outdoors.

- Wet down the street to provide glare and a nocturnal feeling.

- Add colored out-of-focus points of light in the background to provide depth.

- Show darkened windows to quickly reveal it's nighttime.

PUTTING IT INTO PRACTICE

- Shoot a nighttime exterior shot of someone exiting a building.

- Then shoot another shot of the person walking outside. Remember to light the backgrounds and provide a white reference in both shots.

10 WORKING WITH COLOR:
Using Color for Mood and Using Gels

Anyone wanting to master lighting for cinematography should study theatrical lighting design for its use of color. In stage lighting design, we use color extensively for contrast, modeling, establishing time and place, and creating mood and atmosphere. Since the viewing audience sits almost 180 degrees around the subject, color provides the contrast while still allowing illumination for audience members seated on both sides of the theater. Whereas color is blatantly used on stage, it is usually more subtly used in cinematography. I say usually, because there are times when more obvious color may be exactly what is called for in a scene—such as discussed in Chapter 9. The advantage of using color is that it is an international, transcultural language. We all see the same colors of sunrise and sunset, of twilight and moonlight, of fire and streetlights. So color can be used to help communicate visually to everyone, everywhere.

Using color and deciding how rich to make a color are artistic choices that the DP must discuss with the director and often the art director, as it will affect the colors of their sets and costumes. In practice, the use of color in lighting for cinematography is most often for accent, atmosphere, and establishing time and place. But color can also change the atmosphere of the scene.

MOOD

Colors both affect and reflect mood. A blue room seems cold, a green room is more relaxed, a yellow room is more active, and gray is dull. We "feel" color. We also include them in our language. When people feel sick, they "look green"; when they are scared, they are "yellow"; when people are sad, they are "blue." So when creating our lighting, we can use some of these perceptions—whether true to life or not—for artistic and dramatic effect. The trick is not to go too far overboard with the saturation of the color. A little goes a long way. The viewer senses even a slight shift in color from warm to cool. So, the less obvious the better.

> "Color can influence the psychological state the actor is in or the psychological state you want the audience to be in. And sometimes it's just for sheer beauty."
>
> —PETER STEIN, ASC, FEATURE DP

We also associate a location with a color—bright yellow for a hot desert, light blue for a cool ocean, light green for forest, murky tan for a dusty city, neon magenta for a seedy nightclub, pinkish amber for a city streetlight. The cinematographer can use these associations as well.

We also associate color with time. Gold is morning, white is high noon, orange sunset, lavender twilight, deep blue night. Again, moderation is the key—not becoming too cartoonish, unless that is the desired effect.

GELS

To color our lights, we place gels on them. Gels are subtractive—that is, they filter the unwanted color wavelengths and allow the desired color to travel through the transparency. Gels thus get hot and cut intensity. They can fade and melt depending on length of use and the colors being absorbed. The richer the color, the more color wavelengths the gel absorbs. The hotter the gel gets, and the faster it will fade. We can combine gels to create a new color, but that will increase both the heat and the drop in intensity. Sandwiched gels also have a tendency to melt together and can't be taken apart again later, so you can never reuse those gels. Gels are high-heat-resistant polyester film sheets that used to be made from actual gelatin—thus the term. There are four major manufacturers and a few minor companies. The major companies are Rosco, Lee, GAM, and Apollo. Gels will melt before they burn, and are rated for around 356 to 536 degrees Fahrenheit.

Some gels hold their color better than others. Rosco gels have the color infused in the polyester, so they last much longer than Lee gels, which are dipped in color dye. Rosco is an American company, while Lee is British, and their colors are different based on the cultural tastes of the two continents. Both are used extensively in cinematography. The most commonly used colors are the ones mentioned in previous chapters, the various grades of color correction gels, which include CTB (Full Blue), CTO (85), Minus Green (magenta), and Plus Green. But other colors are also commonly used, such as No Color Straw, Light Bastard Amber, True Blue, and Cosmetic Pink.

One must keep in mind that gels don't add color; they subtract all the colors other than the color of the gel. Thus, if your light source is lacking in some wavelengths of light, it will not be able to project the color you necessarily are looking for. This becomes important when working with LED lights and HMIs. Both of these are not full-spectrum lights, which means they are missing various color wavelengths. They both tend to be lacking in the warmer range. So if we put a gold gel on them, we may not get the color we want because the light just may not be producing all the wavelengths needed to create that color.

To compensate for this, Lee has just introduced a new line of LED gels, color matched to cool, white LEDs to render some of their most commonly used theatrical colors. Also, some newer (and more expensive) LED units such as the ARRI LED Fresnel and the ETC LED Source Four have amber diodes added to their array of red, blue, green, and white mix. This allows these units to create a wide variety of colors in the warmer range, without gels.

Rosco makes a cinegel swatch book that contains samples of all their color correction colors as well as all their diffusion gels. Lee combines all their color gels in with their cinema gels in their swatch book. The Apollo and GAM swatch books are only theatrical colors.

COLORS ARE REFLECTED

As discussed before, light bounces and reflects. We see colors by which color wavelength of light is reflected off of something. Paints and fabric dyes absorb the unwanted colors and reflect the wanted ones. That is why black pants get very hot in the sun—they are absorbing all the wavelengths— whereas white clothing is cool, as it reflects all the wavelengths of light.

Cameras can only record the colors that reflect off an object. This means that if we aren't careful, we can totally change the color of costumes, set walls, and even an actor's skin tone due to the color of light we shine on the actor. If the subject is in a blue costume but we only shine an orange light on it, the clothing will record gray, because there are no blue wavelengths of light in orange. If an actress has a rich golden suntan and we light her with a primary blue color as moonlight, her skin might turn gray because there are no orange wavelengths in blue light. This won't produce, say, the image of a sexy woman in a bikini on a beach at night the way the script and the director wanted. A fire will have to be added to motivate some amber light, or she'll look like a zombie. Of course, if the desire is to turn someone into a zombie, a cross fade from one color light to another and working with the makeup department might do just the trick. This effect has been done in several Dr. Jekyll and Mr. Hyde movies.

The gel swatch books have color transmission rates listed for each gel that will help you avoid this problem. Most colors are a mix of all three primaries, with one or more being much more prominent while the others very minimal. Remember that in order to record a color, it needs to reflect at least most of the wavelengths of light that compose that color.

COLORS CHANGE WHEN COLOR TEMPERATURE CHANGES

We also need to recognize that when lights dim, their color temperature changes. For tungsten lights, the color temperature gets warmer. For fluorescent lights, they often turn more magenta. So the color coming through the gel will also change. Light blue gel on a dimmed tungsten light will not produce any blue color—it will only produce white light, as the blue is now compensating for the warmth of the source light.

As mentioned earlier, a colored gel will project one color on a tungsten light and a different color on an HMI light, since they have different color temperatures. Theater lighting designer Christopher Akerlind was working on the design for the Broadway production of *The Light in the Piazza* at Lincoln Center. He wanted a rich golden sunlight to come streaming across the stage. He was using a number of high-output moving lights and couldn't get the rich, warm gold color he wanted out of them. His master electric pointed out that the moving lights were discharge lamps and therefore produced light that has a very high Kelvin degree. There just isn't much gold light in them to project. He recommended renting a few 5,000w film Fresnels and gelling them. They did. Chris won the Tony for best lighting design for that show. (It wasn't because of the 5kW Fresnels, but that sure helped him create his truly beautiful artistic design.)

COLOR CORRECTION GELS

I've touched on this before in several chapters, but there is a standard set of gels used for color correction. Each of these comes in full, ½ intensity, ¼ intensity, and ⅛ intensity.

- CTB—Color correction blue (also known as Full Blue) changes the color temperature of a tungsten light (3,200 Kelvin) to daylight (5,600 Kelvin).

- CTO—Color correction orange (also known as 85) changes the color temperature of daylight (5,600 Kelvin) to tungsten (3,200 Kelvin).

- Minus Green—This is a magenta gel that subtracts the green wavelengths of light to make it more white.

- Plus Green—This is a green gel that enhances the green wavelength of light found in most standard building fluorescent lamps.

MIXING COLORS

Colors mix. So if more than one color of light is hitting the subject, all the colors will mix and produce another hue that will be captured on the camera. If we look at the color wheel, we can learn the color complements. Whatever colors are opposite each other will form white when mixed. A light blue color aimed at the subject from one side and light amber aimed at the subject from the other will produce white light where they mix, only keeping their colors in the shadow areas. Since these two colors lack the color wavelengths of their complements, they also produce a nice contrast when put next to each other.

DIAGRAM 10.1 **Color wheel**

Photo 10.1 illustrates some color mixing and the use of complementary colors to create contrast. Alexandra Landau is lit by warm light from the right and cool light from the left. The lighting units are not at 45 degree angles, but much farther apart, projecting light more from the sides than the front. Where they mix on the center of her face produces more "white" than the sides of her cheeks. We can see this specifically in the shadow of her nose. Compare the color in the small shadow with the color of the mixed light on her cheek surrounding it. Because this scene is a séance in a spiritually possessed house, we have more leeway in our choices of color and how much we employ it.

PHOTO 10.1 **Complementary colors from key and fill on Alexandra Landau as she goes into a trance,** *Dark Tarot,* **DGW Films**

DOMINANT COLORS

Some colors are more dominant than others—which means they visually overpower the other color and make them almost disappear. The red family, which includes lavender, is a recessive color, which means it can fade way, while the green family, which includes yellow, is a dominant one. Designers must be aware of this when planning the colors for their backlight and side lights. We usually don't want the back and sides to dominate the frontal colors unless this is for a specific effect.

All of these are things that theater lighting designers take into account when selecting their gels for a show. In cinematography, we have the luxury of having our lights much more easily accessible, and a production monitor to view what we are recording. So we can more easily swap out gels until we get a look we like. However, the cinematographer still needs to order the selected gels that might be used before production begins. There are literally hundreds of colors of gels, so it's impossible to carry a number of sheets of each of them. DPs and gaffers will almost always have gel swatch books with their kits for easy reference. You can now get an app for a phone that has all the gels from most manufacturers in it. They even list complementary colors and similar colors by different manufacturers. However, you can't hold them up to the light or shine a flashlight through them to see what color they'll actually give you. You can only do that with a physical swatch book (see Appendix 2, "Resources").

THEATRICAL COLORS

Films with theatrical themes often use a wide variety of colors, such as movies like *Chicago* (2002) and *Dreamgirls* (2006), and TV shows such as *Smash* (2013), especially in their theatrical numbers. Musicals, by their very nature, are more theatrical and thus allow everything from acting to art direction to lighting to be more dramatic. But horror and sci-fi movies such as *Star Trek* (2009), *The Shining* (1980), and *Close Encounters of the Third Kind* (1977), and TV shows such as *Supernatural* (2005–2014) and *Doctor Who* (2005–) also employ a range of more saturated colored light.

Cinematographer Vittorio Storaro used color extensively to reveal mood in Francis Ford Coppola's film *One from the Heart* (1982). Colored lights flooded the sets and changed hues during musical numbers—which the characters did not sing—based on the emotions the characters were going through. In *Dick Tracy* (1990), Storaro used colored light in conjunction with the primary-colored production design by Richard Silbert to put the story and the viewer in a Sunday newspaper comic strip come to life. He wrote a very thorough (and expensive) book on the use of color in cinematography. European DPs have a tendency to use more color than American DPs—perhaps a cultural thing.

Ground breaking in his use of color in lighting was legendary British cinematographer Jack Cardiff, especially in his Technicolor work shooting *Black Narcissus* (1947). In this film, he mixed blue and amber colors for great dramatic effects that really set the mood, revealed character, and helped tell the story. This work won him an Academy Award. In *The Red Shoes* (1948), Cardiff used color to add to the surrealistic atmosphere of the film and the growing danger of the story.

American DP Gordon Willis used color extensively in *Pennies from Heaven* (1981) to capture the feeling of the time period, as did DP Conrad Hall in *Road to Perdition* (2002), for which he won the Oscar posthumously. Both of these films were set in the 1930s Depression

era, a time of lavish films that were produced as an escape from the hard realities of the real world. By mixing color with natural lighting, both these DPs were able to merge both of these elements of the time period—one that the modern viewer remembers only through its movies.

The extensive use of green light by DP Tom Yatsko in the TV show *Bates Motel* (2013) helps establish not only the seediness of the location but that something sick is going on underneath. It is motivated by the greenish lights of the hotel and the neon sign out front.

PHOTO 10.2 **Teal-colored light fills on Quentin Fielding, the ghost in *Dark Tarot*, DGW Films**

In Photo 10.2, Quentin Fielding, our ghost, is frontal lit from below by a teal-colored gel on a 2kW softlight (zip light). His key light is a 750w Rifa softlight at a higher intensity. The image was manipulated in post to flare the highlights for this romantic moment. While both sides of his face are lit with soft light, the white light is brighter not only due to its intensity, but its color.

The green-blue teal color was a thematic element, used whenever he appeared. It gave the actor an unnatural presence. We associate green with both the sick and the dead. Mold is green and bruises are a gray/green, and we think of dead things as turning greenish. Teal was selected because it wasn't too rich in the green hue, like a forest green, but had blue mixed with it to "cool" it down.

This use of teal is an example of using color to create a subliminal viewer association. Since it was done from the very beginning of the film with the first glimpse of the ghost, a color language was established with the audience—teal equals ghost. For the rest of the movie, viewers will assume that whenever they see the color teal, the ghost is there. So we must be consistent with our color language and always use teal whenever the ghost appears, and not use it any other time. Otherwise, we risk confusing or losing our viewer.

Since this film was a supernatural thriller made more for TV release, the contrast was created more by the colors than the intensity (we will discuss setting contrast ratios in Chapter 11), the same as is done in theater stage lighting. This method allows illumination into both sides of the face while still providing modeling and contrast. Personally, I love high contrast and allowing one side of the face to really go black. While that would have been appropriate for a more dark and serious thriller, such as something like *Girl with a Dragon Tattoo*, this was a supernatural romance, something geared more toward the Lifetime channel and foreign TV markets. All lighting should be appropriate to both the story and the intention of the project. The decision to use colors can often be part of that.

PHOTO 1 0.3 **Blue and amber colored light on Tina Zoganas, the fortuneteller in** *TV Psychic Party Game,* **MTG Productions**

In Photo 10.3 from *TV Psychic,* a theatrical blue is used on one side of the fortune-teller's face as moonlight and CTO is used to simulate the warmth from the candles and the fireplace on the other. The warm, amber light hitting the background carries out the warm fireplace feeling of the scene.

PHOTO 10.4 Apricot gel forms the starlight hitting Cuyle Carvin and Ashley Taylor, *The Cold Equations,* Ellipsis Films

In Photo 10.4 from the sci-fi festival short *The Cold Equations,* an apricot amber gel was used to give the feeling of a not-so-distant star. Notice the same color coming through the ship's pod door window. Make sure to keep enough sheets of the same color on hand to use on as many lights as might be required.

These are both rather dramatic uses of color on the subjects, but both were called for in their projects. More often than not, color is used more for accent, such as in Photo 10.5 from *The Cold Equations.* Blue light washes the walls, while an inkie with red gel backlights Ashley's shoulder on a

PHOTO 10.5 Colored light accents on Cuyle Carvin and Ashley Taylor, *The Cold Equations,* Ellipsis Films

steep angle. Cuyle Carvin is lit with white soft light from a fluorescent unit above. The red and blue accents were a predetermined visual motif the director Ryan Kelly and I discussed before production began. Almost every shot inside the spacecraft had at least a touch of red or blue light or both. Note the same amber "sunlight" through the spaceship's pod door, which connects to the other scene when the ship is adrift to save power.

Audiences easily accept colored accents in sci-fi due to the idea that high-tech panels are assumed to have various colored lights on them. Viewers also accept colored accents for other high-tech location set stories. In the movie *Hunt for Red October* (1990), DP Jan de Bont used color for accents inside the state-of-the-art Russian submarine in the same manner with rich red and blues. DP Jost Vacano did much the same in the award-winning WWII submarine movie *Das Boot* (1981), but with less-vibrant colors—rather, ones that gave a more faded and worn-out feeling, specifically, faded reds and blues and a few greens.

DP Matthew Libatique used color accents to establish a film noir look in certain scenes in the film *The Number 23* (2007), and obvious colored light was everywhere in *Iron Man* (2008). Superhero movies, like horror films, force the audience to suspend disbelief so far that color becomes more than acceptable. Look at the Batman and Spider-Man movies, and how vibrant the colors are. A lot of that has to do with colored light.

As we discussed in previous chapters, color is more often used in much more subtle ways. In the movie *House of Games* (1987), DP Juan Ruiz Anchia lit the inside of the poolhall with very subtle accents of color that gave it a very real, but also down-and-dirty feeling. In *Memoirs of a Geisha* (2005), DP Dion Beebe used warm-colored light to relay the feeling of rice-paper rooms lit by warm oil lamps.

In Photo 10.6 from *Dark Tarot*, I used a Rosco Colorwave red and orange glass gobo (Photo 10.7) in a Source Four to project the feeling of the rays of sunset on the trunk and the actress.

PHOTO 1 0.7 **Glass gobo courtesy of Rosco**

PHOTO 1 0.6 **Natasa Babic is lit with an orange/yellow glass gobo,** *Dark Tarot,* **DGW Films**

Glass gobos come in a variety of color mixes and styles. They slip into the gobo slot on the Source Four ERS unit, which can project a sharp or defocused image. They render beautiful colors and never burn out, but they do decrease the intensity of the light substantially, which you must take into account when composing the lighting.

MUSIC VIDEOS

Music videos have always used color extensively. This genre of visual storytelling was invented in the early 1980s with the birth of the cable station MTV. I was the gaffer on a number of music videos before MTV even started to air. The record companies began shooting low-budget music videos for virtually every artist they signed as soon as Viacom announced this new outlet for promoting records. Some were very creative, while others were just staged concerts. But all of these relied heavily on the use of colored light. The reason: concerts are lit with a lot of colored light. Bringing the energy and the dynamics that color provides in a live concert to a video of the musicians performing was a natural transition. This was a new venue, and no one was sure if it would catch on or not. The producers, who were all from the record companies and concert promoters at the time, wanted to hedge their bets and appeal as much as possible to their target audience, concertgoers and record buyers.

The colors used by concert lighting designers are more saturated and vibrant. Often the colors are matched with the emotional content of the lyrics of the song, but just as often they are there to accent the rhythm or the energy of the music itself. The lighting and colors in a live concert event are "unmotivated" in that there are no logical light sources. Rather, the lighting and colors are motivated by the desired feelings the artists want to project to their audience. The same is true in music video lighting. There is usually no need to think about motivated light sources. What the project is going for is as far from realism as you can get—no one in the real world carries around musical instruments and suddenly starts playing on the street, and has everyone around him or her start dancing the same dance steps. So virtually anything is acceptable in a music video.

Picking the colors to use when lighting a music video all comes down to the gut feeling of the music and what colors can support and enhance that. Obviously, if the music video is soft jazz, it would call for a different color palette than a salsa band. When I worked on a music video for saxophone jazz musician Grover Washington, Jr., years ago, we didn't use any colored light at all. It was all bright-white soft light in an empty mansion ballroom. But when we shot the New Village People, also in an empty mansion, we used lots of violet, blue, and magenta. To each his own.

DANCE AND ICE-SKATING

Stage lighting designers understand that what is important in a dance recital or an ice-skating show isn't the face of the performers, but the contours of their bodies. These are both movement-oriented performances. Both of these venues are strongly side-lit to rim and highlight the outlines of the body. The ripple of the muscles is best displayed through the highlights and shadows produced from cross lighting, and most often, colored light is used for accent and pictorial design. This all applies when you are lighting dance or ice-skating in a scene.

If two people go ice-skating on a date, the rink must be lit the way a rink would be lit, but also we will light the contours of the bodies of our subjects—as that is how all audiences are accustomed to seeing ice-skating, whether on TV or live. And as these venues always use colored lights, so will the DP. In an ice-skating scene that isn't taking place during a "show," the colors will be more muted. Blue is very common to all ice-skating scenes, as it helps relate the feeling of the cold to the viewer.

But an ice-skating scene without color will read dull and boring to the viewer, which usually isn't the feeling desired for a scene where two people go on a date ice-skating.

We've already talked about musicals and how colored light is not only acceptable, but expected. The same holds true in scenes set in dance clubs or dance competitions. Colored light is common to these locations and helps set the atmosphere. But besides color to support the feeling of being in a dance club, color can be used to create contrast on the subjects' faces and even reveal character feelings during the scene. If a character impresses someone with his or her dancing, side-lighting with color to accent the body movements would be very helpful.

BARS

Bars are also colorful places. The neon signs mixed with the colored lights of the bar itself add a colorful array of light to the walls and the subjects. Which colors the DP chooses to use helps relate to the viewer whether the scene is happy or sad, set in a fun, exciting environment or a sleazy, dirty dive.

PHOTO 10.8 Jonathan Sang, Mike Finkel, Charissa Carfrey, lit by DP Joseph di Gennaro, *Murder at Café Noir,* MTG Productions

In Photo 10.8 from *Murder at Café Noir,* DP Joseph di Gennaro key-lit the subjects with ½ CTB from behind the bar off right and washed the back wall with green. He placed an inkie as an uplight in the back corner with blue on it that mixed with the green to produce a rather ugly color. He placed a slash of ½ blue across the back door and a light outside shining in through the door's top windows with full CTB (Full Blue). A hard white light from off left rims the backs of their heads and gives us a small white reference. The result is a sleazy, dingy-bar feeling. The actual location was a Knights of Columbus social room, which didn't look sleazy at all.

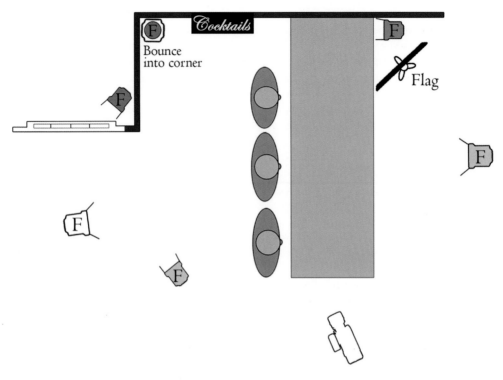

DIAGRAM 10.1 **Light plot for bar by Joseph di Gennaro**

NONFICTION

Color can be put to use in cinematography for shoots other than dramatic storytelling. Photo 10.9 is from an interview of Rich Goldberg, the owner of Ruba Lounge, a popular after-hours club in Philadelphia.

We will look at how this was lit in more detail in Chapter 13 on interviews, but notice the use of colored light both on the background and on Rich's kick. This is an example of how the lighting was created to help communicate the location, which included adding color accents. If the colors weren't added, the environment would have

PHOTO 10.9 **Interview of Rich Goldberg in his bar, the Ruba Club**

looked more bland and empty, which certainly was not the desired look for the piece. His face is still lit with white light, but the bluish edge places him in his surroundings, a nightclub.

I was invited to give a talk at an association meeting of videographers where the majority of the members did a lot of wedding and event shooting. A problem many of them repeated was how dark it becomes during the dancing at these events, and how they didn't want to blast the scene with bright lights just to get a picture. I suggested that they do what we do in fictional cinematography—side-light the area with a few colored lights. These lights will blend in and add to the festivities and bring up the light level to be able to get an exposure. At the same time, it can help edge-light the dancers and make the video their clients get later look all the more "memorable." Which colors they use would depend on the event—a sweet sixteen party would use more vibrant colors such as blue and magenta, while the "first dance" at a wedding reception might be better with more gentle colors such as pink and gold.

Colors to avoid in shooting live events are reds and greens, which will make the skin tones of the subjects either glow or look unhealthy. If the location already has these, use the color wheel and add lights with some of those color's complements to help lower their presence. The opposite of green is magenta, so something in the rose or deep pink family will provide both color and help eliminate the green. The opposite of red is cyan, so a sea blue or an azure blue will counter that and add some color. Gel swatch books are great tools for playing with color. The trick is to have some idea of what to expect and plan accordingly, since, as mentioned earlier, it's not possible to bring gels of every color with you. But you can bring what we often call "party gels," which are a group of colors such as the ones mentioned above that contain rich hues that can stand out. It's a good idea to always bring some pieces of CTB (Full Blue), CTO (85), Plus Green, and Minus Green on a location, as it comes in useful almost all the time. I usually bring ½ CTB, ½ CTO, ½ Minus Green, and ½ Plus Green, since you can always double it to make it full.

STUFF TO REMEMBER

- Color is an international, transcultural language that can help communicate time, place, and mood.

- Color gels subtract light from the source to project the desired color; thus the intensity drops.

- The more subtle the colored light, the more natural and realistic the image.

- The more vibrant the colored light, the more theatrical and dramatic the image.

- When complementary colors mix, they produce white.

- Some colors are more dominant and will overpower other colors.

- Cameras can only record whatever colors are reflected, so there needs to be that color wavelength in the light hitting the subject to reflect the desired color.

- Some lighting units are missing certain color wavelengths, which means they cannot effectively project every color.

- As an incandescent lighting unit dims, the color temperature gets warmer, which will affect the color of the light with or without a gel on it.

- Colors can be used to create contrast while still allowing visibility into the "shadow" area.

PUTTING IT INTO PRACTICE

- Shoot a scene with lots of colors. Have someone sitting at night by a desk lamp. Add a little warmth to the light imitating your desk lamp, and add a little cool gel to the fill. If you can, do this setup with a window behind the subject, and add moonlight and streetlight in through the window. Add backlights with the same color gels as the lights through the window. Does one color dominate the other? Can you move the backlights so that both can register on the subject? If you can't do the setup with a window, place a lamp in the background or in an open doorway with light in the other room, to motivate a backlight but give it a color.

- Now shoot the exact same scene, but just remove all the color gels. Compare how the two images feel—lit exactly the same but one with color and one without.

11 LIGHT THE SCENE, NOT JUST THE SHOT:
High Key, Low Key, Contrast Ratios, Exposure Choice, Chiaroscuro Lighting, Rembrandt, and Butterfly Lighting

When I told my friend DP Joseph di Gennaro that I was writing a textbook on lighting, he said, "Make sure you tell them to light the scene, not just the shot." Hopefully that is what I have been doing throughout this book, by giving examples of lighting setups that help to reinforce the intention of the scene. That is what Joe was getting at. He said all too often he has seen young cameramen get so caught up with the newest lighting gadgets and the perfect balance of color temperature or contrast ratio that they seem to neglect the primary reason for the lighting—to service the scene and its emotional intent. We do this by using everything we've discussed so far—lighting the three planes of action, using color, using texture, using intensity, and using angle. Let's look more closely at how this can be done, once again with a still from *Dark Tarot*.

In the scene in Photo 11.1, these three characters are the last ones left alive in a haunted house that won't allow them to leave. The medium Helena (Alexandra Landau) has just finished performing an exhausting spiritual manifestation that revealed how the first person died. The other two then asked her to perform another spiritual revelation, to discern where the lost key to the house is. She gave a halfhearted try, couldn't, and stormed away when Liz (Jade Elysan, center) claimed she wasn't trying. Bethany (Natasa Babic), the nicer and innocent one, pleads with her to help, but Helena just stands off, by herself, unhappy, even refusing to face them. The scene ends with Liz walking up to Helena and confronting her with the fact that it doesn't matter if they like each other or not, they're stuck here together, in purgatory. The last line of the scene is, "If that's where we are, then you're here with us. So ask yourself this: how long do you want to stay?"

PHOTO 11.1 Natasa Babic, Jade Elysan, and Alexandra Landau, *Dark Tarot*, DGW Films

Now, how does the lighting light the scene rather than just the shot? All that was needed to light the shot would have been to light Helena in the open room and the other two in the doorway. We could have lit them all the same intensity and with the same texture of light, three-point lighting with key, fill, and backlight. The black windows clearly telegraph that it is nighttime, and the camera placement reveals depth with a foreground element and a distant back room visible through the doorway. Throw another light in the back, and it's done. But this is not how the scene was lit.

A theatrical blue-gelled 250w Fresnel (an inkie) was the edge light aimed onto the out-of-focus doorway molding in the foreground. The two actresses in the doorway, Natasa and Jade, are key-lit by a 750w Rifa softlight from camera right, just above eye height and slightly on the far side of their faces from camera. The light was also flagged so that none of its spill light would wash the wall behind Alexandra or Alexandra herself. Alexandra, center, is key-lit by a hard 300w Fresnel with ½ CTB

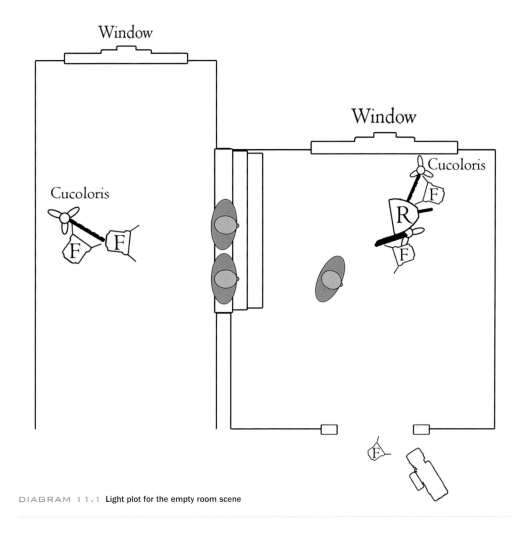

DIAGRAM 1 1 . 1 **Light plot for the empty room scene**

positioned slightly higher than her head level, and on the away side of her face to camera. All three were backlit by a hard 650w Fresnel with ½ CTB on it from the room on the left that catches their hair and helps rim them. The back room was lit with a 650w Fresnel through a cookie (cucoloris) with theatrical blue gel on it, while the gray wall behind Alexandra was lit with a 300w Fresnel with the same blue through a double net and a cookie. Both were aimed at oblique angles toward the walls to give elongated patterns. In order to not be distracting, the pattern on the wall behind Alexandra was made dimmer and less defined with the double net, making a more subtle breakup on the wall.

How does this service the intention of the scene and what the characters are going through?

Alexandra is lit with a hard light and has no fill, which makes her more dramatic and mysterious—the very definition of a spirit medium. Natasa and Jade are both lit with a soft light that wraps around most of their faces; they are the trophy wives in the script.

PHOTO 11.2 **Alexandra hard-lit, harsh contrast on face**

PHOTO 11.3 **Natasa and Jade soft-lit, low contrast on faces**

Photo 11.2 shows how the color of Alexandra's key is colder than the warmer key of the other two women. Alexandra is half in the dark—as is her character about what to do next. She feels lost and alone, disillusioned by something the ghost revealed to her earlier (which the viewer knows). She stands farther away from the other two. Lighting her background darker helps place her more into the "shadows," as does lighting the foreground with a deep-blue edge that helps to transmit the feeling of being in a lonely place—somewhere cold moonlight comes in, rather than warm light from a fireplace or a lamp. The dark foreground and the dark background put Alexandra in a small oasis of light. She is surrounded by darkness and reluctant to step out into it.

Photo 11.3 shows how Natasa and Jade are much more evenly lit. The position of the Rifa allows light on both sides of their faces that is soft and warm. They stand in a doorway with bright light coming from behind them, and while there is a blue pattern on the wall behind them, it is brighter and not as dark somber blue in color as the foreground color holding Alexandra in. This feels like a softer, almost nicer "moonlight" than the deeper blue in the foreground.

Photo 11.4 shows how the strong backlight hitting the floor forms a path that leads the two women to Alexandra, as well as to the viewer's eyes. Thus we are using light to help direct the attention of the viewer to her, but also direct the other two characters to her as their only way out. Thus, this lighting lights the scene and not just the shot.

PHOTO 11.4 **Light streak on floor is path to the character they need help from**

PAINTING WITH LIGHT

This wasn't all planned way in advance, although some DPs, after a scout, will draw up floor plans to give to their gaffers. Floor plans become a good basis from which to begin painting the set with light. But often the crew walks into a set or location that the DP has seen and has an idea of what should be doner, but he or she builds from scratch. Virtually nothing in lighting for cinematography is paint-by-numbers—every situation is different.

This scene was shot a few days prior to the scene that comes just before it, a very common practice in filmmaking. When it came time to shoot this scene, I, as the DP, had to remember the script and the scene that would come before it. What did the characters just go through? Who are they and what are they thinking? What is the conflict in this scene? I checked with the script supervisor and the director about the scene, watched a blocking rehearsal, and set the camera placement. Now it was time to light.

Lighting is a building process. First we add the obvious—bright light from the kitchen, pattern on the background, inkie on the foreground molding. As I ask my gaffer Conor Stalvey to set each light, he asks, which color? It's a few days into shooting, and we've already established the True Blue color for after the mayhem starts. This scene is after the mayhem, so Conor has the True Blue gel with him. He sets the gobo for the back room without being told, puts the gel on, and waits to hear if I want something different. He asks, "What's the key?," and the real build begins. Hard light for Alex—let's make her different than the others—use a soft light for them. He sets them, and I stand by camera and ask him to move them a little this way, a little that way.

This is standard practice in the film biz for how DPs and gaffers work. Lights are moved tiny amounts one way or another until it looks right, it feels right. We all do it, and sometimes it just flows and goes fast, and other times it's a pigsty. All DPs have had those times where after setting light after light for maybe even a half hour, they realize that it just isn't working, and they tell their gaffer to turn everything off and start again. Thankfully this wasn't one of those times. It just came together pretty fast, which was good because it was the end of a long day.

Conor got the Rifa to key the two trophy wives perfectly with just the right amount of wrap. Now it was moving their backlight from in the kitchen. Slide it out—more out—oops, it's in the shot, back it up. Can you aim it down? Can you make it look like a path that leads to Alex—without getting the damn light in the shot? And Conor does. Then we look at it. "The wall behind Alex?" we both ask. "Use the double net cookie, but make it dim, undefined," I say. While he does that I ask the best boy for the party color gels—what do we have in a richer blue? Anything? No—but he can double it. We throw it on the inkie on the foreground molding. Look at it all again, and have the actors move through it. Does it work? Show the director. Shoot the damn thing.

What was needed for the scene was always in mind, both consciously and subconsciously. Making it work and come together is both the fun part and the chore. Taking that last look, with the real actors moving through it and rehearsing, is the moment when you realize what every light's purpose is and how it contributes. And that's when you often have to do some last-minute tweaks—move that light a smidge to the left, drop a double in the pattern on the door frame.

I'm not saying the lighting is perfect or exceptional in any way. But it's right for the scene.

LOW KEY LIGHTING

The preceding text describes an example of what is commonly referred to as low key lighting—which means high contrast and dark shadows. The term low key is part of the vocabulary directors and DPs use when talking about the look for a scene. Some people get confused and think low key means low light. It doesn't. It means that there is a wide range between light and dark within the shot, and very often very little middle ground. Low key lighting is dramatic and in practice used extensively in mysteries, horror, and sci-fi. But it is also a style used in gangster films and spy films, even dramas at times, depending on the scene. Low key isn't necessarily employed throughout an entire film; it can be on a scene-by-scene basis.

Like night exteriors, low key lighting works best when there is a highlight somewhere in the frame—a white reference. But unlike night exteriors, this highlighted area is often lighting the main subject. The contrast between the key side of the face and the fill side is drastic, as well as the contrast between the acting area and the background. Every child is afraid of the dark, and since we were all children at one time, dark shadows produce a universal feeling that transcends ages, languages, and cultures. Low-key-lit scenes are rarely happy ones.

TV shows that employ a lot of low key lighting include *Supernatural* (2005–), *Bates Motel* (2013–), *Doctor Who* (2005–), *True Blood* (2008–), and *Boardwalk Empire* (2010–). Films include *The Road to Perdition* (2002), *Collateral* (2004), *The Girl with a Dragon Tattoo* (2009 & 2011 versions), *Super 8* (2011), *The Number 23* (2007), *Skyfall* (2012), *The Dark Knight Rises* (2012), *Tinker Tailor Soldier Spy* (2011), and so on.

HIGH KEY LIGHTING

The opposite look is high key—which means a more even level of light and less contrast. Some people get confused and think this means bright. It doesn't. It means that the shadows aren't all that dark, and that the majority of the scene is lit in a mid range, rather than very bright and very dark. It doesn't mean a lack of contrast, just low contrast between key and fill, between acting

PHOTO 11.5 **High key lighting on Mitchell Elkowitz, test commercial, Airworthy Productions**

area and background. High key lighting is more often employed in comedies, romances, commercials, sitcoms, and family dramas, since it provides a warm and cozy feeling and often a lack of tension, such as in the woodshop test commercial in Photo 11.5.

But it has also been used very successfully in sci-fi, including *2001: A Space Odyssey* and *Moon*, to create a sterile, antiseptic feeling. TV shows that employ a lot of high key lighting include *Modern Family* (2009–), *Community* (2009–), *Scrubs* (2001–2010), *Psych* (2006–), and every sitcom. Films like *The Hangover* (2009), *Bridesmaids* (2011), *The 40-Year-Old Virgin* (2005), *American Pie* (1999), *Rat Race* (2001), *When Harry Met Sally* (1989), *My Cousin Vinnie* (1992), and *Yes Man* (2008) employ high key lighting.

CONTRAST RATIO

High key and low key are shorthand methods for talking about contrast ratios. The contrast ratio is the difference in light levels between the key side of the face and the fill side of the face, as measured in either foot-candles or f-stops. We measure the contrast ratio by using a light meter. Keep in mind that in most lighting setups, the

> **"I like a certain amount of contrast— it gives the image some depth and drama—but I don't work towards any particular key-to-fill ratio."**
>
> —DAVID MULLEN, ASC,
> TV SERIES/FEATURE DP

key side is also lit by the fill, so the contrast ratio is key plus fill, compared to just fill. Therefore, to determine the contrast ratio, we should read all the light hitting the key side with the meter, and then read only the fill light. Many of us get confused when we talk about contrast ratio, as technically it relates to foot-candles. For example, say there are 100 foot-candles on the key side and 50 foot-candles on the fill side. This would be a 2:1 ratio. It is also a difference in one f-stop between the two sides of the face. But if the foot-candles are 50 on the fill and 200 on the key, the ratio is 4:1, but the difference is only two f-stops, not four, because each f-stop equals a doubling of the foot-candles.

In practice, virtually no one talks about contrast ratios in foot-candles anymore. They use f-stops, because it relates directly to the aperture setting on the lens, and it's just easier to think that way. So instead of talking about a 4:1 ratio, DPs and gaffers will talk about a two-stop difference. Sometimes the DP might want an f-stop difference, to really see the contrast in levels, such as 50 foot-candles on the fill compared to 800 foot-candles on the key. In the old method this would be considered a 16:1 ratio, but today it is a four-stop difference.

While contrast ratio can refer to the difference between key and fill, it also concerns the relationship between acting area and background, and the brightest thing in the shot compared to the darkest area in the shot. The greater the contrast ratio between acting area and background, the more the acting area stands out—which could be what is wanted—or not. Sometimes we want the acting area to blend in with its surroundings; sometimes we don't. And if we're trying to create a silhouette or a shadow effect (which we will discuss in Chapter 12), we need the background to be brighter than the acting area.

In Photo 11.6 from *The Cold Equations*, Ashley Taylor is lit via a chicken coop and a ¾ backlight with a light blue, motivated by the small blue lights on the back panels. A theatrical blue light is aimed into the wall behind her, and uplight from beneath the floor lights the rest of the background. The foreground is allowed to go totally black, which required flags to cut any bounce light from hitting the walls. The extreme contrast between foreground and acting area helps to deliver the theatrical moment the director wanted: her apprehension about what is about to happen as she ventures into the unknown. It's not a moment of fear, which would have been lit differently. This character is a strong-willed, resourceful, and brave woman, characteristics that the lighting helps communicate.

PHOTO 11.6 **High contrast between Ashley Taylor in acting area, and background and foreground,** *The Cold Equations,* **Ellipsis Films**

Basically, the greater the contrast ratio, the more dramatic the image. Dark shadows or dark areas in the shot equals drama. DPs will set their contrast ratios between the key and fill on the subject, but also between the acting area and the background, based on how dramatic the director wants the scene to be. With a light meter aimed at the light, the DP, or the gaffer, will ask the electric setting the light to spot it in or flood it out, or drop

> "I light by eye, then take a picture to see what the contrast looks like. But I would look at the meter also. Generally the subject will always be brighter than the background—unless for some reason you don't want that, such as against a window, which should always be brighter."
>
> —PETER STEIN, ASC, FEATURE DP

a single or double scrim in it, until the DP gets the desired f-stop reading on the meter. Some DPs, such as Peter Stein, will set every light by eye first to a look he likes. Then he asks the gaffer to read the contrast ratios and adjusts the intensity of the lights to nail down the f-stop and the ratio he wants.

Working this way is all based on experience and was done more often when shooting film, where the actual image wouldn't be seen until the next day when the film came back from the lab. Today we have HD monitors on set that allow the DP, and everyone else, to evaluate what the lighting looks like as it's set. Some DPs have virtually retired their light meters, while others loyally use them to check their ratios. It's a working method that is as individual as each DP's lighting.

SELECTING EXPOSURE

Another choice DPs make when lighting the scene, rather than just the shot, is picking what to expose for. In practice, almost everyone in the business uses incident light meters. Everyone is taught to place the meter in front of the subject, turn the hemisphere toward the camera, and take a reading. This method averages fill, key, ambiance, and sometimes even backlight. If we set the f-stop to this reading, the center of the face will be exposed correctly. But often that isn't the look we are going for. By cupping the hand around the hemisphere as we point it at a light, we can read the key light alone, the fill light alone, and the backlight alone. The DP will then make an artistic choice as to which f-stop to set the lens to. Sometimes it will work better for the emotional content of the scene to have the part of the face turned toward the camera be underexposed. This gives the viewer the feeling that they are sad, or hiding something.

In the beauty queen scene in the film *Erin Brockovich*, Erin (Julia Roberts) breaks down crying as she tells her boyfriend how she had once been a beauty contest winner. She's been receiving threatening phone calls and fears for her children and what she's gotten herself into. She sits on a bed in front of a very bright window. DP Ed Lachman underexposed her face, which was lit with soft frontal fill, and set the window light and the kick on her face to become overexposed. The result is a beautiful visual moment of vulnerability, of being overpowered (by the sunlight and much more), and of lost innocence. It's a touching moment that wouldn't have read the same to audiences if he had exposed correctly for her face. The fact that she is underexposed, rimmed by bright burning-out white light, helps support the emotional moment of the scene.

So, the DP picks the exposure not based on the level of light hitting the face, but on what will help make the image better support the intention for the scene. Sometimes this means exposing for the backlight and allowing the front to go underexposed. Sometimes it means exposing for the key side so that the fill will be a little underexposed. Sometimes it means exposing for the fill side and letting the key side of the face go a little overexposed. Sometimes it means

> "When I shoot on digital, I tend to underexpose. I expose for the highlights because you can bring up the image."
>
> —ELIA LYSSY, DOCUMENTARY/LOW-BUDGET FEATURE DP

averaging them both so that the key is slightly over and the fill slightly under. Each will have a subtle but effective emotional context that it will deliver to the viewer.

Photo 11.7 from *The Cold Equations* is an example of letting the faces go underexposed. The scene is after a deadly accident that has trapped several people in an underground research center.

PHOTO 11.7 **Exposure set for highlights on Josh Bragg's face,** *The Cold Equations,* **Ellipsis Films**

The image was exposed for the kick on actor Josh Bragg's neck and face, allowing the rest of his face and that of actor Richard Bell to be underexposed. The side lighting creates modeling, and the shadows create drama. Notice the eye light in Josh's one eye. The added fog lowered the contrast and allowed the light beam from the flashlight to become visible. The backgrounds were not allowed to go totally dark, and the actors are both positioned so that an out-of-focus wall with some light is visible behind them. The dark, negative space is off to the left of frame. As we read from left to right, placing the darkness on the left makes it the first thing the viewer subconsciously sees, thus helping to place the viewer emotionally in a dark and unsettling environment.

Josh's key light is low and warm. His fill is eye level and slightly blue. The rim on Richard is the same blue as is his key light, which is coming at him from the left, 90 degrees from the camera. The white flashlight beam is our white reference, as is the rim on Josh's shoulder. This type of lighting is sometimes called chiaroscuro.

CHIAROSCURO LIGHTING

This term from painting is sometimes applied by film studies scholars to cinematography and lighting. Chiaroscuro is the strong use of contrast between areas of extreme brightness and dim shadows within the frame. While chiaroscuro is a style of low key lighting, it can probably be best described as low key lighting where the blacks are virtually never totally black, and detail is always there in the shadows, just like a Renaissance painting. DP John Alcott's magnificent work in *Barry Lyndon* (1975) stands out as a prime example. Director Stanley Kubrick wanted the film to look like paintings from the period, which Alcott achieved through his use of graduated filters on the lens and Dutch Master's style lighting (discussed further in Chapter 14).

To achieve a true chiaroscuro image for the scenes set at night, Alcott had Zeiss manufacture a special set of super-speed prime lenses with an aperture of f0.7 to allow him to shoot by candlelight. The beauty of Alcott's lighting can be seen in the gambling party scene. The misconception about this scene, and all the other candle-lit scenes in this beautiful film, is that there was "no lighting" and that they just shot under candlelight. At the beginning of the scene you can clearly see how the entire room was filled with candles, including an enormous candle-filled chandelier. Alcott had worked with art director Roy Walker in preproduction to plan for this scene. He made sure there would be enough candles in the art direction of the scene to allow him to paint the lighting, not just get an exposure. Alcott lit each angle just as he would any other scene, but the only lighting units he used were candelabras. In an interview, gaffer Lou Bogue talked about how his electrics were moving very large, dripping candelabras all over the place out of frame to produce backlight, kick, fill, and background lighting. They were also constantly using their light meters to determine the contrast ratios between the acting areas and the backgrounds, adding more and more candles just out of frame, never allowing the background to go too dark. In the next chapter we will discuss how to create "candlelight" lighting.

The new HD digital cameras are very sensitive and can record images under simple candlelight. But keep in mind that in order to deliver an image under candlelight that is comparable to what the human eye sees, with its vast dynamic range and ability to see dim details in the shadows, we cannot rely only on the candles in frame. The most sensitive camera cannot match the human eye, and the backgrounds will drop into a murky darkness that the brain will reject as unnatural. To achieve the chiaroscuro look, the backgrounds need to be dimly lit, and separation between subject and background must be maintained. This means background lights and backlights or kickers for the acting area. If you want to try doing this with only candles, take a cue from Lou Bogue and use really big candelabras with lots of candles—and have several boxes of candles on hand, as they'll burn down and need to be replaced during the shoot.

PHOTO 1 1 . 8 **Chiaroscuro lighting on Tina Zoganas, *TV Psychic Party Game*, MTG Productions**

The lighting of Tina Zoganas in Photo 11.8 for the *TV Psychic Party Game* DVD is an example of chiaroscuro lighting. The exposure was set for her away-side cheek. The candles provide the motivation for the key light, the hair light, and the background light—even though they had no actual effect and everything was individually lit by tungsten units. The star filter on the camera lens provides the flare of the flames, which becomes the image's "white reference."

There are times that people may confuse chiaroscuro lighting with the Dutch Masters look. While it is common to films with a Dutch Masters style such as John Alcott's work on *Barry Lyndon*, Miroslav Ondříček's work on *Amadeus* (1985), and Eduardo Serra's work on *Girl with a Pearl Earring* (2003), there are a number of non–Dutch Masters look films with chiaroscuro-style lighting, such as *The Illusionist* (2006) with cinematography by Dick Pope, *Pretty Baby* (1978) with cinematography by Sven Nykvist, *Memoirs of a Geisha* (2005) with cinematography by Dion Beebe, and *Road to Perdition* (2002) with cinematography by Conrad Hall—all exceptional artists in lighting.

"REMBRANDT" LIGHTING

Rembrandt lighting is a style of lighting a single person, in still photography for portraits and in videography as an interview. This term has been credited to silent film director Cecil B DeMille, who told producer Sam Goldwyn when he complained that the actor's faces in a scene were only half lit, that it was "Rembrandt lighting," which made him much happier. Rembrandt painted portraits with a very strong soft light hitting the subject from mostly one side, because he painted by large windows using overcast sunlight. One side of the face is bright and the other in deep shadows. In most of his portraits there is no backlight or kick. Basically, he didn't add much fill light, but rather allowed the dark side of the face to partially fall off into the darkness of the background. Often he would add a slight glow behind the subject or paint a little lighter background behind the shadow side of the face to provide some separation. Of course, just like cinematographers, Rembrandt changed his style from time to time, but he is best known for this look.

Photo 11.10 from *Dark Tarot* is an example of Rembrandt lighting. The exposure was set for the side of Jade Elysan's face turned toward the mirror (which became the side toward the camera). Her forearm overexposes, and her hair sinks into darkness. All this helps make her eye and her fear to become the center of attention. The aberration of her reflection in the mirror's edge helps convey the feeling of disorientation called for in the script. There is no backlight, but the background doesn't absorb her hair; it has enough fill to separate her from the shadows.

Rembrandt lighting is soft, directional, and dramatic using one frontal light and having a high contrast ratio on the face, generally

PHOTO 11.9 **Typical Rembrandt painting**

PHOTO 11.10 **Rembrandt lighting on Jade Elysan,** *Dark Tarot,* **DGW Films**

producing a triangular shadow from the nose on the fill-side cheek. The difference between this and chiaroscuro is subtle. Rembrandt lighting usually has the brighter side turned toward the camera, and no backlight or kick; while chiaroscuro is more typical of standard film lighting with the key side turned away from the camera, and it usually employs backlight and a touch of fill.

GLAMOUR "BUTTERFLY" LIGHTING

Glamour lighting is an old Hollywood and TV commercial standard. It's a combination of bright backlight and "butterfly" lighting. When someone is supposed to look glamorous on camera, the person is often shot with a lot of direct—not ¾ back—backlight flooding through the subject's hair, giving a halo effect. Sometimes this is achieved by using two backlights, one from each side to sculpt the cheekbones, while flaring the hair. This light is often brighter than the frontal key.

> "For beauty shots you might want the leading lady to have a beautiful backlight all the time."
>
> —PETER STEIN, ASC, FEATURE DP

Sometimes the real sunlight can be used for this hot hair glow, such as when shooting outside or inside by windows. Bright light coming through the hair brings attention to the face it frames, and makes it appear thinner, more sleek.

To even further accent the hair, the backlight can be placed below the shoulders and aimed up into the hair. This angle of lighting rims the shoulders and neck and gives the hair more volume.

> "I'm very fond of 'nuclear' backlighting, as if intense sunlight has come through a window, but only when it looks motivated and believable."
>
> —DAVID MULLEN, ASC,
> TV SERIES/FEATURE DP

I lit a TV commercial for a shampoo, with the standard slow-motion head twirl of the model's silky hair floating through the air. Behind and below her shoulders I added a very bright open-faced light to get the maximum spread and crispness to her hair as it flared out and spun. Lighting from behind and below added a sparkle to the underside of the hair as it spread, which was what the director was going for. This angle also avoids overexposing the top of the head. Is this lighting motivated or natural? Absolutely not. Does it matter? Absolutely not. This kind of hair lighting is used often in dream sequences, in romance films, and in teen comedies when the boy sees the girl of his dreams, but it is also a standard in commercials. It's just glamour.

Something to be careful of when doing this is if the subject moves too much, the hair light might become visible in the frame or glare into the lens. Position the light, then rehearse all the moves/ actions the subject will make while watching through the camera, and see if the light or a glare appears. Always do this before you roll.

The glamour look is additionally achieved with "butterfly" lighting. This comes from still portrait photography and received its name from the small butterfly-looking shadow cast under the subject's nose. A bright softlight is positioned directly in front and above the subject's face, but as low over the picture frame line as possible. The desired effect is a high key look that bleaches out the skin's imperfections with a wash of soft light that comes from the same direction as the lens. You can see this method in the close-ups of Hollywood film stars such as Marlene Dietrich and Greta Garbo, who both had high cheekbones, which this lighting tends to accent. It is rarely used on men, as it can hollow out their cheeks. In fact, glamour lighting is almost exclusively reserved for women.

Butterfly lighting creates a one-to-one contrast ratio on the face—in other words, no contrast. But the sides of the cheeks fall off, providing some couture and modeling, and the contrast between the face and the hair light can be so high as to slightly burn out some of the hair.

The last element to glamour lighting is the eye light. The twinkle in the eye is an essential element to the sexy glamour look. The earlier mentioned ring light was designed for glamour lighting. It adds a nice eye light and washes out the facial features, but it doesn't accent the high cheekbones the same as butterfly lighting does. So, some DPs may use a ring light or an obie light with butterfly lighting and a hot behind-the-shoulders hair light to really sell the look.

Glamour isn't always reserved for just the face of the actress. Rimming the actress's legs and/or backlighting her through her dress are additional accents to the glamour look. When lighting dance, to highlight the shape of the human body, we side-light the figure. If doing a head-to-toe glamour shot, the legs will be side lit, but those units will be cut off the face, which is butterfly lit. Fortunately, when this type of glamour lighting is called for, the majority of the time the woman is standing still, walking down a flight of stairs, stepping through a doorway, or getting out of a car. This lighting look usually only has to carry her for a short distance. If using a bright hard backlight, it's always best not to see too much of the floor, as the shadow of her head might get in the shot, which isn't all that exotic looking. Also, as she moves forward, there is a possibility of either seeing the backlight or getting glare from it in the camera lens. So these are both things that should be taken into consideration when framing and blocking the shot.

Glamour lighting is a resource for commercials, celebrity interviews, TV shows, and movies. It is rarely used in corporate video or documentary, and in reality shows, only for the host or celebrity guests.

PHOTO 11.11 **Classic Hollywood butterfly lighting on Marlene Dietrich**

PHOTO 11.12 **Classic Hollywood butterfly lighting on Greta Garbo**

LIGHTING ANGLES

The angle at which the light hits the subject can subliminally help set location, time of day, and more importantly, the dramatic content of the scene. In life we only see people lit from below when it's coming from candles, fireplaces, TV sets, or low desk lamps. So we associate light from a low angle with darkness and nighttime.

The strange shadows low light produces on a person's face has become a standard look for the menacing killer or mad scientist after years of Hollywood horror films, as these characters always work at night. So placing lights low aimed up helps establish a feeling of night or danger. It might not give the appropriate look when you are lighting a comedy or romance.

It is obvious from Photo 11.13 that this film isn't a comedy. There are shadows and bright spots, and the key light on both actors is coming from low angles. Almost all the lights are coming from a low angle, so it reads serious. Conversely, lights coming from close to eye level and from closer to the lens can give the image a more romantic feeling. Candle-lit dinners are romantic, and candles come from slightly below eye level—so we can see over them and into our date's eyes. A side-lit face comes across more serious and stern, or sexy and sensuous, because part of the face is hiding in the shadows. This can be mysterious, threatening, or even seductive. It all depends on how everything else is lit and the context of the scene.

PHOTO 11.13 Low key lighting conveys the mood desired of the scene with Richard Bell and Andrew Gaul, *The Cold Equations*, Ellipsis Films

DPs say that 90 percent of getting the lighting right is placing the key light in the right place. The best way to learn which angles help produce what sort of feeling visually is to experiment. Slowly move the key light around the subject until it "feels" right. The trick is to find the right lighting feel that helps best communicate the intention of the scene and how the director wants the viewer to feel.

STUFF TO REMEMBER

- High key is not overexposed; rather, it is low-contrast lighting with a wide range of levels of light.

- Low key is not underexposed; rather, it is high-contrast lighting with bright elements and dark shadows, and not much in between.

- Contrast ratio measures the foot-candles or f-stops between the key and the fill side of the subject. The higher the contrast, the greater the dramatic feeling. The lower the contrast, the more gentle, content, or happy the feeling.

- Most DPs light by eye, and then meter later. Some just use the production monitor.

- DPs select the exposure (f-stop) after measuring just the key, just the fill, and just the backlight, and then deciding which to expose for.

- DPs set the intensity of the background after picking the exposure for the acting area, based on the desired contrast ratio between acting area and background.

- Chiaroscuro refers to a lighting design that features a strong use of contrast and has details in the dim shadows which seldom go black.

- Rembrandt lighting uses a bright, soft side light on the camera side of the face that produces a triangular shadow of the nose on the opposite cheek, with little or no fill or backlight, but with subtle separation from the background by having it not go black.

- Glamour lighting is a hot hair light and even facial exposure provided by butterfly lighting, which is a single bright softlight above and in front of the face.

PUTTING IT INTO PRACTICE

- Set up a shot and then shoot it with a 2:1 ratio, key to fill. Now continue to lower the intensity of the fill, holding in a piece of paper showing the difference in f-stops. See how dramatic it becomes as the contrast increases.

- Light a scene, and then set the exposure for the key. Next set the exposure for the fill. Then set the exposure for halfway between the two. Look at the difference, and see how the feeling of the image changes.

- Shoot a person lit with Rembrandt lighting.

- Shoot a glamour shot using butterfly lighting.

- Move a light around the subject and take stills along the way, looking at the feeling each angle telegraphs.

CHAPTER 11 : Light the Scene, Not Just the Shot: High Key, Low Key, Contrast Ratios, Exposure Choice, Chiaroscuro Lighting, Rembrandt, and Butterfly Lighting

196

12 SPECIAL LIGHTING CONSIDERATIONS AND EFFECTS:
Fire, Water, Rain, Fog, Lightning, Poor Man's Process Shot, Green Screen, and Product Shots

There are times that the lighting department has to help make things work. In this chapter we discuss how to address common lighting special requirements and achieve commonly used lighting effects. The exact units used are not as important as how they are used.

PHOTO 12.1 **Backlit steam in lighting class final, lit by Dan Inzitar**

FOG AND STEAM

In order to read well on camera, fog and steam are best backlit. Side lighting can also help, but if the majority of light comes from the front, the fog will become an opaque white and look more like a dense cloud rather than fog. In Dan Inzitar's lighting final, Photo 12.1, the fog was backlit, allowing the camera to see the subject's legs through it. In Photo 12.2 from *TV Psychic Party Game,* the tombstone can be seen through the fog because the fog in the foreground was side-lit, while the fog in the background was side- and front-lit, and thus reads more as a dense cloud.

SMOKE

Like fog, smoke needs to be backlit to appear on camera. In Photo 12.3, the ¾ backlight for Alexandra Landau also was used to backlight the smoke from the incense. If the smoke was only front-lit, it would virtually disappear to the camera.

FIREPLACE/CAMPFIRE

Sometimes there is a scene by an open fire, such as a fireplace or a campfire. Fire is a multiple-source hard light that flickers and emits a limited range of different colors. It comes from below and therefore isn't really very flattering to the face.

PHOTO 12.2 **Side- and front-lit fog with blue and white light,** *TV Psychic Party Game,* **MTG Productions**

PHOTO 12.3 **Backlit smoke, Lauren Muraski and Alexandra Landau,** *Dark Tarot,* **DGW Films**

Viewers accept this and expect fire to be amber and orange in color. To create the effect that light is coming from a fireplace or a campfire, at least two small hard lights, usually 150w Fresnels or 250w inkie Fresnels, are required with slightly different orange/amber-colored gels on them. The lights are placed down on the ground, about 6 inches apart, and aimed up at the subject. The desired effect is to have hard shadows that overlap and slightly "dance" across the face, as the lights flicker or dim erratically up and down. By having the two lights set half a foot apart but aimed at the same place, the shadows they produce will be slightly off, and as the lights alternate their intensities, the shadows will shift back and forth—just as shadows do from a real fire.

Flicker boxes are small devices that can be plugged into a light and then allow you to set a flicker rate. They are usually rented for the days they are needed. However, you can achieve a similar effect using small individual dimmers. Plug each light into a dimmer, and have someone assigned to jiggle the dimmers up and down at an irregular rate. Remember never to dim either light very far down, as fires don't go out and then up again. A little practice, and someone can get the hang of it—although it does become tiring rather quickly.

Variac resistance dimmers are common in the industry, but often we use standard household dimmers that simply have a male Edison plug on one side and female Edison plug on the other. These can be purchased this way from film supply houses, or you can easily make them yourself from supplies bought at a hardware store.

When shooting close-ups, some directors may feel that the moving shadows on the face can become distracting, especially if the shots are rather long or there is a lot of dialogue. In these cases, it's not uncommon to add a low-intensity softlight gelled the same color as the firelights

PHOTO 12.4 **Hand dimmer, courtesy of Cinelease NY**

to fill the face and lessen the shadow effects. This fill is usually positioned around eye height, and not from down below where the firelights are set. The viewer never notices, but the higher softlight placement allows much more flattering facial light. For extended conversations by a fire, it helps to have the characters not looking directly into the fire. This way, the lighting can be arranged with the flickering fire effect as a kicker and the gelled softlight the key, while the other side of the face is allowed to go dark or is lit with blue for a nighttime feel. This provides modeling and a sense of time and place, and eliminates distractions by the flicker effect.

Shadows behind the subject on the background help sell the fire effect. Sometimes it is necessary to add additional small units to create the same fire effect on the background separate from the subject lighting. These can be ganged into the same dimmers as the acting area lights, or can be operated independently by another set of dimmers. Of course, the light hitting the background should be lower in intensity than the acting area lights.

When doing a fire "gag," take into consideration the following:

• The colors on the two lights should be very similar—and not too theatrical. No reds or yellows—stick within the amber/orange range.

• When flickering or dimming, the light from the fire-effect lights should go overexposed when all the way up and only a little underexposed when down—never out.

- If there are several people sitting around the "fire" or they are not sitting near each other, more than two sets of lights will be required to create the firelight effect—plugging lights from each set into the same two flicker boxes or dimmers so that they change together.

Units called scenic projectors are available that have rotating color wheels inside them and can project a firelight effect—as well as rolling clouds, rain drops, water reflections, and so forth. They come in various sizes and intensities. Rosco makes an X-Effects projector that uses two rotating glass filters and can project a really believable firelight effect, and BriteShot makes the Luminator RGBW LED unit that has programmed into it a fire effect. Several LED effects projectors are available that are used in the theater industry that might also be usable for cinema. A concern here, however, is that their base color temperature may be too high (too blue) to read well on camera. Experimentation is always necessary.

Many excellent examples of fire lighting exist, but three that come to mind immediately are *Dances with Wolves* (1990), *Seabiscuit* (2003), and *Stand By Me* (1986). All of these used real fires in their scenes as well as the fire-effect lighting. When you are incorporating real fire, there are some other considerations. Real fire can flare the lens and produce smoke that can obscure the shot if backlit. When real fire flares up, the high light intensity can momentarily burn out the faces on camera.

Keep in mind that when shooting wide shots with a real fire, hiding the fire effects lights is more difficult, but it can be done by hiding them behind logs or rocks that edge the fire. The concern is that the power cables to the lights not get so hot from the real fire that they begin to melt. Often larger-wattage hard lights are positioned low (but not on the ground), off camera right and left with colored gels, crossing their beams up through the fire into the subjects' faces. These units will not have to be plugged into flicker boxes or dimmers, as the real fire will be providing the dancing shadows and be the subjects' key light. These lights are additional fill to help support the firelight color and maintain a certain base intensity. If the scene is a romantic one, it isn't unusual for these off-camera lights to be placed at eye level and aimed through diffusion, such as 4-foot × 4-foot silks, to provide a more glamorous and romantic look to the faces.

RAGING FIRES

Films and TV shows that have scenes with buildings on fire don't rely only on the special effects and the specialty prop people who operate the propane-fed fire jets. Lighting usually creates the effect of the violent flickering firelight on the actors and the set. This is especially true if the fire effects are going to be added in postproduction. If the prop department is adding fire jets, they are usually confined to right in front of the camera's view and a few very contained areas. So the lighting must add the fire effect to the background walls and anything else that is actually flammable and that the fire jets are avoiding. In fact, several films have created convincing fire scenes with no real flames at all. Real fire creates real smoke, which makes it hard to see the actors.

One method to create the light from a raging fire is to bounce a nine-light or a Maxi-Brute into a 4-foot × 4-foot reflector, and have a grip or electric wiggle the reflector. Each of the nine lamps should have different or alternating amber-straw colored gels on them. Spread the beams of the columns so that the lights bounce off in different directions. DP Lisa Wiegand did this very effectively on the TV show *Chicago Fire* (2013). She also augmented the real fire effects by using 1½ full CTS (color temperature straw) to cover a homemade light built by gaffer John Milinac, which consisted of high-intensity bulbs screwed into a board wrapped with chicken wire. Each light was on its own flicker generator to achieve an erratic fire effect.

In the movie *End of Watch* (2013), DP Roman Vasyanov use the reflector/nine-light method to create a house fire, placing the reflectors so they could be seen through the windows of the house, but hiding the lights off to the sides. With smoke pouring out the windows—backlit by the wiggling reflectors—the bright, burned-out, glaring reflectors convincingly looked like fire inside the house.

Smaller productions can accomplish the same kind of effect by using four or five inexpensive PAR can lights bouncing into a reflector. If 4 foot × 4-foot reflectors are unavailable, the shiny silver side of a 4-foot × 4-foot beadboard works as well. To create the effect of a raging fire, more than one lighting/reflector combo is set up, spreading the effect across the entire scene. Add a smoke machine, and you have a convincing out-of-control fire just off camera.

CANDLES

Unlike fire, candles produce a more steady glow without the pops and flare-ups. A single candle has a single hard point source that burns at a rather steady pace, unlike a fire that has bursts of flames that ebb and flow. A candelabra has multiple hard point sources, but while they throw multiple shadows, they all burn at a rather steady pace as well. So, unless there is a wind in the scene, flickering the lights to imitate a candlelight effect is generally distracting to the viewer and therefore unwanted by most directors. Since candle-lit scenes are generally romantic, the audience easily accepts just warm, smooth light that can even be slightly diffused rather than as hard as firelight. To render the effect of candlelight, the practice is to use warm gels and not much fill light.

PHOTO 12.5 Candlelight effect on Joe Molino, Jonathan Sang, Charissa Carfrey, lit by DP Joseph Di Gennaro, *Murder at Café Noir*, MTG Productions

In Photo 12.5, a still from a non-romantic candle-lit scene from *Murder at Café Noir* (2004), DP Joseph di Gennaro positioned the lights to deliberately throw actress Charissa Carfrey's shadow up on the back wall. This helps sell the idea that she is being lit by a candle low on the table. Center,

Jonathan's key light is actually higher than eye level, but still reads as if it is candlelight because it is a hard side light from off right, and the candles are to his right. This same side light catches Charissa, giving her some modeling and contrast on the face, but because she's in the very edge of the beam spread, the intensity isn't as bright as the intensity on Jonathan Sang. The key light on the thug, played by actor Joe Molino, is a hard side light also from camera right, just below his eye level so that light can seep into his menacing eyes. A 650w Fresnel with ½ CTB is hitting Joe's back from off left, adding some definition and modeling to his black wardrobe. Since the room had white walls, no fill light was required. The ambient bounce provided the low fill, as well as the light from the actual candles. So four lights and three candles created this candle-lit scene.

Recently, DPs and gaffers have begun using LED ribbons and rope lights positioned just below frame to simulate the effect of multiple candles or candelabras. These tiny, multiple hard sources shining up can be gelled or can be obtained in warm colors to begin with. This method has been used on many feature films and TV shows and works quite effectively. An electrician hiding below the frame can gently wiggle the ribbon or rope light to give a little flicker effect if desired.

RAIN

In order to read on camera, rain needs to be backlit by hard light. If we front-light rain, it actually disappears on camera. I have been on many shoots where it started to drizzle and we kept filming. So long as there was no backlight and the actors were protected from the rain staying dry, no one could tell. So to get rain to read on camera, it needs to be backlit both in the foreground and in the background.

SNOW

Prop snow can be made from a variety of things from small pieces of Styrofoam to laundry detergent. Prop people also often rent snow machines that spray white foam in the air so that it falls gently in frame. Snow needs to be front-lit. If we backlight it, it will look black and dark on camera—and come off looking more like soot than snow. It is best to front-light prop snow with bright, even soft light, as when it really snows, it is generally overcast, which provides a nice, bright, even soft light all around.

WATER

Water reflects hard light in a random dabbled manner. In Photo 12.6 from *Murder at Café Noir,* actress Tina Zoganas throws pebbles off the dock into the water. In reality, she is standing on a gazebo in the middle of a grassy field, but the set dressing and the water lighting effect sell the scene.

The common practice for achieving the water ripple lighting effect is to place a lot of small mirrors in the bottom of a kiddie pool, and then cover them with water. Shine one or two hard lights down into the pool, aiming them so that the light reflects up into the acting area. A prop or grip gently rocks the pool to allow the water to slosh back and forth, rippling the water, thus creating the rippling water effect in the scene. Since the scene in Photo 12.6 was a night scene, CTB was added to one of the two lights aimed into the mirrors in the kiddie pool. In this shot, blue light directed into the kiddie pool served as Tina's key. She is lit 45 degrees off left by another hard light of a slightly lower intensity with ½ CTB as "moonlight" blue, and backlit by a hard white light.

Rosco makes a "water" projector that will do the same thing, and the BriteShot Luminator LED light has a water reflection effect preprogrammed into the unit.

PHOTO 12.6 Water lighting effect on Tina Zoganas, lit by DP Joseph Di Gennaro, *Murder at Café Noir,* MTG Productions

LIGHTNING

The effect of lightning flashes can be achieved either on set or in postproduction with editing. The latter has become more standard, as it allows the director and editor to manipulate exactly how long the white flash will last and when. But when lightning effects are called for on set, there is a rather cheap method to get a convincing result. Turning a light on and off will not achieve a convincing lightning effect, as the light dims up and down, not instantly on and off as lightning does. Instead, use a bright, hard source light, such as a Fresnel or a Source Four, that overexposes the area in frame where you want to see the lightning flash effect. Have a grip or an electric stand with two showcards or two flags blocking the front of the light. To create the lightning strike, scissors the cards open and closed, allowing three or four bursts of light to flash through. The first few should be short and quick, with the final one lasting a little longer.

Strobe lights can also be used, such as the Martin Atomic 3000 unit, to simulate lightning. and the BriteShot Luminator also has a lightning effect programmed into the unit. For extremely low budgets, people have used old battery-operated still camera strobes, setting them off milliseconds apart. The only problem here is that they usually make a lot of noise both when they trigger and when they recharge.

SILHOUETTES

There are two kinds of silhouettes: the shadow of a person on a wall, and the dark outline of a person standing in front of a wall. What they both have in common is a well-lit wall. I have had several students tell me they had problems creating a silhouette, and when I ask what they had done, they always neglected to light the back wall. Backlighting the subject will not create a silhouette—it can't, because the bounce of the backlight off the floor will illuminate the front of the person. This is the most common mistake. What needs to be done is to light the wall behind the person and cut all light from hitting the subject in front. This is much more difficult than you would think, especially with modern, highly sensitive cameras. The secret is to place the person as far from the lit background wall as possible to make it easier to cut the light off the subject. But often some help has to be added in postproduction to darken the foreground image.

The easier method is creating a silhouette by casting a shadow. The closer the subject is to the wall, the more distinct the silhouette will be, and the more manageable the size; if the subject stands closer to the light, the shadow thrown on the wall will become very large and soft. The best practice is to move the light away as much as possible, and then have the subject stand as close as possible to where the shadow is desired to be seen. A Fresnel at head height will provide the best shadow. An open-faced light is hard and so will also provide a hard-edged shadow; it also falls off faster and spreads faster, so it can't be placed as far from the wall as a Fresnel. A light set low throws a shadow up, and a light set high throws a shadow down. A good example of throwing shadows is in the film *The Third Man* (1949).

In Photo 12.7 from *Dark Tarot*, Quentin Fielding's shadow was made by an open-faced 1kW positioned around chest height. It was about 5 feet from him, and he was about 4 feet from the wall. He had to turn the right direction to allow his profile shadow to fall across the wall, which is perpendicular to the light and not parallel to the wall. The light on Susan was cut so that it only hit her, and none of it hit the back wall; otherwise, it would have washed out his silhouette.

PHOTO 12.7 **Silhouette lighting behind Susan Adriensen,** *Dark Tarot,* **DGW Films**

EMERGENCY VEHICLE LIGHTS

Lights from police cars, fire trucks, and ambulances do not blink on and off. They flash and move back and forth. Sometimes the prop department will bring in an actual police light unit, but these need to be powered off car batteries. So more often if a scene calls for the light from an emergency vehicle to wash across the frame or come in through a window, it is left to the lighting department to rig some sort of police light gag. Two lights are rigged on a double header or on two stands next to each other. Because emergency lights are bright, these lights need to be bright as well, especially since they will have dense-colored gels on them that greatly lower the intensity. 1kW Fresnels or PAR lights work best for this effect.

The color of the gels on the lights will depend on what type of vehicle it is, and should match the colors of the prop vehicle if it is ever shown in the scene or film. In general, police cars today are usually blue and red, fire trucks all red, ambulances white and red, and tow trucks yellow.

To get the flashing light effect, the general practice is to keep both lights on and swing them in and out, overlapping their beams, at a regular pattern and rhythm. People who can play the piano are good at this, as they can make their two hands do two different things simultaneously and can keep time. Sometimes it works better to have two people, one on each light, in order to get a more consistent regular-pattern look. The trick is getting it to be consistent and mechanical.

And, of course, the BriteShot Luminator RGB unit has three different emergency vehicle lighting effects programmed into it—police car, fire truck, and ambulance. There are other LED lighting units that you can program yourself to get these color strobe combinations, but not as easily.

SCREEN LIGHT

When someone watches anything on a screen, whether a TV, a computer, or a movie in a theater, the person is lit by a rolling pattern of colors, light, and shadows. TV and computer screens directly emanate light, and in theaters, light is reflected off the screen onto the audience. So if there is a scene where characters are watching TV, on a computer, or in a movie theater, they need to be lit by the "screen" light.

In the past it was rather standard practice for a TV and a computer screen to use dim, blue soft light shining directly into the subject's face, since TV and computer screens project high-Kelvin-degree light. Like the fire effect, the screen effect light could then be plugged into a dimmer and slowly and slightly dimmed up and down, as if images are moving across the screen. Many times when no dimmer was available, an electric sat next to the light and waved a stick of something in front of the light to create a moving shadow. Not high-tech, but workable.

Now that TVs and computers have moving color images, some gaffers use three tiny lights, such as GAM Stik-ups, in a line; place red, blue, and green gels on them; then dim them up and down. Unlike the fire effect, shadows from screen lights don't move so erratically—unless the subject changes the channel or flips to a new website screen, in which case the light should make a fast change. The same effect is done for subjects watching movies in a theater, except the light should be a wider variety of colors. If you have the time and funds, there are multicolored LED lights that can be programmed to create this effect.

DASHBOARDS

Any scene with people driving a car at night requires the subject to be lit by the dashboard light. Our eyes can see in this dim light, but it barely reads, if at all, on camera. So it is standard practice to rig some kind of small softlight unit either against the dashboard itself or resting on the actor's lap and aimed up. Rosco LitePads are thin, flat, lightweight softlight panels that can be easily gaffer-taped or otherwise rigged to the dashboard. Mini Kino Flo fluorescent units come in 9-inch or 12-inch sizes and are also lightweight. Both of these can run off 12-volt batteries or be plugged into the car cigarette lighter. Other small battery-operated LED units are available, but keep in mind that LEDs produce hard light and multiple shadows, so they may not read as believable dashboard lights. They would need to be gelled with diffusion, which would cut the intensity and spread the light too much.

If the car isn't moving or is fake-moving (which we will discuss next), then extension cords can be run into the car. It is best to use non-tungsten lights in cars when possible to avoid generating so much heat in such an enclosed space. A small softlight could be rigged under the dashboard, such as a 2-foot Kino Flo or some other small fluorescent unit. For lower-budget shooting, Home Depot sells 4-foot two-lamp fluorescent units with a standard Edison plug on the end for around $15. Place two 3,000K T12 fluorescent 40w lamps in, and just set it on the actor's lap. It actually looks pretty good, and it's been used often on professional shoots. Hardware stores also sell under-cabinet fluorescent units that could be usable if you get 3,000K color temperature lamps and use some minus green on them. Remember to place ½ minus green to get some of the ugly green out.

In the real world, only the driver is actually lit by the dashboard light. But in scenes with two people in a car at night, the director and the viewer want to see everyone equally well. While we could just rig a second unit under the dashboard on the passenger side, this will look a little unnatural on camera. All that needs to be done to sell that the passenger is being lit by the dashboard is to place his or her light as close to the driver's light as possible, and then aim it at the passenger. This very slight angle in directionality of the softlight will read subliminally in the viewer's mind that the passenger is being lit by the same dashboard light as the driver and help support the illusion of reality.

POOR MAN'S PROCESS SHOT

Which brings us to lighting the inside of a car moving at night, without actually moving the car. In scenes where the subject is driving a car at night, the majority of the time the car is in a studio or garage, being rocked by the grips as the lighting crew moves lights past the car to simulate it moving. The reason is obvious: it's easier for everyone. The actors don't have to worry about actually steering the car, the producer doesn't have to pay to close down a street, the sound person can get clean sound with no motor noise, the DP can easily light it and set the camera wherever desired, and the director, AD, and script supervisor can all be right there. It's usually so dark outside the windows of a car that you can't see anything anyway, so why not make it easy? We call this the poor man's process shot. Viewers see and accept this as real all the time without knowing it.

First, a dashboard light is rigged in the car. Next, a moonlight backlight is aimed in through the back driver's side windows to add separation and a blue rim to the driver. Usually some kind of frontal light will be added, generally something like a softlight with ½ CTB. Now we add the effects lights. One electric hand holds a 300w Fresnel, standing off right just in front of the windshield. Another electric stands with a 300w Fresnel with red gel on it standing off right just behind the driver's side mirror. These two electrics work together to create the effect of a car passing by in the opposite direction. The ungelled light is swept past the driver first, almost immediately followed by a sweep by the red-gelled light. The effect is the headlights and then the taillights of the oncoming car driving past the subject.

Next rig an inkie or a 300w Fresnel on a double grip arm in a high-boy stand so that it extends out over the windshield of the car. Aim the light straight down, and put on it sodium vapor color gel. Periodically spin the arm so that the downlight sweeps over the car; this throws some light down on the driver, which reflects off the windshield into the camera. This delivers the effect of a car driving under streetlights.

CHAPTER 12: Special Lighting Considerations and Effects: Fire, Water, Rain, Fog, Lightning, Poor Man's Process Shot, Green Screen, and Product Shots

206

Have another electric wear a back ski mask and hold two inkies on a double header or hold two LED flashlights on either side of his or her head. Have the electric crouch a few feet behind the back window and move his or her head as if he or she is another car on the same road. The electric can turn off right or left and then come back again later as a different car during the scene. Out of focus, this will look like the headlights of a car in the distance behind the subject's car.

With a grip gently rocking the car, all this will deliver a totally believable car-driving-at-night effect.

Daytime driving scenes can also be done as a poor man's process shot. For this effect, all windows in the shot are covered with diffusion or a white sheet, and lights are aimed into it from behind to burn out the windows. No dashboard light rig would be used for daytime driving shots. A backlight with ½ CTB would still be rigged to hit the subject as sky bounce, and a side hard light with "sunlight" gel could be aimed in through one of the side windows. A softlight fill would be added to the front, positioned so that the lighting

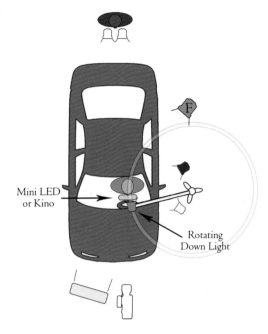

DIAGRAM 1 2.1 **Poor man's process shot lighting diagram**

unit is not reflected in the windshield. Now instead of the passing car headlight gag, grips will sweep branches past the sunlight key and through the beams of the lights backlighting the white material, burning out the back windows. A large tree branch can be rigged on the arm of the high boy and swept over the car to get a reflection of a tree branch moving across the windshield.

The important thing to remember when doing a daytime poor man's process shot is not to have any reflections other than blue sky in the windshield. The viewer will certainly notice if the clouds reflected in the window don't move. So this has to be done either in a garage with a dark ceiling so nothing reflects in the windshield, other than your moving branch, or outside on a clear day.

For either day or night interior car shots, a green screen can be set up a few feet outside whichever windows are in the back of the shot. Second-unit footage, shot out of a moving car, can then be matted into the green screen in postproduction. In this kind of setup, the lighting may have to reflect what is seen outside the window on the green screen.

GREEN SCREEN

Many car, train, plane, and other interior transportation shots are often done with green screen outside the windows. This just makes everything easier, especially the lighting.

In Photo 12.8 from *Stray,* a green screen was set up about 5 feet from the train windows behind Michelle Page. Because it was a nice bright but overcast day, the soft natural light lit the green screen evenly. Outside the windows were two lights—a 1,200w HMI PAR aimed in as her backlight, and a 650w Fresnel with CTB and diffusion right up against the window off right as her kick. Both she and Aaron Lustig were key-lit by 500w daylight LED and filled by another 500w daylight LED off left through diffusion.

Outside, a grip would periodically sweep a tree branch through the beam of the HMI to give the impression of movement. The editor rocked the shot in postproduction and added some erratic sun flares with after-effects to make the entire scene totally believable.

When lighting for green screen, it is important to move the subject as far forward and away from the green screen as possible. There are two reasons. The first is to make sure no shadows of the subjects ever fall on the green screen—as this will cause major problems during the post-effects stage. The second reason is to eliminate any green bounce light from hitting the subject. The green screen needs to be lit as evenly as possible. Never make the green screen brighter than the subject, as this will add more ambient green bounce into the room and possibly be picked up on the subject. Also, try to avoid having the subject stand on a green scene sweep or green floor if the shot isn't head-to-toe. If there are some shots that are that wide and then others that aren't and you can't move the actor off the green floor, throw down black cloth, sound blankets, or black showcards to cut any upward bounce from the floor onto the subject.

When I have lit green screen shots that were showing the subject head-to-toe, I added soft lights, from the floor aimed up, taken down in intensity by adding layers of diffusion over them to wash away the green upward bounce from the floor. The other option is to bounce white light into showcards or foamcore on the floor, and tilt them up to bounce light up into the subject. Adding any light from below must be done very carefully so that it doesn't look like a horror film. It should be virtually unnoticeable, just enough to wash away the green bounce from the floor.

It is common practice to backlight the subject with ½ Minus Green to help reduce any green spill or reflection that might read on the subject's shoulder or head. In green-screen lighting, we often use two or three backlights to totally rim the subject and separate him or her from the green-screen background. In postproduction, the rim will help the after-effects artist to blend the images better.

Sci-fi films are full of green-screen shots, especially outside windows of a spaceship. In Photo 12.9 from *The Cold Equations,* the green screen outside the front window was evenly lit by Kino Flos from both sides, top, and bottom. The actors were side-lit with hard lights to rim them and separate them from the background. The green screen was about 6 feet from the actors.

PHOTO 1 2.9 **Green screen window on** *The Cold Equations,* **Ellipsis Films**

Often when lighting a green-screen shot, we need to light the foreground subject so that the subject matches the lighting of what will appear in the green screen.

In Photo 12.10 from the same sci-fi short, the color used to key-light actress Ashley Taylor was copied and then used by the animator and the after-effects artists so that the planet that would be placed on the green screen would match the color of light hitting the actress. A gel swatch was given to the postproduction team to work with. The actress was also backlit by a ½ Minus Green to help outline her from the green screen and make the after-effects artist's job easier. Notice how the digital artists also matched the angle and the texture of the light on the planet to match the shot.

PHOTO 1 2.1 0 **Ashley Taylor against green screen,** *The Cold Equations,* **Ellipsis Films**

In non–special effects shots, the sequence works the other way around. The background element has usually already been shot, so the foreground subject standing in front of the green screen needs to be lit so that the color, texture, angle, and intensity match that footage.

In Photo 12.11 from *Murder at Café Noir,* actress Debra Lichtenstein is in front of a green screen but lit with the same colors and by the same texture and directionality of light as the green-screen image, which was shot first. Cosmetic pink gel was used on her frontal soft fill to match the color of the sunset sky behind her. Her away-side key light from off left is white and only slightly brighter than the camera-side fill—thus she is lit high key (low contrast), as this is a comic moment in the film. Her ¾ backlight has half CTB on it, which provides a nice light-blue color to her shadows, making it feel like she is outside at sunset, where subliminally we know that half of the sky would be blue. She has another ¾ backlight from the right that helps separate her from the background. This light had ½ Minus Green (magenta) on it, but reads white on camera.

While the intent of this shot wasn't to make the audience think she was at that location—in the film she's on the phone with her boss who is at that location—matching the look of the green-screen image helps smooth the two images together and make the audience more accepting of the visuals. If we had knocked down her frontal fill and added a little shadow pattern across her chest, it might have been able to pass for making her appear to actually be there.

When shooting a green screen, I really can't emphasize how important it is to minimize green bounce from hitting anything in the foreground. Setting the green screen as far back as possible is the best defense against this, and adding Minus Green as backlight helps immensely.

CHAPTER 12: Special Lighting Considerations and Effects: Fire, Water, Rain, Fog, Lightning, Poor Man's Process Shot, Green Screen, and Product Shots

210

PRODUCT SHOTS

In commercials, product shots are the money shot. The product is what it's all about, and the final shot of the product has to make it look appealing and worth buying. Some commercial production companies, known as tabletop companies, have director/cameramen who specialize in product shots. There is a somewhat standard beginning method of lighting a product. The product is usually placed on a sweep—which is a 4-foot × 8-foot sheet of either thin plexiglass, Lucite, or Masonite that is clamped down on the front to a table, and then curved up in the back. The product is placed near the front. A mini chicken coop is then made by flying a softlight overhead, but off-centered to be slightly behind the product. A flag or showcard is then used to cut the light off the back of the sweep halfway up the curve. Fingers and dots are used to net down or cut any hot spots on the top of the product.

Two inkies (250w Fresnels) are positioned on either side of the sweep back by the curve and aimed at the product, rimming both sides and backlighting the product—very important for any liquid product such as drinks, shampoo, perfume, and so on.

PHOTO 12.12 A product shot, done as a class demo, with a 2kw softlight above flagged off the back of the sweep, two 150w inkies as backlights, a double dot scrim over the bottle cap to take it down and two white cards to provide bounce and reflection in front.

You might have noticed that so far there are no lights coming from the front. Often, there never will be. Instead, just outside the camera framing, two slivers of showcard that have been cut and bent to stand up are used in front to provide the only frontal light necessary (along with the bounce up from the softlight on the sweep). The reason is that many products will have a reflective surface, and the spot of the light will appear in the reflection. The white cards will provide both a frontal soft fill and a white glint that will be reflected in the contours of the bottle, glass, or plastic elements of the product. If the product is a box, an inkie with a snoot is typically added coming from beside camera, masked to only highlight the product name on the label.

There are many variations, various accents, and minute adjustments that each individual tabletop cameraman makes, giving the cameraman his or her own style. If the sweep is translucent, patterns of lights can be made on the sweep by lighting from under the plexiglass or Lucite. Of course, not all product shots are done on sweeps. Coffee product shots are often shot on marble counters or other places, but the lighting approach remains pretty much the same. In fact, no matter what the product is and where it is placed for the shot, this lighting method usually works well.

I was called to light a commercial with a company I only worked for occasionally. When they hired me, they merely asked if I knew how to light products, and I said I did. I had had the pleasure of getting my first production assistant jobs working for Bernman/Steinberg Productions, who was one of the top Table Top commercial houses in New York City, so I was introduced to the art of product lighting by one of the best. I worked my way up through the TV commercial industry, where every shoot ended in a product shot, and I had lit a fair number of them. When I showed up at call time, I walked into a large, empty, freshly white-painted sound stage with a car sitting in the middle. That was the product. I had never lit a car before. The grips and my electric looked at me, waiting for instructions.

Acting like I knew what I was doing, I asked them to hang six 5,000w open-faced skypan lights on the grid over the car, and then stretch a 20-foot × 20-foot silk butterfly under them. We then took two 5kW Fresnels (known as Seniors) and set them up as the two back rim lights off to either side of the car and all the way to the back wall. Then we set up an 8-foot × 8-foot butterfly and two sheets of 4-foot × 8-foot foamcore on stands, and wheeled them around in front of the car to catch the light from the 5kWs and get the reflection off the white surfaces onto the shiny surface of the car. In other words, I just did standard product lighting, but on a more grand scale. It looked good and everyone seemed happy—and my check didn't bounce.

When shooting a product shot, keep in mind that if the product is reflective, the lights, camera, and crew might all be seen reflected in the product. We threw black cloth over the camera and crew for that car commercial so no one would be seen in the surface of the car. The more shiny the object, the harder the job. Steel is particularly troublesome, if the surface is stainless. I was shooting pickup shots for an infomercial for a cleaning cloth, and I had to talk the director out of shooting a close-up of a toaster, as its sides were so mirrored they reflected the camera, lights, and everything else. We shot a brushed-steel coffeepot instead.

One way to cope with reflection is to use silks or white cloth to build a tent over the entire object, which is what we had to do when I was hired to light the Super Bowl XVI trophy. That thing was a mirror that reflected everything 360 degrees around it. So I sent out for three 12-foot × 12-foot silks, and we spent several hours using a dozen or more grip stands building a tent around the trophy, which was on a turntable in the center. The camera lens was poked through where two of the silks met in the front, and the lenses of the two backlights poked through where the other silks met on either side behind the trophy. I then added a few open-faced lights to wash the silk from all around the outside, to make it as even a white light source as I could get it. As the trophy rotated, all that was reflected was the glowing white silk spherically surrounding it, which brought out the bronze. The backlight lenses did reflect and glare off different edges of the trophy, but Neal Marshad, the cameraman, added a star filter on the camera that made the lens reflections sparkle. It was the first time I worked with Neal, and he was so happy with how it turned out he hired me many times after that.

STUFF TO REMEMBER

- Backlight fog, smoke, and rain.

- Front light snow.

- Firelight has multiple hard sources, so use at least two slightly different-colored lights that flicker.

- Candles are single hard sources that do not flicker unless there is a breeze.

- Water effects are created by light reflecting off multiple mirrors under moving water (in a kiddie pool).

- There are some lighting units that project these special effects, such as scene projectors and the BriteShot Luminator RGBAW.

- Many night interior car driving shots are done without the car actually moving—the lights move instead.

- Green screen requires that the screen be evenly lit, that no shadows from the subject hit the green screen, and that the subject is well rimmed, optimally with ½ or full Minus Green gel.

- When lighting subjects in front of a green screen, it is best to match the lighting of the image that will appear in the green screen later—the same angle, texture, color, and intensity.

- Reflective-surfaced objects need something white to reflect, such as white cards.

PUTTING IT INTO PRACTICE

- Shoot two people being lit by either candlelight or firelight.

- Shoot a shot with man-made fog, steam, or rain in it.

- Shoot a poor man's process shot of someone driving at night. You will need several people to help you—one to rock the car, one to do the passing car headlights/taillights sweep, and one to be the headlights of the car in the background. If you have a high-boy stand, add the passing streetlight.

- Shoot a daytime poor man's process shot by tenting the windows with a sheet or silk and then moving branches past the lights as the car "drives."

- Shoot a 30-second commercial that ends with a product shot that combines all of the above.

13 NONFICTION LIGHTING:
Interview, Corporate, Newsmagazine, Documentary, Reality

Interviews are the most common form of nonfiction shooting. Interviews are in documentaries, corporate videos, training videos, educational videos, news segments, and even commercials. Interviews can be a person talking directly to the camera, or to an interviewer who is slightly off to the side of the camera lens.

INTERVIEW LIGHTING

How we light the interviewee is very much determined by the desired feeling the producer wants us to have about this person and what he or she is saying. The look may also vary depending on whether the interview is for a corporate video, a documentary, or TV newsmagazine. We always want to make them look their best, which means never using hard lights on the subject.

The person being interviewed is almost always a normal person, which means they will have the normal wear and tear on their skin and face that we normal people have. So if we light them with a hard light, we will accent every flaw in their skin. If all you have are hard lights, it's best to bounce them into a white card or off a white wall. While an option is to cover hard lights with heavy diffusion such as Lee 216 White Diffusion or Rosco Grid Cloth, it still isn't as soft and complimentary as a true softlight. To convert a hard light into a soft light, we can place a Chimera or Westcott softbox on them. Since these cut the intensity of the unit quite a bit, it's best to use an open-faced 1kW or 750w light for this. Of course, the easiest method is to use a softlight fixture, such as a Lowel Rifa light, a Kino Flo Diva, or a zip light.

When lit by softlights, people don't tend to squint as much as looking into a hard light, even one with diffusion on it. So, the softer the better when lighting interviews. Also, we tend to try to keep the lights out of the direct eye line of the subject, so he or she can look naturally at the interviewer without squinting. There are lights made to be attached to the front of the camera and ring lights that look like a donut through which the camera lens is placed. These lights add a soft white light directly on the face, which helps wash out any skin imperfections by bleaching them with light. While actresses, models, and news anchors may not have a problem staring straight into a bright blinding light, that doesn't really work for the average subject of an interview. They are painful on the eyes and extremely disorienting to the normal person.

Interview lighting is basically a return to the three-point lighting formula—key, fill, and backlight. One thing we think about in interviews is getting light under the eyes. In dramatic stories, darkness under the eyes can add mystery, sexiness, or sadness—none of which are usually wanted in an interview shot. As we've discussed before, people don't tend to trust someone whose eyes they can't see. So an important thing to consider is the height of the key light. Deep-set eyes are a concern. The key light should be set higher than the subject's eye level, but not so high as to throw dark shadows under the eyes. The way to avoid this is to use a very soft light source, such as a fluorescent unit with opal diffusion on it, and back it up so that the radiant light wraps in under the eyes and bounces up from the floor.

The desire is to throw the nose shadow into the crease of the fill-side cheek below the eye, where it can hide naturally without calling attention to itself. For a person whom the viewer is to respect or look at as an authority, another soft light can be placed on the other side of the camera, but at a slightly lower intensity and at a slightly more severe angle to create a little modeling. A ¾ backlight is added for a rim and kick, but at a subtle intensity so that it doesn't call attention to itself.

Before lighting the interview, the LD/DP needs to talk to the director/producer about the desired feeling of the interview, just like in a fictional movie scene. Is this a happy story the interview will discuss? Is it a near-death experience? Is it a very sad story? Are they an authority on the subject? Are they someone we are to trust or not trust? The way the interview is lit will help relay these feelings, and lighting it differently than the intention of the piece may hurt the visuals and the story that is being told. Most interviews are lit high key, unless the interview is with a criminal or is about a deadly serious subject. So the first thing to determine is the subject of the interview.

I was hired to shoot a training video series for EMTs on how to respond to a hazardous material accident. Besides the dramatic re-creations, we shot interviews with emergency responders who arrived at chemical accident sites. Obviously their stories were ones of caution and drama. So the lighting was more dramatic than when we were shooting the experts talking about safe practices and procedures, who were shot with standard three-point lighting.

The EMT interviews were done in a small room against a seamless blue-paper background. They were lit with a softlight 45 degrees off camera right, with only a bounce card as their fill. Since we read from left to right, key lighting them from the right gave a more dramatic feeling subliminally to the image, since the viewer's eye looks first into the dark side of the subject's face. The EMTs all addressed an off-camera interviewer, who sat with her head right next to the lens. This is standard practice when shooting interviews, in order to get the interviewee's eye line as close to camera as possible without looking directly into the lens. We tend not to trust someone who doesn't look us in the eye when talking to us, so in serious interviews, the producer strives to get the eye line as close to the lens as possible. The interviewer sat on the key side of the camera, so the EMTs would all be turning into the key light, and the camera would be shooting into the darker side of their face, adding a feeling of drama to what they were saying.

Opposite the key was placed a ¾ back hard light to outline their shoulders and head and get a kick off their dark cheek. Another light was placed on the ground directly behind the stool the EMTs sat on for the interview. This light was aimed up into the blue background behind them, but only enough to allow a halo of light to be seen on the backdrop around their shoulders. The rest of the backdrop fell off into a dark blue. The result was a very moody, very serious feeling that matched the subject of the interviews. This was a variation on Rembrandt lighting.

Photo 13.1 is a still taken off the production monitor of the interview lighting done by LD Gus Dominguez for *Project Runway Allstars* (2013). Local 600 camera assistant Jamie MacPherson sat in while we tweaked the lights. The setup is rather simple and could be considered a variation on

PHOTO 13.1 **Still off the production monitor of Local 600 AC Jamie MacPherson sitting in during lighting for the interviews on *Project Runway Allstars 3*, lit by LD Gus Dominguez**

PHOTO 13.2 **Negative fill surrounds Jamie**   PHOTO 13.3 **Background and backlights for the setup**

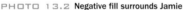

Rembrandt lighting, in that there is only one frontal light on the subject, in this case a 1kW open-face through a Chimera on a dimmer.

This key light is off left, and a 300w Fresnel is her ¾ backlight opposite it (behind her off right). She is turned to face into the key light so that the dark side of her face is toward the camera, thus providing modeling and contrast. There is no fill light and no bounce card used in this setup. A 300w Fresnel on a dimmer is aimed sideways at the two dress forms, and a 650w Fresnel with three layers of ½ CTB is aimed through a metal grate to throw a pattern on the seamless white-paper backdrop.

Notice that besides the 4-foot × 8-foot black flag cutting the key light off the background, there are also cloths taped up to the walls. This is called "negative fill," even though it is physically impossible to add or bounce darkness. Adding negative fill means preventing bounce light from hitting the subject. This interview location was a white room. Gus wanted to add a little drama to the interview to fit the show—contestants talking about their concerns, fears, hopes, and so on. Gus feels shadows add drama: "The minute you see shadows, you're interested—the darkness adds mystery." Even though we used only one frontal light, there was a lot of bounce off the white walls, ceiling, and floor that lowered the contrast. To combat this, and try to get the contrast a little more dynamic, black cloth and sound blankets were taped to the wall to cut the ambient light created by the bounce. The sound mixer put a sound blanket on the floor to help cut the echo, which also helped cut the bounce light that came off the floor.

BACKGROUNDS

The background in an interview is important and should be lit in some way to add some depth and an interesting visual. Often interviews are shot in a place where the background is relatively close to the subject—such as in an office or off in a corner of a conference room, or against a backdrop of some kind. An interview against a dark background may subliminally say to the viewer that the person on-screen is hiding something, not to be fully trusted. When people are interviewed who want to hide their identity, they are filmed in the dark. So lighting your background is very important in interview lighting.

Bright backgrounds can be more acceptable in an interview than in a fictional piece, so long as the background helps to place the subject in their environment.

As seen in Photo 3.1, Gus lit the background both artistically and to place the subject within the context of the show. The designer forms are lit and defined, while the background has a pattern and a graduated color that becomes slightly lighter behind the subject. In the TV show *Project Runway,* there is no pattern on the background; rather, Gus lights the backdrop with two Kino Flos and allows the white seamless paper to totally burn out, allowing the dress forms to become silhouettes with no side edge lighting.

If we look at Photo 13.5, we can see how a background can easily be lit with very few lights. A 300w Fresnel with magenta gel was aimed into the back of the bottles on the back shelf of the bar, and a blue LED strip was placed on the shot glasses shelf. The rest of the background lighting comes from what was already there—three yellowish lights over the mirror, a small blue light inside the top of the glasses shelves, and a blue-color disco ball above the bar. The 650w Fresnel that we bounced into a far corner of the bar provided some ambient light for both the background and the foreground.

PHOTO 13.4 Magenta minus green gel added to an inkie for bar light

PHOTO 13.5 Rich Goldberg lit in his environment

PHOTO 13.6 **Interview lighting setup in the Ruba Club**

The subject was lit with a 4-bank × 4-foot Kino Flo lamp with diffusion taped over its center, which diffused the light hitting the subject, but allowed the rest of the light to disperse and add ambient fill. The ¾ backlight has blue on it and kicks off the side of his face without any light hitting his nose. It comes from the same side as the blue color in the background, so it helps to place the subject in his environment. Other than the ambient light, there is no fill—none was needed. (Photo 13.6 was overexposed so that the light placements can be seen.)

SPECIAL CONSIDERATIONS

On some interview shoots a makeup artist will be on the crew. While this is rather common on corporate videos, reality, commercials, and TV newsmagazine shoots, it often isn't the case with documentaries. In cases where there isn't a makeup artist, a compact of face powder, triangle sponges, and a can of hair spray should be brought to set by the producer. If the subject is a woman, chances are she will have her own makeup. For either a man or a woman, face powder can be used to take down any glare off the nose or the forehead. If the subject has any fly-away hairs, the producer can spray his or her own fingers and then use the hair-spray-moistened fingers to straighten the subject's hair or pat it into place. The DP should consult closely with the makeup artist as soon as the subject arrives, especially if there are any visual concerns. Along with the makeup artist, the lighting is responsible for making the subject look as flattering on-screen as possible—often while still making the subject look authoritative.

As the lighting director for a major energy company in the mid-1980s I was called in to light the CEO for a network news interview. The CEO didn't want the news crew lighting him because the last time he did an interview for the news, he felt he looked almost guilty. He wanted his own in-house makeup artist and lighting person. Phyllis, the makeup artist, had worked with the CEO before. She warned me he had bags under his eyes. Not just bags—"shipping trunks," I believe is how she phrased it. So before we went up to the penthouse office with the location gear, I grabbed a small 1kW baby softlight and a short rolling stand from the studio. I pre-lit the office for a person sitting on the edge of the desk (never have people sit behind a desk; they look distant and trapped and are harder to light). When the CEO walked in, Phyllis asked him if it was alright for her to do some makeup. He said yes. She had him sit on the edge of the desk while I tweaked the backlight a bit. When she was done, I added the baby 1kW softlight, on a dimmer, down low right in front of him. The warm softlight filled in under his eyes. Phyllis did some touch-up with a lighter makeup to diminish the shadows from his bags. He wasn't very happy with the bright light below his eye line, until he looked in the monitor. For the next two years, every time he had to do a news interview, Phyllis and I were called in. He always asked if I had his "little blue light"—it was a Colortran brand unit, which were always blue.

This also brings up the three B's of interviews, which all need special attention:

- Bags
- Bald
- Blond

Bags

As we discussed above, the trick with deep-set eyes and bags is to get as much soft light into the eyes as possible without creating an upward nose shadow or an awkward look. Often a simple white card held just below frame will be enough to bounce light up into the subject's eyes, but for some people, this can be distracting. A low softlight as discussed previously also works. It isn't uncommon to find Fresnels with diffusion or softboxes on them set low to ground in sets for talk shows where the host and guests sit around a sofa. A Fresnel is used because it has a longer throw than a softlight unit such as a Rifa or a Kino, so the units can be set farther away and out of both the subject's direct eye line and the camera framing.

Keeping the key light very soft and just above eye level can also help. Again, so as not to blind or distract the subject in an interview, when a unit is placed near eye level, the light should be moved off to the side.

Bald

Bald heads and the temples of someone with a receding hairline have a tendency to reflect the backlight. Dimming the backlight will lower the glare but not remove it. Moving the backlight will not reduce or eliminate it either, as a bald head or large temple are spectacular reflectors. Shooting with it will often become distracting to the viewer and be unflattering to the subject. The most common method of dealing with this issue is to tilt down the backlight and aim it at the subject's neck and shoulder, then close the top barn door so no direct light hits the top of the subject's head. This method will still allow a bit of a kick off the subject's chin and to rim the shoulder while eliminating the glare off head or temples.

Blonds

Blond hair explodes in backlight. It reflects so much light it can sometimes look like it's glowing and the top of the head can often overexpose. For subjects who are blond, the backlight needs

> "I always rim the shoulders. It works even if you can't light the hair because they're blond or bald."
>
> —RAY BRIBIESCA, CAMERAMAN,
> *60 MINUTES*

to be dimmed considerably. Also, the light itself can be lowered so that not as much light strikes the top of the subject's head. Similar to dealing with bald subjects, the backlight can also be tilted down and aimed more at the subject's ear to reduce the hot spot of light on the top of the subject's hair. Rimming the shoulders by aiming the backlight at the neck and barn-dooring off the head works as well. A standard method is to forego the backlight and instead make it into a kick light glinting off the cheekbones and highlighting the ends of the hair. In this case, it is important to make sure the kick doesn't glare off the subject's nose.

Glasses

A common problem in interview lighting is dealing with a subject who is wearing glasses. Depending on the manufacturer, the lenses of some glasses will reflect the lights, which will become very distracting in the shot. The first attempt in removing this reflection is to ask subjects if they can slide their glasses down their nose a little and/or tilt their glasses down a fraction. Doing this in combination with raising the key light up a little can remove the glare. Sometimes, however, this doesn't work or the subject just can't keep his or her glasses tilted this way without it looking unnatural.

Raising the key light until the reflection disappears can work, but sometimes this will cast dark shadows under the eyes. The next approach is to move the key light more to the side of the subject until the reflection disappears. In this case the key needs to be very soft and bright to allow the light to wrap around the face, and another soft light will need to be placed on the other side of the

subject's face. The concern here is throwing the shadow of the glasses' arm over the eye. So a certain amount of small, fine adjusting will be required.

In Photo 13.7, soundman Tyler Cartner grudgingly stands in for lighting adjustments for an interview in a corporate video. (It was early and he was just getting his first coffee.) Notice there are no reflections of the two lighting units in his glasses.

Both the key, a 4-bank × 4-foot Kino Flo, and the fill, a Rifa light, are positioned enough to the sides to light his cheeks and wrap into his eyes. A 300w Fresnel, with diffusion, was rigged on the end of the arm of a grip stand, providing the backlight.

PHOTO 13.7 Soundman Tyler Cartner stands in for interview lighting adjustments

The contrast ratio is low, almost even. The high key look was created because the video was about promotion. Keeping the lights to the sides allowed some modeling. This was shot-balanced for daylight, with half blue on the Rifa and daylight lamps in the Kino Flo.

CORPORATE VIDEOS

At least just as many, if not more, crew people are employed in making corporate videos yearly as in TVs shows and movies combined. Corporations worldwide produce in-house videos for meetings, new product introductions, training, and educational purposes. Top among these are the financial, pharmaceutical, and telecommunications industries. One drug company alone in New Jersey makes between 500 to 700 videos every year. While the majority of these are shot TV-style with multiple cameras in TV studios, a good portion are also shot on locations, such as in conference rooms,

PHOTO 13.8 **Kino Flo fill with a Rifa key light on Tyler**

offices, and hallways. The subjects being lit in most corporate videos are busy executives who have tight schedules. So while the shooting crew usually has ample time to come and set up, once the subject arrives, the shots are fast and limited, and there is little room for rehearsals or many angles. Often the subject has to leave within an hour after arriving, so having everything pre-lit and ready to go is essential.

Sometimes two cameras are set up so that there is both a wide shot and a medium shot done at the same time. This allows the director and editor the ability to cut between takes and edit out the things they don't want. It is important when doing this that the lighting look just as good for both cameras. Always remember to keep the camera angles around 30 degrees apart, have at less two lens sizes difference between them, and have both cameras shooting into the same side of the subject's face, so that the subject is looking in the same screen direction in both shots. This will make the shots match better and the lighting work better for both angles.

The subjects in all corporate videos are people in authority and should come across on the video as highly trustworthy. So interview lighting in corporate videos must reflect and reinforce this. Often this means a high key look with a low contrast ratio on the face. Often the subject is looking directly into the camera, reading from a teleprompter. In these cases, it is important not to overlight them or let light glare into their eyes that would make them squint or become uncomfortable reading the teleprompter. When the subject is looking slightly off camera, it is often the practice to have them slightly turn into the fill, so that the camera is shooting into the brighter key side of the face rather than the shadow side, as we do in dramatic scenes. They are in the know, they are "enlightened," and while the viewer may be in the dark about the subject, this person is the light at the end of the tunnel.

If the project is trying to be a little more artistic in nature, or is trying to look more like a TV commercial than an in-house video, the subject may be turned into the key light so that the camera is looking into the fill side of the face, thus making the image more dramatic. The contrast will still generally be low with plenty of mid-range levels of intensity. Otherwise they might come across as a doomsday sayer.

Good corporate video producers/directors often search for locations with interesting backgrounds that don't have to be lit, or require minimal lighting, such as a muted slash of light or a little side light to model the background. Often the producer will select locations that have windows behind the subject. Just as we discussed in Chapter 8 on daylight, there are several options for how to deal with the windows. The advantage of working in rooms with windows is using the light from the window. As the interview will be less than an hour, the sun will move only a little. But we still need to know how far the sun will move during that time—will it disappear behind another building during the first five minutes of the take? Will it come out from the clouds and burn out the background outside the window? There are inexpensive mobile device apps that will chart the movement of the sun, which every cameraman and director should have (see Appendix 2, Resources).

Most corporate buildings have blinds that can lower over almost all their windows, which can help us in many ways. But it is a very good precaution to always take with you ND6 gel and black cloth, or black showcards and lots of gaffer's tape, when shooting any corporate video outside a studio.

This shoot was in a corner conference room high up with a view of New York City. Two walls were composed of floor-to-ceiling windows, and we had several interviews to do. The room was selected by the producer so that we could get as many different looks as possible without leaving the location. We did one interview looking into a corner with the blinds closed (Photo 13.9), another looking out the one set of windows, another looking out the other windows, another with the windows on just the edge

PHOTO 13.9 Tyler gets his coffee; blinds help dim the background

of the frame, and so on. Whichever windows were in the background were gelled with ND6, taking the exterior down two f-stops. This worked fine when we were shooting into the shady side of the buildings outside the windows. But at one point the sun moved, and direct sunlight hit the buildings outside the window.

We didn't have HMI lights on this shoot, only daylight Kino Flos, a Fresnel ARRI kit, and a Rifa. As the sun hit the outside buildings, I needed to bring the exposure up on the subject so that I could stop down the camera and not have the background burn out. If I had the time, I could have put another layer of ND gel over the windows. But there were no grips on the shoot, and the interviewee had a very limited window of time to talk with us. This meant bringing the lights as close as possible to the subject without getting them in the frame, but also moving them more to the side so that they didn't blind the subject, which made the image a little flatter. I had to add a 650w Fresnel with diffusion to bring up the key side, but I also had to add CTB to it to make it daylight, which cut the intensity greatly. This was a case where we really should have had small HMI lights, such as a 575w Fresnel and a 1,200w PAR light aimed through a 4-foot × 4-foot frame of diffusion. With this combination, we would have been able to adjust for the changes in the light outside much easier and keep the f-stop and limited depth of field the director wanted. Unfortunately, this shoot didn't have the budget to rent those lights, and we did the best we could, which satisfied the producer.

Budgets on corporate videos vary greatly. Some companies own their own lights and cameras, and some rent equipment. Some hire people who own their own equipment, which is how many cameramen have gotten their start—owning a camera and a few lights and then doing industrials, documentaries, and music videos. Most of the time a corporate video, outside of a studio, will have to travel light with easy-to-roll cases, as the crew will be moving through busy office buildings and hallways. LED lights, Diva Kino Flos, and Rifa lights have become the darlings of the corporate video world, as they pack up into nice small cases.

Extension cords, ground lifters, and cube taps are essential tools in any lighting kit, but invaluable in corporate video shooting, as is gaffer's tape. Never go anywhere without gaffer's tape.

NEWSMAGAZINES

Most of the time the cameraman will have some time to light the interview segments for TV magazine shows. However, the shooting schedules for magazine shows are often unpredictable. People show up late, the location gets changed, and so on. The host and the interviewee are usually shot at the same time by two cameras cross-shooting, so cross key lighting is often the choice. Longtime *60 Minutes* cameraman Ray Bribiesca liked to use 4-bank × 4-foot Kino Flos as the cross key lights, extended out on grip stand arms to keep the stands out of the shot. Then he would add a bounce card as the fill for the interviewee. The lighting for the interviewer would change depending on which correspondent was hosting the segment. Sometimes extra lights would be added for the host, such as a kicker or a very diffused fill. But basically, he would light them a little flat—high key. Ray always tried for a "warm and fuzzy" feeling during his interviews, which he said were 90 percent of the time shot in hotel rooms.

Ray also strived to make the two shots match in their contrast ratio and their background lighting so that the viewer would feel that both subjects were together in the same room. They always were, but if the guests had a more severe contrast ratio than the host and there was a window behind one and not the other, the images could look like they were shot at different times—which would be a breach of journalism ethics. So the cameras had to be arranged to either have pieces of a

> ### "Make sure both cameras are in the same room."
>
> —RAY BRIBIESCA, CAMERAMAN, *60 MINUTES*

window in the background of both host and interviewee, or no window behind either. Ray's standard background lighting, which is common to most newsmagazine shows, was to use a 300w Fresnel through a cookie to add a soft breakup on the background. He would also often try to place a table lamp (on a hand dimmer) out of focus in the background, giving the image some depth.

Because he would travel shooting in a wide variety of locations, all of Ray's lights were balanced for daylight. This allowed him to shoot outside, in rooms with windows, and even in rooms that had no windows. When he went to Afghanistan, he took along four Frezzi 400-watt HMI units, which are 5-inch open-face parabolic reflector units. They are lightweight, and two could fit in one case. Outside he could use them bare to fill in the daylight, and inside for the interviews he would add softboxes or Chimeras on them. The lights could run on either AC or DC, so they could be operated off batteries in the field, which is a must for newsmagazine production, as one never knows where one will be shooting and where the closest electricity might be.

Many LED lights that are also AC- and DC-powered are currently available and are used frequently by TV news, reality TV, and documentary shooters. The most common manufacturers include Litepanel, Lowel, Frezzi, and Ikan. These require less power but can pack a pretty good punch from the daylight-balanced units. Keep in mind that many LED lights are also available as bicolor, which means you can dial the color temperature between daylight and tungsten. In these units, half the diodes on the unit's surface are tungsten-balanced and half daylight-balanced. So when it is set to just tungsten or just daylight, it is only half as bright as a non-bicolor unit. For this reason, many cameramen prefer to go with full daylight units.

On-board lights that attach to the top of the camera are common in news and often in lower-budget reality shows. These are small but bright little lights that are powered by the camera battery or another small battery attached either to the light or to a belt worn by the cameraman. They are primarily designed as news segment lights to light a reporter at a news scene. This is commonly referred to as "deer-in-the-headlights" lighting, as the light is coming straight in at the subject from just above the lens. These lights are designed with the intent of hiding the subject's shadow directly behind the subject so that the camera won't see it. While illuminating the subject, they also wash out the subject's features and diminish any modeling. Diffusion over the light is common practice, often in the form of a plastic diffuser panel that slides or clips over the light, or a tiny softbox can be added to soften the light and flatter the subject a little more.

With these types of fast-moment situations, it helps to try to position subjects so that they are also getting some light from a natural source such as a streetlight, store window display, bounce of sunlight off the side of a building—anything to add an edge or another angle of light to help add dimensionality to the image. This isn't always possible, and certainly the average TV viewer is well accustomed to seeing TV news lit with only one straight-forward light. This lighting is imitated often by movie and TV shows for scenes in the script that are supposed to have been shot by a news crew.

DOCUMENTARIES

There are a variety of documentary styles. Some have interviews and some don't. Some allow the subject and the audience to be aware of the camera, and others strive for the opposite. What they all have in common is going into a real location and having to shoot immediately something that is happening live, without rehearsals, that will never be repeated.

Documentary crews are usually very small and often don't include a gaffer. With the advent of more-sensitive digital cameras, the intensity of the units needed to shoot a documentary has diminished. Lowel, Fiilex, and several others make LED light kits specifically to fill this need: they usually include three units, softboxes, and stands. Since they are shot on the fly, lighting for a documentary is basically used for interviews, while everything else is often shot with available light. Adding lights to a real location where the director is trying to capture people unnoticed may call attention to the camera and defeat the purpose. Also, there often isn't any time or ability to light due to the limited time and space.

But there are times when the crew can arrive early and get a few minutes to do whatever pre-lighting that might be possible. Swapping out the bulbs in preexisting fixtures such as floor lamps, desk lights, and hanging lights with brighter/whiter lamps is always a good thing to do. Putting hand dimmers on any lamp in the shot will allow the cameraman to adjust the intensity of the light so that it won't burn-out on camera and distract the eye of the viewer. Hiding lighting units on the top of cabinets or behind furniture and bouncing them into the ceiling will work to bring up the overall ambiance in the space for better exposure and a softer look.

In documentary shooting, you cannot always place the subjects where you want them—that sort of goes against the entire ethics of documentary—but you can place the camera wherever you want it. Good documentary shooters pick the angles they will shoot from based on the existing light in the room, so the subjects are in the best light possible. Perhaps that's by the windows so that the skylight coming in becomes the image's main source. Or putting the camera where the subjects will be ¾ backlit by an out-of-frame window, or side-lit by light coming in through the open doorway to the next room.

Documentary interviews strive to place subjects in their surroundings and pick an interesting visual background, which requires either lighting the background or picking a location where the background is naturally well lit. Interviews are one of the times that allows lighting in documentary production. Different from TV news or a corporate video, the subject being interviewed in a documentary is usually an ordinary person rather than someone "important" or in authority. Thus the look should be different. The subject in a documentary interview should look more natural and "everyday" rather than the glossy "professional" look of corporate videos and newsmagazines.

> "A lot of times in documentaries, you are dealing with locations you have no choice over. So the location inspires you. You come into an old workshop and it has old lights that are warm and I love it. That will give me an idea of what I can add to keep the look of that location."
>
> —ELIA LYSSY, DOCUMENTARY DP

In the non-interview shooting sequences of documentaries, usually the best we can do is add ambient fill light to offset the contrast and fill in the shadows of the faces. I shot a documentary about a special children's school. We were shooting during school hours in the classrooms and hallways, so it was virtually impossible to do any lighting. When we went into one room in which we were going to film, the students were still at lunch. I quickly set up two open-faced lights and bounced them into the ceiling to bring up the overall ambiance in the room and help balance out the light from the overheads and the windows. The lights were set behind where the director and producer were standing; thus we knew no children would be going near them. Placing lights where no one will trip over them is a very important thing to remember when shooting fast. Because the lights were on when the students first walked into the room, they just accepted the brightness and weren't put off by it. This is a good method to follow when the occasion arises that you can add some light—always try to have the lights on before the subjects walk into the room.

When I was the DP on a series of educational documentaries for seminary college use, we had more of a budget and a much more relaxed time schedule that allowed us the luxury of doing some lighting. The producer flew us to various churches around the country where we would shoot two Sunday services back-to-back with three cameras. We would come in on a Friday afternoon and scout the church location, then shoot B-roll of the local area. The producer usually hired a local gaffer and grip with lighting gear who would meet us on Saturday morning. We would watch the natural light coming in at the time that the services would be, and then light the church, hiding 5kW Fresnels and nine-light Fays in the choir loft and on balconies, imitating the feeling of bright, heavenly sunlight descending on the worship area. No lights were ever on the floor of the church itself so as to avoid tripping hazards, lower our "invasion" of their sacred space, and not get into any shots. While the cable was being run, I would light an interview spot off in another part of the building where the producer and director could rotate various interviewees through. After I did the lighting, these would be shot by a local cameraman we hired for the project while I continued lighting the church with the gaffer and grip.

Sunday morning we would turn on all the lights well before any of the parishioners walked through the door. Every time, they all accepted that it was just bright sunlight coming in from the windows, even though several times we were lucky and it was overcast—which meant we didn't have to worry about real sunlight coming in and going away during the shooting. For one church in Las Vegas, we even gelled the stained glass windows from outside with ND6 and created our own patterned rays of sunlight from the organ loft. The concept was to light it bright enough for multiple cameras to shoot the action happening from three different angles, but allow it to still look natural and somewhat "unlit." And this brings us to lighting for reality TV.

REALITY TV

Reality TV is a stepchild of the documentary in that it shoots real people doing things in real time, but is manipulated for the purposes of entertainment. Another difference is that it has multiple cameras, the ability to redo something, more time to set up, and a bigger budget. Also, unlike documentaries, which often attempt to be a fly on the wall, reality TV is blatant about there being cameras around all the time filming everything. Some reality is lit; some isn't. *The Bachelorette* looks like a soap opera because it's selling romance, while *Cops* looks like bad home video because it's selling voyeurism.

Setting the camera white balance to 4,300 Kelvin allows it to get an acceptable color when shooting in rooms with mixed light from both windows and tungsten lights, which is common to most reality shooting.

Lighting for reality is striving for an "unlit look" that provides a nice exposure for the multiple cameras that are moving all around and shooting in almost all directions. Usually this means no lights on stands on the floor. In practice, reality shows will pre-light their primary reoccurring locations, often with fluorescent units and small Fresnels with diffusion (and usually ½ CTB) rigged to the ceiling, and LED lights hidden in various places. The diffusers from any preexisting fluorescent fixtures in the space are usually removed and the units relamped with all the same color temperature lamps, usually 4,100K (TL841), and wrapped with ½ Minus Green. Doing this will provide a very even, bright, soft ambiance throughout the area. The brighter the ambient light all around, the easier it is for the many roaming cameras to get good shots. Reality shows are, in general, high key.

> **"On reality it's a broad open look. No flagging, lots of soft light, and color corrections to get to 4,300K, and using preexisting fixtures."**
>
> —TIGRE MCMULLAN, GAFFER, PROJECT RUNWAY, CHOPPED

If there are any practicals, such as hanging lamps, bedside table lamps, or floor standing lamps—these will also be relamped usually with compact fluorescent lamps (CFLs) that are the same color temperature as the overhead fluorescents, or with "Reveal" bulbs, which are daylight blue bulbs that can be purchased in any hardware store. The advantage of using Reveal bulbs is

CHAPTER 13: Nonfiction Lighting: Interview. Corporate, Newsmagazine, Documentary, Reality

228

that they are dimmable, whereas most CFLs are not. Reveal bulbs are also often placed in mirror lights in bathrooms. The idea is to make all the lights in the location the same color temperature and consistent from room to room.

Extra attention is sometimes placed on entrances and places where the sponsor's logo may appear. So lights will be rigged to the ceiling, using scissor clips, to hang small Fresnels with diffusion and ½ CTB to make it 4,300K. Scissor clips are very cheap and can hold up an inkie to a 650w Fresnel hanging from the suspended-ceiling tile frames.

For hallways, wall spreaders are put up onto which two Kino lamps, one tungsten and one daylight (which creates 4,300 Kelvin light), wrapped in diffusion are attached by plastic zip-ties. The poor man's wall spreader is an expandable pressure curtain rod or shower curtain rod sold at any hardware store. Just remember that these are made to only support the weight of a curtain, so it's best not to attach anything too heavy on them. The advantage of Kino Flo units is that the "guts," meaning the wiring, can be stripped out of the housing, which allows the lamps to be taped or zip-tied almost anywhere. It is important that the lamps be encased in the clear plastic tubing, which protects them from breaking. Otherwise they might shatter while being rigged without the housing to protect them.

In Photo 13.10, three of the lights are Kino Flo lamps outside their housing. Only the last unit in the back is still in its housing, which makes it larger and heavier but more directionable.

While fluorescents generate a soft light already, adding additional diffusion gel around them allows the light to wrap more, which will help fill in below the subject's eyes.

This same combination is often rigged above windows (directly to the curtain rod) for a more directional "motivated" light look that remains soft and not overpowering.

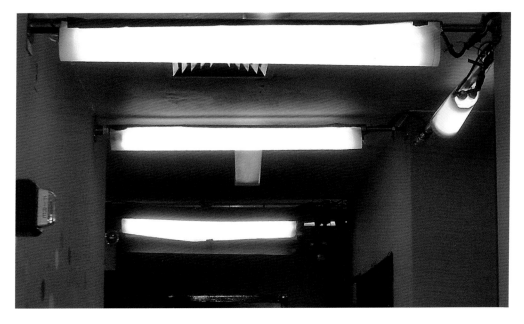

PHOTO 13.10 **Stripped Kino Flo lamps on wall spreaders for *Project Runway***

On locations, small lighting packages are brought along, usually mixed lamped Kino Flos and bi-color LED lights, which are used to add ambient fill under the eyes of the subjects, and can mix with the existing location fixtures. The challenge is finding where to position the lights in order to allow the cameras' maximum mobility, yet still be effective in bringing up the faces of the subjects. Whenever possible, adding a small kick to the cheek or hair helps to add some modeling, but it is always at a low intensity so as not to call attention to itself. Subtlety is key in reality lighting.

> "Mornings and evenings are the only times reality shoots inside the apartments—so the lighting is balanced for morning sun and late night with mixed 32 and 56 lamps. Morning sun is warmer, so adding the mixed color temp light helps cool it down so it can mix with what is seen outside the windows. The outside still goes a little blue, but it's acceptable in reality TV. At night, everything outside the windows is no longer tungsten—the street lights, signs etc. are all LEDs or other colors."
>
> —GUS DOMINGUEZ, TV LIGHTING DIRECTOR/DP

On *Project Runway Allstars 3* (2013), we had a scene where four contestants visited a successful designer in her office. It was a corner office with windows that faced south and west. The shoot was first thing in the morning, so we knew we wouldn't have to deal with direct sunlight coming in. I ordered two 575w HMI PAR lights to augment our location package, which was four 2-bank × 4-foot Kino Flos (with mixed lamps) and two bi-color LED 1 × 1 Litepanels. My intention was to aim them through 4-foot × 4-foot opal frames to augment the skylight and provide some direction. Instead of the sun, we had overcast on the shoot day. This meant there was much less ambient fill coming in through the windows, which made the HMI lights look too sharp and bright compared to what the cameras saw out the window. So we bounced the two HMIs into the ceiling from the two corners of the room behind the three cameras. By focusing where each beam hit the ceiling, I was able to direct the bounce from one unit onto where the guest designer would be standing and the other onto where the contestants would end up standing.

We then made use of the track light units in the office. On the track over the desk, we focused one unit to backlight the guest designer and the others to place highlights on the walls of fabric swatches behind her and on a dress form by her desk. The other track light was behind where our contestants would stand, so we focused four of those as backlights and the rest to highlight the fabric and fashion sketches behind them on the back wall.

The cameras were going to "carry them in," which means shoot through the open office door as the contestants stepped off the elevator and walked in through a short hallway. One Kino Flo was positioned out of frame to throw some light into the elevator foyer, and another was just outside the office door to side-light the contestants as they came up to the door. This Kino was set to come from the same side as the windows inside the office, so it would match the directionality of the light inside the office.

This setup looked totally natural and "unlit," while allowing the three cameras shooting to work without restriction, adding ambient fill light to everyone's faces and some small backlight to each person as well.

For another episode, we shot at the United Nations in a large room with 20-foot ceilings. The downlight from so far up produced "raccoon eyes" (shadows under the eyes) on everyone, so we rigged two mixed-lamp 2-bank × 4-foot Kino Flos as cross keys. The units had to be placed rather far back because the wide shot would be done on a floating Steadicam while three other cameras were shooting close-ups. So we had to rig the Kinos on the ends of grip arms to get the stands out of the wide shot. After the cameras were in place, we lowered the Kinos as far down as we could without getting them in anyone's shot to get the light as much under the eyes as possible. Because the units were moved back for the wide shot, I added two bi-color LED 1 × 1 Litepanels to boost up the intensity. We added Chimeras, but then pulled the diffusion in order to get more throw.

The Kino Flo in Photo 13.11 was rigged on the end of a grip arm in order to back the light stand out of the floating Steadicam shot. To help support and counterbalance the light, a grip knuckle was put on the back end of the grip arm from which sash cord was tied down to a sandbag on the ground. The LED light with a Chimera under the Kino Flo was moved back before shooting.

The result was a very subtle fill under the eyes and a nice little kick to both the guest and the contestants. The softness and the low intensity made it look "unlit," but adding the lights was essential to making the faces look nicer on camera. That's basically what lighting does the majority of the time in reality—it makes the faces look a little nicer than the real lighting does.

PHOTO 13.11 **A Kino Flo rigged on the end of a double grip arm for reality shoot at the UN**

STUFF TO REMEMBER

- Always use soft light for both key and fill for interviews.

- In documentaries and reality TV, have the interviewee turn into the key to shoot into the fill side and add some modeling to the face.

- In corporate video, have the subject turn into the fill to allow his or her brighter side toward the camera. It is also almost always high key.

- For interviews, keep the key light as close to eye level as possible, but without blinding the subject.

- Add a small, below-eye-level, low-intensity softlight to fill in bags under the eyes.

- For bald men and blond-haired subjects, aim the backlight into the subject's shoulders, and barn-door light off the top of their heads.

- Always add some light to the background—usually through a cookie or broken up somehow.

- For subjects with glasses, move key and fill to the sides to avoid reflections.

- For a TV newsmagazine, the correspondent is usually lit flat and flattering.

- In documentary, bounce lights into ceilings to bring up the ambient light, and always have the lights on before the subject enters.

- Reality TV lighting is adding soft light to fill in under the eyes and bring up the overall exposure—making faces look better than they would under the existing light.

PUTTING IT INTO PRACTICE

- Light an interview of someone in his or her natural surroundings.

- Light a scene using as many available light sources as possible.

- Then add softlight (bounced, or direct) to bring up the faces as subtly as possible, and look at the emotional difference.

14 INSPIRATION AND LIGHTING LOOKS

DPs finds inspiration for the look of a project from various sources. When DPs take on a project, they read the script and talk with the director to get ideas on how they should approach the visual design. If it's a period piece, they will look at the popular culture of that time period—the paintings, the clothing styles, any photographs, and movies, if any. They may also watch other movies with similar settings or plots to the one they will be taking on to see how others handled the material. DPs and directors will often reference paintings and films as a shorthand form of communication to describe how they see something appearing in camera.

DP Gordon Willis found inspiration for his talented work on the film *Pennies from Heaven* (1981) from the paintings and the movies of the era. In the musical number "Love Is Good for Anything That Ails You," Willis paid homage to the lighting and cinematography of Sol Polito on the Busby Berkeley extravaganzas *The Golddiggers of 1933* (1933) and *42nd Street* (1933). For the song "Let's Misbehave," Willis took visual cues from the paintings of Archibald Motley, Jr., and for the "Pennies from Heaven" sequence, the paintings of Edward Hopper. Conrad Hall studied the work of Edward Hopper as well for his Academy Award–winning work on *Road to Perdition* (2002). Laszlo Kovacs said he studied the Depression-era photographs of the Midwest to create his wonderful deep-focus, black-and-white cinematography for *Paper Moon* (1973). Depression-era photographs were also the inspiration for Haskell Wexler's work on *Bound for Glory* (1976), which won him an Oscar. For *Days of Heaven* (1978), DP Nestor Almendros worked to achieve a look inspired by the paintings of Andrew Wyeth, and he also won an Oscar. John Alcott found inspiration in the paintings of the Dutch Masters for his Oscar-winning work on *Barry Lyndon* (1975), and obviously the lighting of DP Donald M. McAlpine in *Moulin Rouge!* (2001) was inspired by the garish colors and lighting from the paintings of Toulouse-Lautrec.

Often the source material itself will become the inspiration for the lighting. DP Vittorio Storaro made the film *Dick Tracy* (1990) look like a Sunday newspaper comic, and John Leonetti worked to make *The Mask* (1994) look like the comic book it was based on.

Inspiration can come from things totally unconnected to the time period of the story as well. It can be a feeling or an atmosphere—almost anything.

LIGHTING LOOKS

There are some classic looks, or styles, for lighting that a DP can employ that have been established through time. These looks are the result of inspiration from paintings, movies, and even nature itself. Each DP will put his or her own stamp on how to create or interpret these styles, using them as a starting-off place or an inspiration for the look of a project. But using the terminology can help form a shorthand language between the DP and the director, just as *high key* and *low key* does. Not all films and TV shows fall into one of these categories; many are well shot but don't have any kind of classifiable "look." That doesn't mean there wasn't some form of inspiration for the style of the production.

PHOTO 14.1 **Dutch Masters look, *Barry Lyndon*, DP John Alcott, Warner Bros.**

The Dutch Masters Look

This look is inspired by the work of such master painters as Vermeer and Rembrandt and the other Dutch Masters who painted near windows to let in bright, soft light. The northern part of Europe is famous for its fog, overcast skies, and long days where the sun barely rises above the horizon, thus sending sunlight bouncing off the clouds in the sky and providing a bright, soft, diffused light coming in through the window at a treetop-low angle. Buildings were made with large windows, either very wide or floor-to-ceiling high to allow in as much natural light as possible. So this style of lighting is large, bright, soft sources with very little backlight and somewhat midrange contrast ratios. It can be seen in most costume dramas; exceptional examples include *Barry Lyndon* (1975), *Amadeus* (1984), *Dangerous Liaisons* (1988), *The Other Boleyn Girl* (2008), *The Duchess* (2008), and, of course, *Girl with a Pearl Earring* (2003).

PHOTO 14.2 Dutch Masters look, *Girl with a Pearl Earring* (2003), DP Eduardo Serra, Lionsgate

PHOTO 14.3 Dutch Masters look, *Marie Antoinette* (2006), DP Lance Acord, Columbia Pictures

The standard method of achieving the Dutch Masters lighting look is by placing big lights outside, usually on scaffolding, aimed through 4-foot × 4-foot frames of diffusion that floods light in through the windows. The ambient bounce off the floor and walls becomes the fill. On the features mentioned, this was often achieved with large arc lights, or on the more recent films, with 20kW HMIs. But lower-budget productions can achieve a similar look with only a few lights.

As discussed in Chapter 8, "Working with Windows," if the shot is limited in view, a 2kW Fresnel or a cluster of PAR lights can be placed outside the window(s) to provide the bright flood of light. Placing the diffusion on the lighting units themselves will diffuse the light before it reaches the window, lowering the intensity. So it's best to either allow the light to go undiffused, or place the diffusion on 4-foot × 4-foot frames positioned closer to the window, or put diffusion over the outside of the window. Placing white cards on the flood and then aiming lights down into them to bounce light up will help augment the Dutch Masters look.

PHOTO 14.4 Dutch Masters look, FDU cinematography in-class shoot

However, if the shot is wide, good planning and utilizing the real daylight is required. Photo 14.4 was from a cinematography in-class project. The desire was to light and frame the images in the Dutch Masters style. The class used only one 4kW baby softlight, inside the ballroom, positioned off left, and then used the light from the windows themselves. The wide shots had to be shot first, before the sun moved too far across the sky and would no longer create the desired glaring bounce off the floor.

Notice there is a hard shadow on the floor of the window frames and glare on the floor from the skylight coming in through the windows. The light hitting the floor bounces up, illuminating the walls and everyone in the room, with the tops of the walls falling off in intensity just as we discussed in an earlier chapter.

PHOTO 14.5 Dutch Masters look, FDU cinematography in-class shoot

In Photo 14.5, the baby 4kW softlight used three lamps and was positioned off right. Skylight from the window on the left provided the key light kick, and the light through the sheers on the window off right provided the hair light. The 4kW softlight not only fills in the maid's face, but also brings up the shadow area behind her in the corner, lowering the contrast ratio, which is desired in this style of lighting.

In Photo 14.6, only two lamps were used on the 4kW softlight set off right and at eye level to provide the soft key as if it were coming from the window.

PHOTO 14.6 Dutch Masters look, FDU Cinematography in-class shoot

This project was shot on 16mm Kodak film with very little done in terms of image control in postproduction. The shadows are not deep, and the overall tone of the image is in the midrange. Getting the softness provided by the film would require diffusion filters over the lens with today's high-definition digital cameras. What helps to give this the Dutch Masters feeling is the amount of detail outside the windows. While the outside is overexposed by two to three stops, it isn't blown out or washed out. The film was balanced for daylight (5,600 Kelvin), but the 4kW softlight was used without any color correction gel on it, thus providing a warm, soft glow.

PHOTO 14.7 Hollywood look, *War Horse* (2012), DP Janusz Kaminski, DreamWorks

The Hollywood Look

Hollywood means glamour. The Hollywood look is based on the way classic Hollywood spectacles were shot—films like *Gone with the Wind* (1930—Photo 14.8), *Doctor Zhivago* (1965), *Cleopatra* (1963), and *The Wizard of Oz* (1939). There is a beautiful, high-gloss look generally for stories that are larger than life. The lighting is larger than life as well—sometimes over-the-top or melodramatic, but still appropriate for the story and the project. Sometimes the director and the DP will agree on a Hollywood look for a scene or an entire film. What exactly defines this look isn't that easy to identify. A lot has to do with the camera work, but in the lighting it often includes employing textbook three-point lighting, heavy backlight and kickers, colored light, and hard light sources, and embracing a more theatrical approach to the lighting. Because the stories themselves are rather epic, the lighting not only can be, but is, expected to be epic as well. Films that embraced the Hollywood look include *Hugo* (2011), *War Horse* (2012—Photo 14.7), *Pirates of the Caribbean* (2003 + sequels), *Harry Potter* (2001 + sequels), *Peter Pan* (2003), *Raiders of the Lost Ark* (1981 + sequels), *Star Wars* (1977 + sequels), *Star Trek* movies, and *Alice in Wonderland* (2010), and TV shows such as *Boardwalk Empire* (2010–) and *Game of Thrones* (2011–).

Film Noir

Film noir is a term started by French film critics to describe a certain genre of American films that were made during World War II that didn't make it to France until after the war ended. These were pessimistic, lower-budget, mystery genre "B" movies made by the studios often based on the pulp fiction of the 1940s, such as *The Maltese Falcon* (1941), *Murder, My Sweet* (1942), *This Gun for Hire* (1942), and *Laura* (1944). The cinematographers of these films had short shooting schedules, but were also allowed to do things that the higher-budget main title films weren't allowed to do—such

PHOTO 14.8 Hollywood look, *Gone with the Wind* (1939), DP Ernst Haller, Selznick/MGM

PHOTO 14.9 Film noir look, *The Big Combo* (1955), John Alton, Allied Artists

PHOTO 14.10 **Film noir look, *Night of the Hunter* (1955), DP Stanley Cortez, United Artists**

as allow their stars to be half in darkness—mainly because no one at the studio really paid much attention to them. These were the second freebie movies shown in double features, and used actors, writers, directors, and cameramen who were under contract, so they couldn't say no.

The stories were dark mysteries where the line between good and evil was always gray. The lighting reflected this in its harsh contrast ratios of black shadows and bright highlights produced with steep hard lights. Not using a lot of fill and not trying to make everyone look glamorous allowed the production to do more setups per day and meet the tight schedule. Also the stories were all set in dark nightclubs and back alleys—where the underbelly of society mingles with the upper crust—so the higher contrast and deep blacks were part of the story.

The film noir look is low key, but never underexposed or too dark that you can't see what's going on. Puddles of light are common, as are kickers and ¾ hair lights, shadows, and a lot of darkness in the backgrounds. DP John Seitz is often considered one of the innovators of this look starting with his lighting work on such films as *This Gun for Hire* (1942) and *Double Indemnity* (1943) and through *Sunset Boulevard* (1950). Many other cinematographers added to the style, most notably Harry Wild (*Murder, My Sweet*—1944; *Macao*—1952), John Alton (*I, the Jury*—1953; *The Big Combo*—1955), and Stanley Cortez (*Night of the Hunter*—1955).

Noir lighting is fun and allows you to be very selective in what you light and creative in your angles. Photos 14.11 and 14.12 are from the short *Joker's Wild* (1985), which I shot on 16mm as part of A&E's Short Subjects series. It was a two-character mystery in the film noir tradition, about two actors

PHOTO 14.11 **Film noir look, *Joker's Wild,* Nancy Richards and Douglas Ballard, Mallinson Media**

in a theater finding a body and accusing each other of murder. This was a very low-budget production, so we used some of the theater's stage lights with our small tungsten film light package.

To accent the noir feeling, we cut the light off actress Nancy Richards' eyes and forehead, giving her the Veronica Lake femme fatale look whenever we could. This allows her to be mysterious and alluring at the same time. This shot was exposed for her cheek, allowing her eyes to fall almost two stops below. Actor Douglas Ballard in the foreground was also almost two stops below, thus providing a subliminal connection between them. We should have used an eye light to pick up her pupils, but we didn't have any inkies or dimmers. The strong hair light and the slash on the painting help separate her from the background and continue the noir-inspired look. While hard light from the right hits her hair and cheek, a soft light from the left adds a much lower-intensity fill so that we can see her eyes. Doug is lit with another soft light, but rimmed with a hard source from off right.

In Photo 14.12, Nancy holds a gun on Doug, stopping him from leaving. Nancy is side-lit by the magenta-colored light coming in through the venetian blinds. That is the motivation, but it is augmented with a white hard light from off right, which is again cut off her eyes. A strong hair light from behind left helps her out-of-focus presence dominate the image, as well as the fact that her white blouse is slightly overexposed. Meanwhile, Doug is slightly underexposed and lit with a hard light with ½ blue from the left and just slightly above eye level, throwing his nose shadow under his left eye. One lamp on a 2kW zip light with thick diffusion fills in his face from very close to camera. He has a hair rim light from behind left to continue the feeling from the hair light for Nancy. The contrast between

PHOTO 14.12 Film noir look, *Joker's Wild*, Nancy Richards and Douglas Ballard, Mallinson Media

the magenta light through the window and the ½ blue on Doug's face places him in the cold shadows, almost as if he's dead already—foreshadowing of what's to come in the story.

Many modern films have used film noir lighting, and not all are mysteries or set in the 1940s. These films include *The Number 23* (2007), *House of Games* (1987), *Chinatown* (1974), *LA Confidential* (1997), *Kiss Kiss Bang Bang* (2005), *The Black Dahlia* (2006), and the black-and-white sequences in *Memento* (2000).

Natural Realism

Trying to go as far from the old Hollywood studio look as possible, natural realism in cinematography really grew out of the work of such DPs as Laszlo Kovacs on *Easy Rider* (1969) and *Five Easy Pieces* (1970), and Vilmos Zsigmond on *Deliverance* (1972) and *The Long Goodbye* (1973—Photo 14.14). Not coming from the Hollywood studio system, and shooting on real locations rather than sets, these two revolutionary cinematographers strove to make their images as natural as possible. Their lighting was to imitate on film the image the human eye would naturally see, rather than the more glamorous images Hollywood produced. They found beauty in motivated lighting and delicate lighting ratios. The idea was to subtly lull the viewer into the world of the film.

PHOTO 14.13 Film noir look, *Skyfall* (2012), DP Roger Deakins, Columbia Pictures

PHOTO 14.14 Natural realism look, *The Long Goodbye* (1973), DP Vilmos Zsigmond, Lionsgate

Natural realism look, *Up in the Air* (2009), DP Eric Steelberg, Paramount

Other DPs, such as Conrad Hall (*In Cold Blood*—1967, *Cool Hand Luke*—1967, *Butch Cassidy and the Sundance Kid*—1969), and Michael Chapman (*Taxi Driver*—1972, *Raging Bull*—1980) continued to develop the look through their work. Again, what characterizes this look is hard to pinpoint, but could be said to be a heavy reliance on the concepts of motivated lighting, key lighting from the sides, extensive use of soft light, and a natural logic to the lighting ratios. Films that typify this look besides those mentioned above include *Silver Linings Playbook* (2012), *Up in the Air* (2009), *Away We Go* (2009), *Little Miss Sunshine* (2006), *Juno* (2007), *Fargo* (1996), *Sideways* (2004), *Collateral* (2004), *One Flew Over the Cuckoo's Nest* (1975), and *Midnight Cowboy* (1969).

The "Home Video" and "Unlit" Look

This look is a more recent style and appears often in "found footage" movies, basically started by *The Blair Witch Project* (1999), shot by the late Neal Fredericks, and continued with such films as *Paranormal Activity* (2007), but also applied to some serious dramas such as *Margot at the Wedding* (2007) and *Frances Ha* (2012). These are usually typified by shaky handheld camera work and what appears to be available light. At times, the DPs will go out of their way to make the lighting actually look bad in order to sell the "home video" look.

On the feature film *End of Watch* (2013), DP Roman Vasyanov achieved a convincing "available light" look to simulate dashboard cams and police chest cams by adding large banks of fluorescent tubes above the acting areas, with ½ Minus Green on them, to create a dreary top-down lighting look. This became the only lighting in several scenes. He carried out the same lighting concept in the police

PHOTO 14.16 **The unlit look,** *End of Watch* **(2013), DP Roman Vasyanov, Exclusive Media**

cars by taping LED strips on the ceilings. For a few scenes inside dive buildings the cops storm into, he used 12,000w HMIs shining in through the slants of the boarded-up windows.

On *Zero Dark Thirty* (2013), DP Greig Fraser took a similar approach when trying to achieve the moonless night, no-light look during the compound raid scene. He used 48 Kino Flo lamps suspended by cranes above the entire outside area.

All this can be done on a much smaller, less expensive scale. Hardware stores, such as Home Depot, sell "shop" 4-foot strip fluorescent units with a plug on them. You can get them in two- and four-bulb units and in various sizes, such as T8 and T4, for $20 to $40 each, as well as a variety of under-cabinet lights. All of these can be easily rigged above acting areas. Lamped with 4,000K bulbs wrapped with ½ Minus Green gel will produce a soft top light for very little expense. This lighting allows the actors and the camera(s) to move around freely and allows the image to look "unlit."

Other things that might typify this lighting look would be wide contrast ratios within the shot with some things burning out and others deeply underexposed, as well as a lack of backlight or separation from the background. Downlight from real ceiling fixtures (often augmented by additional sources such as those just mentioned or with bounced light), as well as replacing the location's household lights with higher-intensity lamps, generally becomes the motivation and method of lighting. Michael Bonvillain's work on *Cloverfield* (2008) is a well-constructed found-footage look. The shots were well composed and lit, even though it was supposedly all "home video." One of the most creative variations on this look was done by DP Matthew Jensen in *Chronicle* (2012), who was also one of the DPs on HBO's high-quality productions *True Blood* and *Game of Thrones,* where he did Hollywood-style lighting. The lighting he did in *Chronicle* transforms from "home video" to "unlit" to natural realism to Hollywood as the characters and the story transform. The changing-lighting look worked to help reinforce the progression of the story, rather than just attempting to look "real."

Documentary

The documentary look isn't the same as the home video look. No documentary filmmaker would ever wants his or her film to look that amateurish. As discussed in a previous chapter, documentary cameramen try to shoot using available light, but position their subjects in the best light possible and often use bounce cards and a few small lights. Most times, in documentaries it doesn't matter if the shot looks like some lights have been added.

Documentaries often include interviews, which we discussed in Chapter 13, which is a staple of the sitcom documentary-style TV shows such as *The Office* (2005–2013) and *Modern Family* (2009–) They also shoot a lot of B-roll, which is footage of the subject working or of what the subject is talking about, which is often shot under available light. But again, documentary cameramen do strive to make the image look appealing, generally by positioning the subject in the best natural light at the right time.

The documentary look can be achieved by bouncing lights into walls and ceilings out of frame and replacing the location's household lights with higher-intensity lamps, but also striving to use natural and available light to add modeling, depth, and backlight to the subject. It is generally a more soft, low-contrast look. *Project Runway* (2004–) has this documentary look, as do the TV show *Parks and Recreation* (2009–) and *Arrested Development* (2003–2013) and films such as *This Is Spinal Tap* (1984), *Best in Show* (2000), *A Hard Day's Night* (1964), and *Zelig* (1983).

PUTTING IT INTO PRACTICE

Find a painting with great lighting. It's best to select one with only one or two people and a rather simple setting that you can easily re-create. Shoot a still of it. Now imitate the scene, including the lighting, framing, color, and so on. Shoot the shot that matches the painting, then make the painting come alive. Shoot two more angles and carry out the lighting.

PHOTO 14.18 The Documentary look, *The Office* (2005), DP Randall Einhorn, NBC/Universal TV

PARTING WORDS

I hope you have found this book inspiring and enlightening. Hopefully this book will be more than just a beginning for learning the art and craft of lighting for cinematography—the photography of moving images. We are always learning throughout our career and throughout life. Every setup provides its own challenges and opportunities. Remember what works, and have the courage to recognize what doesn't—and then consider how to do it better next time. Without setbacks, there is no progress; without risk, no reward. Failure at times is not an option, but rather a necessity. For without it, how can we realize what doesn't work and what does? Most of all, don't forget to play—because that is how great things are often discovered. Here are a few words from some of my colleagues, who have agreed to share more of their insights and experiences in Appendix 1, "Advice from the Field."

- Play now—who cares if it's underexposed? Do it now. You can't experiment with other people's money. If I had had to light the exact same thing today, I would light it differently. Cameramen are storytellers—it has to be part of the story whether it's the framing or the lighting; it has to further the story. It's good to know the rules, but in the world I work in, it doesn't matter how many sit-down interviews I've done; it's always something new. So I've learned to never come in with a plan on exactly how to light it. Instead, I come in and see the room. —Elia Lyssy, documentary and low-budget feature DP

- Don't let anyone tell you lighting is not important. It's a "visual medium." Don't develop bad habits; otherwise, when you get into a situation where you really need to light, you won't know how. —Gus Dominguez, lighting director, reality TV, awards, and game shows (Local 600)

- The more you think about it, the better you get; the more experience you have, the better you get—so shoot as many varied types of films to get experience to see what works and doesn't work. Experience is a great teacher. And don't be afraid to take chances. —Peter Stein ASC, feature film DP (Local 600)

- Just look at light. The more you look at what light does in nature, the more you'll see it. Notice just the little touches of light. The difference between ho-hum and [lighting] that blows you away will be a tiny addition or subtraction that makes the scene pop. The only way to find those things is to look at light. —Tigre McMullan, gaffer/LD (Local 52)

1 ADVICE FROM THE FIELD:
Interviews with Cameramen and Gaffers

A number of really good books are available that interview famous, big-time feature directors of photography (see Appendix 2, "Resources"). Their stories are always informative and inspiring, but often don't relate well to someone working with a very small crew, limited equipment, and restricted time. For this section of the book, I wanted to include a cross section of DPs, ranging from Hollywood and TV to low-budget films, newsmagazines, and documentaries. I am very thankful that these talented cinematographers and gaffers all agreed to answer some questions and share their experiences for this book. They are as follows:

Peter Stein, ASC—DP, feature films and TV movies, IATSE Local 600, http://petersteinasc.com/

David Mullen, ASC—DP, feature films and TV series, IATSE Local 600, http://www.davidmullenasc.com

Gus Dominguez—Lighting director, reality TV, awards and game shows, IATSE Local 600, www.gusdominguez.com

Joseph di Gennaro—DP, low-budget feature films, IATSE Local 600

Elia Lyssy—DP, documentaries and low-budget features (www.Elialyssy.com)

Ray Bribiesca—Award-winning *60 Minutes* and *48 Hours* cameraman, IBEW

Tigre McMullan—Gaffer, reality TV and sitcom TV shows, IATSE Local 52

Bill O'Leary—Gaffer, major Hollywood feature films, IATSE Local 52

What do you feel is the most important thing lighting does for the film/scene/shot?

To create a feel that furthers the story that wants to be told. —Elia

Setting a mood without setting a mood—without being obvious. —Tigre

Light is the chisel that sculpts the mood of any image on-screen. —Joe

The lighting has to establish the emotional tone of the scene, though sometimes it can be in counterpoint to the emotions of the characters in the scene. —David

Control the look of the scene—we can't control Mother Nature. —Ray

Everything a DP does is in service to the story. The lighting is to service the story. You shouldn't make the audience aware of the lighting; rather, it's there so that they can lose themselves in the story. –Peter

Helps you see it. LOL. It adds to the story—paints the picture. —Gus

Lighting helps to shape the director's ideas and vision about what each scene means, and therefore, the film as a whole. —Bill

What is the first thing you think about when you walk into a location or set you have to light?

First thing I look at are the interesting architectural aspects and how do I use them. Then windows and what do I think the best angles would be. Look for the most architecture of the room—height of the ceiling, how to rig lights, how can I hide lights, bounce lights, wall stretchers—what about a floor for lights through windows? Are there fixtures that we can attach to? General feeling of that location. —Peter

A lot of times in documentaries, you are dealing with locations you have no choice over. So the location inspires you. You come into an old workshop, and it has old lights that are warm and I love it. That will give me an idea of what I can add to keep the look of that location. What do I have to do to be in control of the light? Do I like the way it looks—why? What do I have to do to keep that look? So, I look at what I like and how can I enhance, keep, and control it. —Elia

How can I give this a warm and fuzzy look? I'm doing interviews and have to light the correspondent nice. But 90 percent of the time, I'm working in hotel rooms with limited space and power. So I have to think about making the most of it. —Ray

During a scout, I'll arrive with an idea of how the scene should look based on discussions with the DP and the script. From there, logistics and compromise rule. —Bill

For an interior on location, I look at how it is normally lit with natural and artificial sources and decide whether the story demands a certain honesty about how the location is visually represented. For example, a supermarket often has a high-key look with a lot of bright soft top-lighting from fluorescents. So, even if I could change that look, maybe I shouldn't lest it no longer feel like a supermarket. But assuming that different lighting approaches are justified dramatically, then I might see how the location looks with just the window light or just the overheads—I turn selective fixtures off and on to adjust the look. Beyond manipulating what is actually there, I may have to consider rigging additional lighting inside the room or outside the windows, and I also may consider changing or adding to the practical fixtures in the room. So I look at a location in terms of the ease of rigging, if that will be necessary. Can I get lamps outside the windows, and at what height? Can I change the bulbs in the practical fixtures to different wattages or color temperatures? A lot of these discussions will involve the gaffer, key grip, production designer or set dresser, etc. —David

First thing I think about when entering a location or set is what type of show it is. Lighting on a sitcom is different than drama or reality. What is the show's established look? On reality, it's a broad open look. No flagging, lots of soft light and color corrections to get to 4,300K, and using preexisting fixtures. On sitcom, it's a closed environment with multiple angle cameras and one or more booms that extend far into the set. You have to contend with large sticks coming out over the actors. So the lighting is from the back and sides with softlight frontal light. ¾ back from both sides with 2kWs with Lee 250 (diffusion) and bobbinet [a kind of tulle netting] on the bottom. Key the entry ways and through windows. 2kW softlights from both sides in the front, and a long bounce along the entire front. Drama lighting is more dictated by the script/scene and trying to match the location style/look with the interior studio look. —Tigre

How often do you use a backlight? Do you consider it necessary or unnatural?

I love a good backlight. A strong backlight adds drama, character, and depth while separating the subject from the background. —Gus

I always rim the shoulders. It works even if you can't light the hair because they're blond or bald. —Ray

I love having backlight. Without it, they will blend with the background. A backlight makes it two levels. —Tigre

I think using backlights is part of the palette of the cinematographer. You use it for psychological aspects besides separation. Bright backlight for happy—maybe no backlight for tense scenes, if you want them to fade into the background. It says something to the audience whether or not you use a backlight. But they take the most time to rig and to cut. —Peter

Backlight for me can have two reasons—purely esthetics and for separation. I can use a direct backlight, or a background light to separate the subject from the background. Sometimes the director says, "I don't want the 60 Minutes look—I want it to look natural." So sometimes I shy away from a kicker or a rim and instead add a slash or pattern on the background, keeping it behind the shoulders for separation from the background. That said, sometimes there will be a window farther back. Rather than block it, I keep it—it adds a little backlight. It is an esthetic question. I shot an interview with one soft key light that wrapped around, but the subject fell off into the background, and that's what the director wanted. As a DP you are there to bring a vision of the director to the screen. So the final word is the director. I did an interview with just a backlight because we couldn't show the face. I did put a kicker on the person and added a little background light. —Elia

I tend toward a naturalistic, "motivated" style in my lighting approach. If a source for a backlight can be justified, I will, of course, jump at the opportunity to use it as a way to separate my subject from the background. However, unless it is motivated, I will avoid the use of such an artifice. Instead, I will enhance the tonal separation of my subject by using a low-angle edge light, or will find some reason (perhaps a practical lighting source visible in the background) to place a "slash" of light across the scenery. As long as a tonal separation exists, my subject will be isolated and enhanced as the focal point of the shot. Unless I achieve this effect, the subject has a tendency to blend into the scenery, and the point of focus in the frame can become confused. —Joe

An unmotivated backlight is unnecessary and unnatural. Without a motivating source in frame or one that's been established, it will only serve to draw the audience out of the story. In a superhero film OK, but in a character-based drama, no go. —Bill

If I am aiming for a natural look in general, I only use backlights when motivated by sources in the room, so often the backlight will be quite intense if it's supposed to be sunlight; otherwise, it will be a soft backlight coming from a window, and the reverse angle opposite the windows won't be backlit at all. I'm very fond of "nuclear" backlighting, as if intense sunlight has come through a window, but only when it looks motivated and believable. In day interiors, I don't like backlight coming from the opposite direction of the established natural light source of the room; it looks artificial. For night interiors with practical room lights on, one can justify a backlight more easily. However, if you use the same backlight on everyone no matter what direction the camera is pointing or where the actor is standing, it starts to look theatrical. I don't think backlight is always necessary; even for separation, you can sometimes frame dark hair against a lighter background, for example. Occasionally, however, a little backlight may help a dark object from disappearing against a dark background. When possible, I prefer soft backlighting so that it feels like some practical source is bouncing off of the ceiling and onto the hair. However, sometimes a hard backlight can come from practical sources like track lighting. —David

Do you have a light or lighting tool that you just love, and if so, why?

I like Kino Flos and pancake lights because they are very soft and wrap around. I'm used to working [on] docs and in different countries where they may not have a Kino Flo, so I'll use a Chimera or whatever they have.—Elia

Whenever possible, I like to use a dimmer system. It offers me enormous flexibility with both intensity and color temperature. It is the closest I can get to actually "painting" with light. If a multichannel dimmer system (which I own and offer to my clients as an extension of my tool kit) is not available to me, I will endeavor to use Variacs and homemade dimmers (known in the parlance as "hand squeezers") to achieve the same effect. In any case, the end result can achieve all sorts of great lighting effects, from a firelight glow to an urban rave, very quickly. —Joe

Bucket lights—which is a porcelain socket in the bottom of a white plastic bucket. They can be hidden behind furniture and they can't crush it. They provide a nice, soft glow. They also work as something to hand off to the PAs when setting up craft services and work lights. —Tigre

No, not really. I may have my habits but nothing I "love." —Bill

I love new tech and old tech. Big soft sources—the bigger the Fresnel the better, blasting through a silk. —Gus

I like softlights—Chimeras, Rifa lights, china balls, any kind of softlight unit, like a 2kW zip, softened even more with diffusion. —Peter

I'm fond of the ETC Source Four Leko, mainly for bounce lighting, because it is so easily cut to whatever pattern is needed. I also use them for creating hard-focused slashes of light in the room. I also like small Chimera units like Lowel Rifas or the WoodyLight because they are lightweight and fast to set up.—David

A 4 × 4 Kino Flo or a Diva with a dimmer in it. I can light anywhere with those.—Ray

What do you think of the new LED lights—color, multiple shadows, texture?

I wouldn't say I'm a hardcore advocate yet. It's a smart way to go, because they are so more energy-efficient. Tungsten has certain warmth, especially in skin tone. The LED light is a little clinical on the skin tone. When you underexpose skin tone a little bit, it becomes nicer. I don't know what it is. LEDs don't get hot, so that's a big plus. But when I shoot concerts, a lot of LEDs are there; the blue ones start to create lines on the video, so you have to adjust the shutter. —Elia

LED is not there yet. Has its place, right now as an accent. It's so flexible, but not quite there yet as a key. —Gus

LEDs? Don't think they don't get hot. Great for reality because they can operate off batteries, and use so little power they work on any breaker. Multi-shadows is an issue and color, but you're not going to notice them in most situations. You're not gonna stick an LED outside a window and say it's sunlight coming through. They're not a big source, so they have to play close. The new Chimeras make the LED work, as they are usually too spotty/hard. —Tigre

I'm not sold yet on LEDs. Until there's a focusable Fresnel that can be cut and produce a hard shadow, they're a specialty tool. [LED] ribbon is good for setups in cars, as undercounter lights, etc.—good for setups that can only be run on battery. —Bill

I used the 1 × 1 Litepanel a lot as an eye light; it's easy to dim and can be powered with a battery. I also use the Litepanel Micro on the camera when I have to do Steadicam shots and need a little eye light. Most of the daylight LED fixtures work fine when mixed with HMIs, fluorescents, and natural daylight; the tungsten versions are a little more problematic, color-wise, but some have gotten pretty good. For now, I tend to use LEDs as eye lights or back and edge lights, but rarely as a key light . . . but that may change. —David

The way of the future. So small, compact profile, and give you a good punch for so little electricity. They are to lighting what digital was to film. Perfect for documentary, but stay with the same manufacturer, as units from different companies have different diodes, and they don't mix well. Good as obie lights. —Peter

How important do you feel it is to separately light the background?

I pay a lot of attention to the background. I like to hit the background with a 300 through a cookie. Adds some depth and dimension to the shot. —Ray

I always pay attention to the background. I look to see what I can do—is there too much light in it? A lot of time it's about taking light out of the background. I like to work with low depth of field, so I feel I need something in the background. The background can help you—if your front is a little dark because you want it moody, you can add something brighter in the background which creates a more dark and moody feel—it makes the front more silhouette without becoming muddy. —Elia

Lighting the background is one of the factors in creating a mood. I don't believe in three-point lighting. I believe in four-point lighting—key, fill, back, and background. To create the mood, you need to light different planes of the set separately. —Peter

This question implies that there is a luxury of space. In many practical situations, the spatial constrictions of a location make it impossible to treat the background as a separate element in the frame. In cases where there is enough distance between the middle-ground subjects and the scenery, it is often desirable to add "accent" lighting to elements in the background. In the more claustrophobic environment of location shooting, it is more often the case that one needs to take light AWAY from the wall behind the subject, in order to cancel shadows caused by the key light and to offer tonal separation of an oatmeal-colored cubicle from a pale-faced office worker. —Joe

Ideally you light the room, and the actors move through that lighting, you light "spaces not faces," rather than the older method of lighting the actors separately from the room. However, sometimes you need more precise control over how the light falls on the actor versus the background, and have to separate the two. But if it works, I'm more than happy if one light source can work for both the actors and the background. —David

You have to remember what show you are on. In reality TV you may not do it. In sitcoms the set is lit separately. In reality you light for the talent more than the background. "Light the money." Reality adds more light and is more creative with lighting when we're shooting the hosts and judges—the show's stars.—Tigre

Generally, if you light the background, you've got most of the foreground done, other than cleaning up the faces. —Bill

Lighting the background is mandatory. Shooting in depth means lighting in depth. —Gus

Do you have a preferred contrast ratio between key and fill? Between subject and background?

Not really. I love to light an old person with an incredible face, to get those beautiful wrinkles that's part of the personality—so I like to have it fall off a bit. I'm not big on fill light. But some directors will say it's too contrasty, so you put a little white board in. I tend to stay away from fill light and let the contrast be a little higher. But it totally depends—you are working to create the vision of the director. Sometimes they want it a little flatter. It has to feel right. There's plenty of dark comedies—such as the Coen brothers, so high key for comedy and low key for drama doesn't apply as much anymore. I don't mind contrast when I shoot digital. Maybe 4 to 1. —Elia

I like a certain amount of contrast; it gives the image some depth and drama, but I don't work toward any particular key-to-fill ratio. Sometimes it's necessary to be more precise in levels when doing something like a very underexposed moonlit sequence where you want the minimal amount of light in the shadows to see detail; to your eye, the key-to-fill ratio may seem very low, but once it's all underexposed, you will have a dark feeling, but retain some openness to the shadows. —David

2½ to 1 on the face—but it depends on the scene and the script. I light by eye, then take a picture to see what the contrast looks like. But I would look at the meter also. Generally the subject will always be brighter than the background—unless for some reason you don't want that, such as against a window, which should always be brighter. —Peter

Contrast? Don't be afraid of shadows. —Tigre

Low contrast, sort of flat light for the correspondent, and make them match the interviewee. But I keep the subject brighter than the background. That's where I put in the contrast. —Ray

How blue do you think is acceptable to indicate night when lighting?

It's fun to push the envelope with blue gel, but normal would be full CTB, when you want it natural.—Gus

For night blue I tend toward ¾ CTB, something very light. But I also add warm gels to lights imitating the practicals, like ¾ CTO. Maybe some sodium vapor light color coming in through the window if it's a city location. —Peter

Usually ½ CTB for on locations. On a sitcom set, full CTB—perhaps even Rosco 80 (gel) for outside and through the windows. Everything is an adjustment to the eye and the camera lens. —Tigre

I've come away from night is blue; that becomes too self-conscious of the cinematography. If you are in the city, there is no blue light—everything is glowing orange from the mercury vapor. But if you are in the country, it would be cooler. I would use ½ blue or ¾ blue and put a ¾ or ½ CTO on the inside lights, so that the moonlight is a little cooler, rather than "blue." I would use CTB instead of theatrical blues. —Elia

If you mean how blue should moonlight look, it depends on whether you are going for a natural look or a stylized look, because the color may also serve a symbolic effect; it may be part of the visual design for the movie where you want the color to stand out and make a statement. But if not, then my feeling is that moonlight should feel cooler than other sources like tungsten practical lamps (since technically it is daylight in color temperature, the moon just reflecting sunlight). You may also have to factor in whether the blue will be in contrast to other colors from other sources, or if the moonlight is the only source of light for the scene. For example, in a campfire scene, the moonlight doesn't have to be very blue because it's in contrast to orange firelight. With digital color-correction today, it is easy to adjust the intensity of blue lighting because it is the opposite color of flesh tone, and thus easy to isolate in the frame; therefore, if for practical reasons you are using HMI lamps for moonlight and cannot easily gel them to reduce the blue effect, it's not hard to make the blue less saturated in post, to create something more like a pale blue moonlight effect. —David

Other than color, how else do you make the scene appear nighttime?

More contrast. Areas of total shadow and areas of a white reference. Less fill light. In the frame, have one area exposed correctly and the others underexposed. —Elia

A lack of light in the background; reduce fill, but not eliminate it. You still need a little fill; otherwise, it feels dishonest. —Tigre

Contrast and dark, unlit areas. And choice of source. If headlights are the brightest and motivational source in a scene, then it appears to be night. Or make the refrigerator light the source, and the kitchen seems suddenly dark. —Bill

You try to frame visual indicators that the scene takes place at night; that may mean a practical lamp is on in a dark room, it may mean establishing windows with a dark view outside, it may just be indicated by the darkness of the scene. —David

Underexpose a little and create super-high contrast. But, you can't light every subject the same. Each situation will be different. —Gus

Show a dark window, and that will show it's night. Add less fill light at night. Add color to the fill light. —Peter

How often and why would you add color to your lights?

Use it for time of day, time of year, location—is it a period film, a sci-fi film? It can influence the physiological state the actor is in or the psychological state you want the audience in. And sometimes for sheer beauty. We may want the audience to look at a certain actor, so we may put a certain color of light on that actor. —Peter

I look at it and I say, hmm, let's warm it up. I have a director that always would like some color in the background. So we'd block some of the windows and shoot with an HMI, and then use a tungsten in the back. Or do the reverse and use ½ CTO on the HMI in the background. Maybe a straw at times. I'm not big on theatrical colors. I like to be "white," but by underexposing a little, you bring in a little warmth. —Elia

Other than color correction, not any on reality TV. On sitcoms, very little chance to add color. TV is unlike theater. Adding color needs to be very specific and clearly motivated by an obvious source. —Tigre

Add color when it strikes you as appropriate. Sunset, sunrise, a night interior with lamps, a night exterior with storefronts or streetlights. —Bill

There are only two reasons to add color to the light in a scene: either for technical correction or for aesthetic effect. Since I am apt to use a dimmer system quite often, I am constantly shifting the color temperature of my tungsten lighting, which creates a very flexible aesthetic approach. However, there are times when the intensity I am striving to achieve puts the color temperature out of range for the film stock or digital sensor I am capturing with. In such cases, I will add color correction gel (CT Blue) to the lighting instrument to help retain a sensible color balance. This is purely a technical adjustment. I am still reliant on the dimmer to create the aesthetic effect. In cases where I do not have the luxury of a dimmer system, I will add CT Blue or CT Orange to my instruments, in an attempt to imitate the aesthetic I would normally achieve by voltage manipulation. Thus I am now using the same technical correction gel for an aesthetic purpose. —Joe

Just on the background, just to make it warmer. —Ray

For live events, it's all about mixing colors—seeing colors mix and thinking how fun it would be to try that—especially contrasting color tones. —Gus

CTO and CTB gels are commonplace on any set to warm up or cool off a lamp, either to match a practical source in a room or to re-create a natural effect like a setting sun; and color may be used for symbolic effect, though it is best if this is motivated by a light source in the scene. In other words, if you want a strong green lighting effect for symbolic reasons, it doesn't hurt to establish a green neon sign out the windows so that the effect is also logically justified. In real life, we encounter many light sources of different colors, so we use colored lighting partly because it may be more realistic to match this natural phenomenon. Also, we may have to re-create the shifting colors of daylight from sunrise to sunset through twilight, for story reasons. And finally, you occasionally have scenes in nightclubs and other locations where colored lighting is commonplace. —David

What is your relationship with your gaffer/DP?

I strive to maintain good communication of my aesthetic intent for every scene in the film. I insist that my gaffer, my camera operator, and my camera assistant all read the script and understand the story we are trying to convey. Whenever possible, I try to bring my keys to all location scouts, and I will have discussions with them in advance of the shoot about aesthetics as well as technical rundowns. In many cases, my gaffer is working as my lead team supervisor . . . pre-lighting a set in advance of the camera crew. Unless that person really understands my creative intent for the scene, including camera angles, there is little they can do besides empty out the truck and stage equipment until I arrive on set to give instruction. Even a detailed lighting plot does little to inform my colleagues of my creative approach. It is my job to inspire my gaffer as a fellow artist to help me by making informed decisions that are based upon previously discussed aesthetics in advance of my arrival on set. This approach has innumerous benefits. It speeds up the day. It keeps my support team creatively involved and emotionally committed to the project. It often teaches me new technical approaches to lighting design, and proves the adage that moviemaking is the ultimate collaborative art form. —Joe

I love lighting, so I tend to be very specific with my gaffers as to what I want; however, I will listen to their ideas too, and I rely on their professional skills, their level of organization, and the ability of their crews to pull off the lighting in a fast and efficient manner. As a gaffer becomes more familiar with my lighting approaches to scenes, it becomes easier for them to anticipate what I might need; in fact, thinking ahead is one of the primary things I need from my keys, because often I have to focus on the scene at hand. They can't wait for me to tell them everything because sometimes that will be too late; they have to keep in mind what was planned in prep, they have to prepare for upcoming scenes and locations, hours, days, or weeks to come. . . . Often during breaks between setups, they will be asking me questions about these scenes down the road. But even creatively, it's important that the gaffer be an artist and understand or share your aesthetic sensibilities, to think about the needs of the story and the actors. It's important that the key creative people are all on the same page. —David

I like my gaffer to run the show for me—my right-hand person. I like for my gaffer to speak up for lighting concerns to the key grip. I like to come up with my own game plan, and then I always appreciate whatever the gaffer can add to it. If it's a great idea, terrific—I use it. If not—nawh, let's do it my way. —Peter

Barely ever get a gaffer. I love the fact that a gaffer has been on more films than I have, so he brings a whole bag of tricks. I like the collaboration. He has input. We could do this or that—maybe something I hadn't thought of. It's one other person that brings something to the table. When we do films, we improvise. On a film set it's a jazz combo, the director, cameraman, gaffer, grip. We play together and feed off each other. And sometimes it works and sometimes, well. . . . —Elia

It's all based on previous working relationships. On the *Sheri Show* and *Are We There Yet?,* I would have Bill Berner's plot, prehang it, then he'd come in and tweak and aim it. He trained me to do it his way. On *Project Runway* with Gus Dominguez, I do all the standing locations—the workspace, sewing room, hallways, apartments—based on the established look Gus created in past seasons. It's their design that I re-create, and can sometimes add to, but they always have the final look and say. —Tigre

The DP sets the vision; the gaffer is the execution. Sometimes I'm nonspecific—I just say, "Give me a bright soft thing here," and I let the gaffer come up with it. Other times I'm very specific. A good gaffer is incredible. —Gus

What's the biggest problem you encounter when lighting a location?

Contrast control. Basically because I don't work with big lighting packages and large crews, how to control the contrast in the environment with limited gear. If you're in an exterior or a roomy place with lots of windows, and I don't have a crew to gel the windows or fly a silk in, to keep the contrast I want is sometimes a challenge. —Elia

Placing the generator. I need the power, but where do I put it out of the shot and out of the soundman's range, and still be able to get to it? After planning long and hard where to hide the thing—they change the shot and see or hear it. —Tigre

Sometimes you light a stand-in, only to discover when the actor steps on set that they are wearing some big hat or wardrobe piece that is shadowing their face from your light. Sometimes the actors end up standing in a spot where there is no possible source of light, or it's a light that is wrong for the mood of the scene. —David

I never have problems. I have challenges. My approach to a complex situation is, wherever possible, to simplify the technical intervention. I always strive to light an entire scene, rather than focus upon lighting individual setups. I try to give my director at least a 280-degree field of view, to minimize the number of lighting re-sets to get through a typical scene. This may require hanging instruments in the ceiling to avoid light stands encroaching on the set, but that extra effort is well worth the payoff. The director experiences less delay between setups, and the actors are better able to stay in character to give a more consistent performance on camera. This is the essence of moviemaking. Artful lighting of a mediocre scene is a waste of aesthetics. —Joe

I lit a scene, which took a long time to achieve, and I looked at it and I hated the way it looked, and I came up with a whole new concept. The hardest part was telling my crew I changed my mind and I wanted to do it a different way. We all make mistakes. —Peter

Tell me about a time that a lighting setup just didn't work or accidently did work.

I've had to light where there's no stand-in; you get someone from the crew to sit in or stand in and you light it, and suddenly the subject walks in and they [have] dark skin or white hair, and you have to quickly adjust. I came in once and had a preconceived notion of how to light it. I did the scout and went home and planned out a whole lighting plan, and when we got there, it was totally different. It was a bar and it was different because I saw it during the day, but it was a night scene. So I had to scrap the entire plan and just went for some bounces because the location looked great. Sometimes the location will tell you what looks good. —Elia

I remember once in a location with a lattice over the windows, I was trying to get the pattern of the lattice to fall across the room from moonlight. I couldn't get a sharp pattern from my HMIs outside because I couldn't back them far enough away due to space restrictions. Frustrated, I told the electrician to pan the light off of the room for a moment, and as he did, the lattice pattern appeared due to the sharp light spill from the edge of the lens in the HMI—it was very dim but usable, exposure-wise, so I lit the scene with HMIs pointed away from the room at a 90-degree angle. —David

On the kids' TV show *Between the Lions,* we lit a puppet with my mag light for a close-up. Later I switched to an LED mag light, and when the DP called for it again and I gave it to him, he threw it across the room yelling, "Get me a real mag light." I always carried both from then on. —Tigre

I was trying to achieve a night effect using a very large HMI unit. We were short on time, and the scene required my lead actor to carry a kerosene lamp as his key light. I needed an ambient glow of "moonlight," but the only suitable unit my gaffer had on hand was simply too powerful. We set up a 12 × 12 with two layers of diffusion material, but the light was still too directional for my taste. I asked my key grip to fetch an additional 4 × 4 silk to further diffuse the light. As he trotted toward the very white grip truck that was parked behind the setup, he tripped over the header cable and spun the lighting unit. It landed focused on the side of the grip truck, creating a perfect bounce surface. I congratulated my grip on his profound solution to the problem, and we set out to capture a beautiful night scene. —Joe

I went on a scout with the director to a long hallway with windows along one wall. I said, "If we shoot it so that we don't see out the windows, we can almost shoot it as is." He said, "Great; that's what we'll do." So, on the day of the shoot we arrived and the director says he wants to shoot this against the windows. I told him that on the scout he said we wouldn't see the windows. He said, "I never said that." I said, "I have it on tape." He said, "I don't care what you have on tape, I never said that." You always have to be resourceful. I used a traveling softlight at the right angle so we didn't see it in the window and let the windows burn a little bit, and it was fine. —Peter

Where do you get your inspiration from?

I keep a mental tool box of images I've seen—something on TV or art or even a streetlamp. I can't wait to use that later. —Gus

I have spent many hours at museums, studying the painting style of masters like Georges de La Tour, who has done with oil on canvas what I can only fleetingly hope to achieve with actual light sources on my set. —Joe

I get inspiration from nature. Something about a sunset—the blue in the sky with the clouds, and then watching the shadows move. —Tigre

Watch movies—lots of movies. —Ray

Other movies, still photography, the other visual arts like painting, and of course, nature. —David

Other films of a similar genre or different genres, and watch the scenes that are relevant to this film. See what they did, where they put their lights and the quality of light, and what the ratios are. Look at art—paintings are how DPs and directors talk to each other. —Peter

One of my favorite painters is Edward Hopper, and favorite DPs are Gordon Willis and Roger Deakins. I'll think, "How did he do it?" I'm not going to copy that—I'll make it my own thing, original thing. Inspiration comes from music, paintings, a nice sunset somewhere. My inspirations come from every shoot—when I see it done I say, "That I liked." Or when I see a film and see a scene that I say, "Oh I like that"—so it gets stored in my brain. When I'm at a party, my wife says I'm a little boring because I sit there and watch this guy on a couch where the light is slightly behind him and it looks cool. Then maybe I have to shoot a person on a couch with a lamp beside him—but I'll move the camera over so that the light is behind him a little like at that party. —Elia

Just keep looking at movies and at what surrounds you. —Bill

2 RESOURCES

Web instructions on how to set color bars on your production monitor.

From ProductionApprentice.com
http://www.productionapprentice.com/tutorials/general/
using-color-bars-to-set-up-your-equipment/

From Apple
http://documentation.apple.com/en/color/usermanual/
index.html#chapter=A%26section=2%26tasks=true

From VideoUniversity.com
http://www.videouniversity.com/articles/color-bars-and-how-to-use-em/

APPS

There are a number of apps for digital devices such as smart phones and digital tablets that are useful for lighting. Most, if not all, are available in both iOS and Android versions. Following are the ones I've found to be the most useful:

* Barbizon—Lists lamps, electrical data, color information, and so on

* Cine Meter—RGB waveform monitor, false-color picture, and shutter-priority reflected light meter; using the camera in your device

* CineCalc—Separated into Camera Depth of Field and Lighting Unit Throw calculators

* Pocket Light Meter—A digital reflected light meter using the camera in your device

* Gel Swatch Library—Catalogue of gels made by Rosco, Lee, Apollo, and GAM

* iGobo—Catalogue of gobos made by Apollo

* myGobo—Catalogue of gobos made by Rosco

* theGripApp—Covers knots, grip gear, dollies, cranes, and so on

* Light Calc Lite—Calculates lighting throw and falloff

* set Lighting—Catalogues of lighting manufacturers, lamps, and lighting tools

* StageHand—Catalogue of Rosco, Apollo, and Lee gels

* Sun Tracker—Tracks the sun

* Sun Seeker—Tracks and predicts the sun's path

* SkyView—Tracks the stars and the sun

* TechScout—Lighting gear ordering app

BOOKS

A number of available books include interviews with cameramen and directors of photography. They are all interesting and inspiring. The few I have listed here seem to devote more coverage to lighting than others.

* *Painting with Light* by John Alcott—A classic by a master of lighting from the golden days of Hollywood

* *Film Lighting* by Kris Malkiewicz, Simon & Schuster—Covers lighting and cinematography by compiling interviews with big-time feature film DPs

* *Reflections: Twenty-one Cinematographers at Work,* edited by Benjamin Bergery, ASC Press—Interviews with big-time feature film DPs

* *New Cinematographers* by Alexander Ballinger, HarperCollins publishing—Interviews with big-time feature film DPs

* *Shot in the Dark* by Jay Holben, Course Technology—A creative do-it-yourself guide to making your own lights and basic lighting

- *The Grip Book* by Michael Uva, Focal Press—The training guide for being a grip

- *The Set Electrician's Handbook* by Harry Box, Focal Press—The training guide for becoming a film electric

MAGAZINES

- *American Cinematographer Magazine*—Interviews with feature film DPs about new films

- *British Cinematographer Magazine*

- *Australian Cinematographer Magazine*

- *Canadian Cinematographer Magazine*

- *ICG Magazine* (International Cinematographer's Guild, Local 600)—Interviews with DPs, camera operators, camera assistants, and so on, and union business

- *Sound & Picture Magazine*—Articles about both cinematography and sound

- *MovieMaker Magazine*—Mainly about indie filmmaking, occasionally has articles about cinematography and lighting

- *Student Filmmaker Magazine*—Mainly about low-budget filmmaking, occasionally has articles about cinematography and lighting

WEBSITES

- www.theASC.com—American Society of Cinematographers

- www.bscine.com—British Society of Cinematographers

- www.AbleCine.com—Camera/lighting rental/sales company has educational programming

- www.Motion.Kodak.com —About motion picture cinematography

- www.rosco.com/tutorials—All about using color in theater

- www.leefilters.com—Lee Filters' website with interviews with DPs

- www.fstopacademy—Variety of interesting stuff

- www.crafttruck.com—Interviews with DPs

MAJOR LIGHTING MANUFACTURERS

- ARRI—Tungsten, HMI, LED, all kinds of lights

- Lowel—Small open-faced and collapsible softlights in tungsten and small LEDs (no Fresnels)

- Mole-Richardson—Tungsten, HMI, LED, fluorescent—all kinds of film lights

- DeSisti—Tungsten, fluorescent studio lights

- k5600—HMI lights

- Hive—Plasma lights

- Kino Flo—Fluorescent and LED lights

- Litepanel—LED lights

- Creamsource—LED lights

- Cool Lights—Tungsten, HMI, LED, fluorescent—all kinds of film lights

- BriteShot—LED lights

- Chimera—Softboxes

- Westcott—Softboxes, collapsible flags

- The Rag Place—Silks, nets, butterflies, flags

- Matthews Studio Equipment—Grip equipment, flags, nets, butterflies, reflectors

- American Grip—Grip equipment, flags, nets, butterflies, reflectors

- Cineo TruColor—Remote phosphorus lights

- Nila—LED lights

- Frezzi—On-camera lights

- Sunray—HMI lights

- Kobolt—HMI lights

- ETC—Ellipsoidal and PAR lights

- Airstar—Balloon lights in tungsten and HMI

- Dedo Lights—Small unit lights

GEL AND GOBO MANUFACTURERS

- Rosco—Also makes small LED lights

- Lee

- Apollo

- GAM

GLOSSARY

Following are some terms and industry jargon commonly used in the lighting profession.

4 × 4—(n) A 4-x-4-foot frame that can have either diffusion or other materials stretched across it.

18 × 24—(n) A flag or a net that is 18 × 24 inches

24 × 36—(n) A flag or a net that is 24 × 36 inches

85—(n) Slang for orange color correction gel, known as CTO, converts 5,600K light to 3,200K

86—(v) To get rid of, take down, remove. East Coast slang term originating from Chumley's, a New York City speakeasy, which had its main unmarked entrance in an alley but had a backdoor onto the street with the street number 86 Bedford Street. When it was raided, the owners would yell "86" and everyone would run out the back door.

Amps—Amperage. Measurement of the current, i.e., the electrical flow of the electrons (speed). Breakers, fuses, and wire are rated by how many amps they can support before beginning to melt. Amps can be determined by the equation: Amps = Watts/Volts.

Apple box—(n) A wooden rectangular box used on sets for a variety of things.

AWG—(American Wire Gauge) A number rating of wire thickness as to how many amps of electricity it is capable of carrying safely before melting.

Baby—(n) Common slang term for any Fresnel-lensed 1,000-watt lighting unit. Originated by the Mole Richardson lighting company.

Back—(n) Slang for a backlight. (v) To add a light from behind the subject.

Backlight—(n) A lighting unit aimed at the subject opposite the camera. (v) To add a light to backlight a subject.

Bag—(n) A sandbag or shotbag. (v) To place a sandbag on something.

Balloon light—(n) A large, white, silk balloon that is filled with helium and contains one or more lamps inside, either tungsten or HMI, which can be flown above the acting area to provide overall soft ambient light.

Barn doors—Hinged metal leafs that frame the sides, top, and bottom of the front of a lighting unit, used to direct and block the light coming out.

Bead board—(n) Usually comes in 4-x-8-foot sheets is silver on one side and has Styrofoam-type white material on the other, usually about 1½ inches thick. Used to bounce light

Best boy—(n) The second electrician on set, under the Gaffer, in charge of distributing the electrical power and keeping track of all lighting equipment.

Black—(n) Also known as a flag. A solid black material stretched across a frame that can be mounted in a grip stand. They come in various sizes, with the standards being 18 × 24 inches, 24 × 36 inches and 4 × 4 feet.

Black wrap—(n) Aluminum foil painted black on both sides, used to wrap lights to cut light leaks and spill, also to extend the barn doors. (v) To cover with black wrap.

Bounce card—(n) A white cardboard used to bounce light.

Butterfly—(n) A large metal frame upon which is stretched a silk, black, net, or other material that comes in various sizes, including 6 × 6 feet, 8 × 8 feet, 12 × 12 feet, and 20 × 20 feet. Primarily used to filter the sunlight, but can also be used to shine lights through or into for a large bounce light surface.

C47—(n) Wooden clothespin, used to attach gel to the barn doors of a light

Cable—(n) Electrical cable that comes in various thicknesses. (v) To run electrical power to a unit.

Cameraman—(n) Nickname for cinematographer or director of photography, but also used for camera operators in television.

Color temperature—(n) The color of light as measured in Kelvins.

Cookie—(n) Nickname for a cucoloris. A wooden panel with shapes cut out of it used to throw a breakup of shadows when a light is aimed through it.

Chicken coop—(n) A softlight box hung from above. Black on four sides with white diffusion on the bottom through which light is aimed.

Chimera—(n) A company that manufactures a variety of a collapsible softboxes made to be affixed to the front of a light; has become generic slang for any such device.

Cinematographer—(n) Same as director of photography. Person in charge of photographing the moving image, which includes designing the lighting.

Coming up to speed—(v) The action of HMI lights, after being turned on, to build up to their full intensity and color temperature. This can take several minutes.

Coney Island—(n) Old New York film slang for a sandbag, named for the famous beach in Brooklyn. Sand comes from beaches.

CTB—(n) Color correction blue gel, also known as Full Blue, converts 3,200K light to 5,600K.

CTO—(n) Color Correction Orange gel, also known as 85, converts 5,600K light to 3,200K.

Cucoloris—(n) A wooden panel with shapes cut out of it used to throw a breakup of shadows when a light is aimed through it.

Cut—(v) To block light, usually using a flag.

Cutter—(n) Also called a flag. A solid black material stretched across a frame that can be mounted in a grip stand. Cutters come in various sizes, although the standards are 18 × 24 inches, 24 × 36 inches (also called a 2 by 3) and 4 × 4 feet.

Daylight—(n) The color of outdoor light during midday, the accepted standard being 5,600 Kelvin.

Diffusion—(n) Translucent material, usually in a polymer gelatin sheet, that softens the texture of the light when placed over the front of a lighting instrument.

Diffuse—(v) To add diffusion to a light.

Dimmer—(n) Electronic device used to lower/raise the intensity of a light. Can be an entire system of dimmers and a dimmer control board or a single outlet dimmer.

Director of photography—(n) Same as cinematographer. Person in charge of photographing the moving image, including creating the lighting.

Distribution (n)—The division of the electrical power using cables and outlet breaker boxes called distribution boxes. (v) To run distribution—To run extension cords and outlet boxes to various areas of the set and to specific lighting units.

Dot—(n) A small round net or flag used to block or diminish the intensity of light.

Edge—(v) To create an outline of light on one side of the subject with a lighting instrument.

Edge light—(n) A unit used to provide an outline or edge of light on a subject.

Electric—(n) A member of the lighting crew.

Eggcrate—A thick black frame with multiple dividers designed to focus soft light.

Ellipsoidal spot—(n) An ellipsoidal reflector spotlight (ERS) is a focusable spotlight with an ellipsoidal reflector, a lens system, and shutters for controlling the beam. Designed for pattern projection and creating sharp beam edges, the ellipsoidal is the most commonly used type of instrument in theatrical lighting in the United States.

Eye light—Low-intensity light placed just above the lens to provide a twinkle reflection in the subject's eye.

Extension—(n) An electrical extension cord, usually 25 feet long, AWG 12, made to carry 20 amps.

Fill—(v) To add light into a shadow area.

Finger—(n) Small, thin rectangular flag or net.

Flag—(n) Same as a cutter. A solid black material stretched across a frame that can be mounted in a grip stand. They come in various sizes, although the standards are 18 × 24 inches, 24 × 36 inches (also called a 2 × 3), and 4 × 4 feet. (v) To block light using a flag.

Flexfill—(n) A collapsible round reflector with silver on one side and gold on the other. The outer lining can be removed, and the Flexfill then becomes a circular silk.

Flicker box—(n) A device that controls lighting units plugged into it and can make them flicker or strobe at various rates and intensities.

Flood—(n) A wide beam of light. (v) To adjust the lighting unit so that the beam of light widens.

Flying in—(v) To bring something to the set that was asked for.

F-stop—(n) Setting of the iris of a lens that controls how much light passes through the lens.

Foamcore—(n) Lightweight, ½-inch-thick poster board, white on one side and black on the other. Usually comes in 4-x-8-foot sheets.

Fresnel—(n) 1. A stepped convex lens. 2. A lighting fixture with a Fresnel lens with a spherical reflector that provides an even, variable spot-to-flood field.

Gaffer—(n) Chief lighting technician. Implements the lighting design determined by the cinematographer

Gaffer's tape—(n) Cloth-based adhesive tape, commonly 2 inches wide, but also comes in various widths and various colors, although usually in black, gray, or white. Often used by crew members.

Gel—(n) A thin, colored polymer filter used to change the color of the light. (v) To place a gel over the front of a light.

Generator—(n) A gasoline combustion engine that generators electricity. Come in various sizes and electrical output ranges.

Gobo—(n) A pattern cut into a thin piece of metal that when placed inside an ellipsoidal spotlight will project a pattern. Also, a pattern cut into a showcard or foamcore.

Grip—(n) A crew member in charge of securing light mounting hardware in strange places as well as handling butterflies, grip stands, flags, and nets. The grip also moves the camera and is in charge of safety on the set.

Grip stand—(n) A three-legged collapsible stand with a "gobo" head and a "gobo arm."

Ground—(n) 1. Where all electricity wants to go, back to the earth. 2. The round prong and the wire attached to it in three prong extension cords that allows any electrical leak from the lighting unit to safely go directly to the ground. (v) To run a wire from a lighting unit or generator that is clamped to something that stretches deep into the ground, such as a fire hydrant, metal fence post, or a metal rod pounded into the ground.

Gauge—(n) The number rating of a wire as to how many amps of electricity it is capable of carrying safely before melting, as measured by the AWG.

Hair light—(n) Same as a backlight. Light that rims the hair of the subject.

Hollywood—(v) To hand-hold a flag or light, usually to follow the camera or a subject as they move. (n) A small town in southern California to which Biograph and Paramount Pictures moved from New Jersey in the early 1900s to avoid lawsuits from Thomas Edison for using his patented motion picture camera device. The rest, as they say, is history.

HMI—(n) A lighting unit that emits daylight color-balanced light.

Inkie—(n) Common slang term for any small in size and wattage Fresnel lens lighting unit. Originated by the Mole-Richardson Lighting Company, whose inkies are 250 watts. ARRI brand inkies are 150 watts.

Joker—(n) A small, low-wattage HMI par light, comes in various intensities.

Junior—(n) Common slang term for any Fresnel lens 2,000-watt lighting unit. Originated by the Mole-Richardson Lighting Company.

Kelvin—(n) The measurement unit of the color of light.

Key—(n) The brightest light aimed at the subject. (v) To light a subject with a bright source.

Kick—(n) The glare or reflection of light off a surface.

Kicker—(n) A light that is aimed at the subject's side.

Kino Flo—(n) Brand name for a fluorescent lighting unit made for film lighting. Comes in various sizes and wattages. Has become a common slang term to refer to any fluorescent lighting unit.

Lamp—(n) The bulb in a lighting unit. (v) To place a bulb inside a lighting unit.

Light—(n) 1. The visible spectrum of radiant energy. 2. A unit that produces light.

Lighting director—(n) The designer of the lighting in television, who does not operator or control the camera framing.

Load—(n) The amount of electricity being used or running through a wire. Measured in amps.

Magic Gadget—(n) Manufacturer trade name of a flicker box.

Maxi-Brute—(n) A light with nine 1,000-watt PAR lamps arranged in a pattern of three columns of three.

Meat axe—A flag that is at least three times longer than its width.

Mickey—(n) Common slang term for any open-face 1,000-watt lighting unit. Originated by the Mole-Richardson Lighting Company. Also known as a redhead.

Mighty—(n) Common slang term for any open-face 2,000-watt lighting unit. Originated by the Mole-Richardson Lighting Company. Also known as a blonde.

Negative fill—(n) Positioning something to block bounce light from hitting the subject.

Net—(n) A thin screen material stretched across a frame that can be placed in a grip stand, used to cut the intensity of a light beam. Nets come in various sizes, but the standards are 18 × 24 inches, 24 × 36 inches (also called a 2 × 3), and 4 × 4 feet. Also comes in larger sizes to be used on butterflies. (v) To lower the intensity of light using a net.

Obie—(n) A small light positioned above the camera lens, named for actress Merle Oberon, who was lit this way by cinematographer Lucien Ballard.

Open-face—(n) A lighting unit without a lens.

PAR—(n) Short for parabolic aluminized reflector. PAR fixtures are a wash light often used for live entertainment applications. These lights are available in various beam spreads: WFL (wide flood), MFL (medium flood), NSP (narrow spot), and VNSP (very narrow spot).

Pins—(n) Wooden clothespins, used to attach gel to the barn doors of a light.

Power—(n) 1. Electricity. 2. Where the electrical service is or where the electrical cables end. (v) To run electrical cables or extension cords to an item.

Profile Spot—(n) Another name for an ERS or other spot light unit.

Reflector—(n) Any of a variety of items with at least one shiny silver side used to reflect light from collapsible round to 4-x-4-foot hard square designs.

Rifa—A collapsible softbox light made by Lowel that comes in various wattages.

Rig—(v) To affix, fasten, or otherwise attach something.

Rim—(n) A light that outlines or produces a halo around the subject from behind. (v) To aim a light from behind to add a halo of light around the subject

Safety—(v) To add a safety chain, wire, or rope to a light's yoke and fasten it around something permanent in the ceiling to stop it from falling in the event it comes loose from its mount.

Sandbag—(n) A two-pouch saddle bag filled with sand, used to weight things down such as light and grip stands. (v) To place a sandbag on something.

Scrim—(n) A circular metal screen used to lower the intensity of a lighting unit by being placed behind the barn doors. (v) To lower the intensity of the light by adding a scrim.

Senior—(n) Common slang term for any Fresnel lensed 5,000-watt lighting unit. Originated by the Mole-Richardson Lighting Company.

Shiny boards—(n) Stiff 4-x-4-foot reflectors that have a soft side and a hard side.

Shotbag—(n) A two-pouch saddle bag filled with metal shot pellets, used to weight things down such as light and grip stands.

Showcard—(n) A white cardboard sheet usually black on one side and white on the other, usually 24 × 36 inches in size, used to bounce or cut light.

Silk—(n) A translucent white material stretched across a frame used to soften the texture of light. They come in various sizes; standards are 18 × 24 inches, 24 × 36 inches, and 4 × 4 feet. Also comes in larger sizes to be used on butterflies. (v) To soften the texture of the light by placing a silk in front of it.

Side light—(n) A lighting unit aimed at the subject from the side, at least 90 degrees from camera.

Sky pan—(n) A large open-faced silver saucer-like lighting unit with a 5,000-watt lamp, usually hung high up in studios to shine down through a stretched silk or a butterfly or to light a backdrop.

Slow down—(v) Slang for lowering the intensity of a light, usually by placing a scrim in it or adding a net in front of it.

Source Four—A trade name for a commonly used ellipsoidal spot light unit. Has become a common slang term to refer to any ellipsoidal spot lighting unit.

Softbox—(n) A black cloth and wire collapsible, four-sided, tent-shaped device with white translucent cloth over the front that when attached to the front of a lighting unit produces soft light.

Soften—(v) Place diffusion on something.

Softlight—(n) Softlights provide soft, virtually shadowless light over a large area. They can be used for a soft fill where shadows must be washed out. Accessories are available to modify the light such as scrims, diffusion frames, and eggcrates.

Solid—(n) A black flag.

Spacelight—A lighting unit designed to have anywhere from two to six lamps configured like spokes of a wagon wheel, pointing down into a white diffusion silk cylinder with a round diffusion ring on the bottom. Can have a black "skirt" added to cut light from the sides.

Spill—(n) Light that leaks out of a unit from the back, sides, or edges of the barn doors.

Spot—(n) Nickname for an ellipsoidal spotlight. (v) To tighten the beam of light, allowing it to throw farther before its intensity drops

Stinger—(n) Slang for an electrical extension cord.

Strike—(v) To take something down.

Striking—(v) To turn on an HMI light or an arc light. Said by an electric because these units will emit a bright flash when first ignited, which can be mistaken for a lamp burning out, and then take a few minutes for their intensity and color temperature to come up to its final setting.

Sun gun—(n) A small, handheld, battery-operated tungsten or HMI light, invented for news crews.

Swing—(n) A crew member who works for both the electric crew and the grip crew.

Take down—(v) 1. Lower the intensity of a unit, either with a dimmer or with scrims or nets. 2. To remove.

Tenner—(n) Common slang term for any Fresnel-lensed 10,000-watt lighting unit. Originated by the Mole-Richardson Lighting Company.

Top—(v) To add a top chop flag in front of a light.

Topper/top chop—(n) A flag that is positioned horizontally just above the front of a light to block light from going upward.

Tungsten—(n) 1. The metal used inside a lamp that glows when heated and produces light. 2. The color of light put out by a tungsten lighting unit, the standard being 3,200 Kelvin.

Unit—(n) Nickname for a lighting unit

Volts—(n) Measurement of the potential of alternating current electricity, which is the difference between the + /- (strength). In the United States, the standard voltage of the electricity in standard wall outlets is 110 volts. In Europe, the standard is 220 volts.

Wash—(n) A wide spread of light over an area. Example: "Give me a wash of red here"

Watts—(n) Measurement of the usage of electricity, how much is needed to operate something. Every electrically powered item should have the wattage listed on it.

Wrap—(n) The end of the shooting time/day. (v) 1. To put everything away. 2. Allow light to spill around to the side of the subject turned away from the lighting unit.

Zip light—A lighting unit that emits soft light, designed with the lamps hidden below that shine up into a white coved reflector. Comes in various wattages and sizes. Invented by New York City gaffer Willie Meyerhoff, who gaffed over 30 feature films, including *Midnight Cowboy* and *Serpico.*

INDEX